P9-CDW-728

Celebrate *Country Woman Christmas 1999*

Bright tins bursting with fresh-baked cookies…festive packages piled under the tree…friends and family coming together in cheerful celebration…these merry signs can mean only one thing—it's Christmastime!

There's nothing quite like this happiest of holidays. To help you make the most of it, we've once again bundled up the season's very best and bound it into this fourth annual edition of *Country Woman Christmas*.

What makes this book truly one-of-a-kind is its heartwarming country focus. You see, most of the recipes, stories, crafts and photos have come directly to us from the rural readers of *Country Woman* magazine. Here's a quick look at what's inside…

Festive Foods. Tempting treats, from appetizers to sweets, complete meals and more, abound in this keepsake publication. You now have more than *100* never-before-published, soon-to-be-favorite recipes to add to your files.

Each dish had to pass rigorous tests in the *Country Woman* kitchen to ensure it is tasty *and* timely.

After all, busy country cooks often don't have spare moments for trips to town. So, every recipe in this book can be made with ingredients you likely have on hand.

Merry Makings. Also contained within these pages are dozens of original Christmas projects.

The crafts all come with easy-to-follow instructions, charts and patterns and take only a few hours to finish. But they'll make your home and gift-giving sparkle well beyond December 25.

Plus, you'll enjoy insightful profiles of ladies who've found fun ways to share the spirit of the season, glimpses of gals who deck their halls in down-home styles you can try, sentimental poems, true tales of Christmas joy…and lots of other merry features and photos.

More in Store. With a colorful new edition being added to this series every year, you can look forward to many more country-flavored holiday celebrations. But, for now, simply settle back with *Country Woman Christmas 1999*. We hope you enjoy it as much as we enjoy bringing it to you!

Executive Editor
Kathy Pohl

Editor
Kathleen Anderson

Food Editor
Coleen Martin

Associate Food Editor
Corinne Willkomm

Senior Recipe Editor
Sue A. Jurack

Test Kitchen Assistant
Suzanne Hampton

Craft Editors
Jane Craig
Tricia Coogan

Associate Editors
Sharon Selz
Kristine Krueger

Editorial Assistant
Sarah Grimm

Art Director
Maribeth Greinke

Cover Designer
Julie Wagner

Art Associates
Claudia Wardius
Vicky Marie Moseley
Linda Dzik

Photographers
Scott Anderson
Glenn Thiesenhusen

Food Photography Artist
Stephanie Marchese

Photo Studio Manager
Anne Schimmel

Production Assistant
Ellen Lloyd

© 1999 Reiman Publications, LLC
5400 S. 60th Street
Greendale WI 53129

International Standard
Book Number:
0-89821-259-6
International Standard
Serial Number:
1093-6750

All rights reserved.
Printed in U.S.A.

INSIDE...

8 Welcome to My Country Kitchen

FOOD
10 Holiday Brunch
14 Christmas Breads
20 Appetizers
24 Christmas Dinner
30 Holiday Cookies
36 Seasonal Sweets
40 Festive Desserts
44 Gifts from the Kitchen

CRAFTS
48 Sugar Cookie Sleigh
58 Bright Lights Garland
59 Speedy Sock Reindeer
60 Appliqued Tablecloth
62 Santa and Mrs. Claus Mugs
63 Cheery Pinecone Trim
64 Fabric Candy Canes
66 Cross-Stitched Santa Trim
67 Candy-Striped Santas
68 Crocheted Star Place Mat Set
69 Shining Star Ornament
70 Appliqued Snowman Sweatshirt
72 Mini Tree Skirt
73 Pinecone Angels
74 Noel Bell Pulls
75 Card Puzzle Magnets
76 Snowman Candy Jar
76 Country Claus Trim
78 Spool Nativity
79 Sequin Snowflakes
80 Painted Tree Trims Sweatshirt
81 Evergreen Door Decor
82 Signs of the Season Quilt
84 Santa Claus Napkin Holder
85 Poinsettia Napkin Ring
86 Knit Sweater and Hat
87 Tree Slice Ornament
88 Jumbo Stocking
90 Festive Hot Pads
92 Fabric Stocking Trims
93 Merry Plant Pokes
94 Quilled Bear Ornament
95 Dancing Gingerbread Toy
96 Plastic Canvas Gift Bag
98 North Pole Pins
99 Christmas Card Barn
100 Woven Sleigh Basket
102 Kris Kringle Tea Towel
103 Crocheted Slippers
106 Kountry Klaus

AND MUCH MORE!

PICTURED ON OUR COVER. Clockwise from top left: Bright Lights Garland (p. 58), Cardamom Almond Biscotti (p. 34), Snowman Candy Jar (p. 76), Festive Hot Pad (p. 90), Gingerbread Rings (p. 35), Golden Fruitcake (p. 45), North Pole Pin (p. 98), Fabric Stocking Trim (p. 92), Candy-Striped Santas (p. 67).

Photo Contributors: pp. 8-9—Joy Davis; p. 51—Gene Paulson, Anne Redfield; pp. 56-57—Midwest of Cannon Falls; p. 104—Woody Woodard; p. 108—Tom Dusard.

Holiday Delights

Evergreen trees and cinnamon spice—
The scents of Christmas are ever so nice!
Warm country kitchens, cozy and near,
Filled with memories of all we hold dear.

Shiny new shoes and perky red bows,
Dressed in our best from our heads to our toes.
Little round faces, eager and bright,
Waiting for Santa and Christmas delights.

Candles aglow in each window tonight,
Lighting our way as *His* star did that night.
Christmas is more than presents and songs,
It's His love in our hearts all the year long.
                                —*Brenda Moore James*
                                Livermore, California

A Berry Merry Christmas Stems from Her Top Crop

COME CHRISTMAS, Carol Hop's active green thumb lands her in the red …and she's glad as can be about it.

The nursery she tends with her father near Fennville, Michigan is brimming with all sorts of holly—more than 150 different varieties at last count.

"We've been growing crab apples, magnolias, dogwoods and other landscaping materials here since my dad started back in 1959," Carol says. "But the holly's our most abundant crop.

"It's by far *my* favorite—those crimson berries and shiny green leaves are a combination that can't be beat!"

While most hollies here feature foliage in shades you'd expect, some surprises sprout up…such as blue and almost black. The fruit also varies, from red to white, yellow and even black.

"As far as size and shape go, the sky's the limit. We raise diminutive creeping shrubs, 30-foot-tall trees and everything in between," Carol describes.

Jolly Holly's Hardy

"Our spread gets lots of moisture and warmth from nearby Lake Michigan, making it ideal for growing many plants. However, holly isn't as delicate as most folks think. It can be found all over, from polar regions to the tropics.

"It's just a matter of finding the kind that's best suited for a particular locale. We pride ourselves on cultivating a wide selection to fit almost any need."

Propagation does require patience, notes Carol. Ends of branches snipped from mature holly are first rooted, then tucked into small containers. After 2 years, they're either sold in their containers or replanted out in the field, where they continue to grow for several years more.

But that doesn't mean Carol leads a leisurely life, waiting for tender shoots to toughen up. "From spring to fall, we handle holly that's sized right for folks to take home," she details. "Come midsummer, we're also pruning and shaping shrubs and trees. The 100-year-old barn we turned into a garden and gift center keeps things lively, too."

Of course, the pace doesn't slow once the mercury drops. "In November and December, we trim branches daily for use in swags and wreaths," Carol comments.

To keep the branches fresh, Carol and crew apply a special antidesiccant spray before bundling the sprigs onto wire forms, along with bunches of evergreens. "Our workshop sure smells good this time of year," she reveals.

Many of the berry-bright adornments—along with packets of fresh holly boughs—are shipped far away. A good number stick close to home, however. "My parents and I adorn our abodes with the wreaths we make," Carol grins. "It just wouldn't be a holiday around here without holly!"

Editor's Note: *If you'd like to see the holly and other pretty plantings Carol offers, stop in at Wavecrest Nursery and Landscaping Co., 2509 Lakeshore Dr., Fennville MI 49408 (call 1-616/ 543-4175 first for hours). A mail-order catalog is also available by sending $1 to that address.*

The Barn Owl Gift Shop, located on the nursery grounds, is open from mid-March until Thanksgiving. Hours are 9 a.m. to 5 p.m. Monday-Friday and noon to 5 p.m. Sundays and holidays. ●

HOLLY-DAYS happen year-round on berry merry acres Carol Hop works with father (pictured above left)! Crop, gift shop keep her busy cultivating, crafting Christmas wreaths.

WELCOME TO MY COUNTRY KITCHEN

By Mary Ellen Moison of Tilbury, Ontario

GATHERING GLAD TIDINGS. Mary Ellen Moison and clan (pictured above)—husband Paul and kids Ashley, Aaron, Alicia—enjoy congregating in spruced-up kitchen to enjoy sweet flavor of holidays!

ALTHOUGH it is warm and welcoming year-round, the heart of our home is especially inviting during December. That's when I flavor my kitchen with Yuletide flair…and folks flock there to share in the spirit of the season!

Unlike most gatherings that end up in the kitchen, the ones my family—husband Paul and kids Aaron, Alicia and Ashley—help me host start and stay right there, so decking everything just right is a big priority.

What better place to start than at the top? I turn attention toward the handsome oak cabinets by twining a pine garland adorned with beads, blooms and bows along the upper edges.

The trio of windows surrounding the sink gets the same green treatment, while the generous sill below turns lively with a collection of ceramic Christmas village pieces. The quaint buildings, trees and tiny townspeople populating that spot enhance the view of our country acreage beyond.

Dishing Up Holiday Hospitality

In anticipation of company coming, I sweeten my antique table in the adjacent dining room with a glowing fir centerpiece, crimson place mats, a plaid runner and matching napkins rolled into pine rings. Everyday plates are tucked away in a handy double-tiered rack near the sink and replaced with special white china budding with poinsettias and ribbons. For an added touch of luxury, I swathe the ceiling fan light fixtures in velvet bows.

Another favorite gathering spot, the spacious island we constructed in the kitchen, is brightened by a sack-toting Santa and pairs of green candle holders bearing cheery tapers. Seasoning the array neatly is a country fruit basket and handy wooden rack filled with Noel napkins.

These simple accents all have one thing in common—they're merrily mobile, allowing me to quickly make room for trays of cookies and other goodies I turn out each December. With its built-in dishwasher, storage drawers and shelving, my kitchen island can't be beat. It's situated perfectly, too—just steps away from cupboards, the sink and appliances.

Best of all, the island's sized right for eager elves to lend a hand…or, more likely, sneak some home-baked treats!

Additional green and red accents crop up all over, richly enhancing the woodwork we installed in both the kitchen and dining room. Look around and you'll find Santa mugs sitting on shelves near the stove, a Nativity scene animating the old-fashioned buffet, festive tins atop the cupboards and an evergreen display crowning the dining room's china cabinet.

Shades of the Season

These traditional Yuletide hues also complement my country color scheme—blue counters, mauve and green print wallpaper, tan kitchen tiles and warm wood floors in the dining room.

Even my almond refrigerator's tied into our holiday happiness, thanks to the strips of vibrant ribbon and fluffy bow I attach to the doors and the jolly Santa Claus sign taped alongside.

All this trimming sets the stage for our many get-togethers, including the most important occasion—the annual dinner I prepare and serve to our extended family each December 25.

How delightful it's been having you join in our cheery kitchen-based Christmas celebration. I hope this visit has helped make your holidays more merry—and maybe even given you a festive decorating idea or two to try!

ALL WRAPPED UP. Festive fir garlands festoon kitchen and adjacent dining room in natural beauty. Poinsettias and bows also add bright notes on light fixtures and tabletops, while a scenic ceramic village (below) enlivens sill behind sink. Even fridge (right) is prettily packaged. "You'll find doves, my favorite seasonal symbol, perched all around, too," notes Mary Ellen.

JINGLE-BELL BRUNCH! Starting clockwise from top left: Bacon Potato Omelet (p. 11), Special Long Johns (p. 11) and Christmas Breakfast Casserole (p. 11).

Holiday Brunch

BACON POTATO OMELET
Nancy Meeks, Verona, Virginia
(Pictured on page 10)

For a fun way to present basic breakfast ingredients—potatoes, eggs and bacon—try my recipe, a family favorite I inherited from my mother-in-law.

  3 bacon strips, diced
  2 cups diced peeled potatoes
  1 medium onion, chopped
  3 eggs, lightly beaten
Salt and pepper to taste
  1/2 cup shredded cheddar cheese

In a 9-in. nonstick skillet, cook bacon until crisp. Drain, reserving drippings. Set bacon aside. Cook potatoes and onion in drippings until tender, stirring occasionally. Add eggs, salt and pepper; mix gently. Cover and cook over medium heat until eggs are completely set. Sprinkle with cheese. Remove from the heat; cover and let stand until cheese is melted. Sprinkle with bacon. Carefully run a knife around edge of skillet to loosen; transfer to a serving plate. Cut into wedges. **Yield:** 3 servings.

CHRISTMAS BREAKFAST CASSEROLE
Debbie Carter, O'Fallon, Illinois
(Pictured on page 10)

Spicy sausage, herbs and vegetables fill this egg casserole with hearty flavor. I like to make it for my family's Christmas breakfast…but it's delicious anytime of day!

  1 pound bulk Italian sausage
  1 cup chopped onion
  1 jar (7 ounces) roasted red peppers, drained and
    chopped, *divided*
  1 package (10 ounces) frozen chopped spinach,
    thawed and well drained
  1 cup all-purpose flour
  1/4 cup grated Parmesan cheese
  1 teaspoon dried basil
  1/2 teaspoon salt
  8 eggs
  2 cups milk
  1 cup (4 ounces) shredded provolone cheese
Fresh rosemary sprigs, optional

In a skillet, cook sausage and onion until sausage is no longer pink; drain. Transfer to a greased 3-qt. baking dish. Sprinkle with half of the red peppers and all of the spinach. In a mixing bowl, combine flour, Parmesan cheese, basil and salt. Combine eggs and milk; add to dry ingredients and mix well. Pour over spinach. Bake at 425° for 20-25 minutes or until a knife inserted near the center comes out clean. Sprinkle with provolone cheese and remaining red peppers. Bake 2 minutes longer or until cheese is melted. Let stand 5 minutes before cutting. Garnish with rosemary if desired. **Yield:** 10-12 servings.

SPECIAL LONG JOHNS
Beverly Curp, Festus, Missouri
(Pictured on page 10)

My husband and I have been making these doughnuts regularly for years. He does the frying and I whip up the frosting.

  3 packages (1/4 ounce *each*) active dry yeast
  1/2 cup warm water (110° to 115°)
  1/2 cup shortening
  1 cup boiling water
  1 cup evaporated milk
  1/4 teaspoon lemon extract
  2 eggs
  1/2 cup sugar
  2 teaspoons salt
  1/2 teaspoon ground nutmeg
8-1/2 to 9 cups all-purpose flour
Oil for deep-fat frying
FROSTING:
  3/4 cup packed brown sugar
  6 tablespoons butter *or* margarine
  1/3 cup half-and-half cream
  3 cups confectioners' sugar
  1 teaspoon vanilla extract

In a mixing bowl, dissolve yeast in warm water. In a small bowl, combine shortening and boiling water. Stir in milk and extract; cool to 110°-115°. Add to yeast mixture. Beat in eggs, sugar, salt and nutmeg. Add enough flour to form a soft dough. Turn onto a floured surface; knead until smooth and elastic, about 5 minutes. Cover and let rest for 10 minutes. On a floured surface, roll out dough to an 18-in. x 12-in. rectangle. Cut into 6-in. x 1-in. strips. Cover and let rise in a warm place until doubled, about 1 hour. Heat oil in an electric skillet or deep-fat fryer to 375°. Fry dough strips in oil for 2 minutes or until golden brown, turning once. Drain on paper towels. For frosting, combine brown sugar, butter and cream in a saucepan. Bring to a boil; boil and stir for 2 minutes. Remove from the heat. Stir in confectioners' sugar and vanilla; beat with a portable mixer until creamy. Frost the long johns. **Yield:** 3 dozen.

CINNAMON CREAM SYRUP
Vera Reid, Laramie, Wyoming

The sugar 'n' spice flavor of this syrup enhances waffles, griddle cakes, even cooked oatmeal. I often fix it for brunches.

  1 cup sugar
  1/2 cup light corn syrup
  1/4 cup water
  3/4 teaspoon ground cinnamon
  1 can (5 ounces) evaporated milk

In a saucepan, combine the first four ingredients. Bring to a boil over medium heat; boil and stir for 2 minutes. Cool for 5 minutes. Stir in milk. Serve over pancakes, waffles or French toast. **Yield:** about 1-2/3 cups.

FLUFFY PINK FRUIT SALAD
LaDona Merwin, Hamilton, Montana

Pastel marshmallows give this salad a perky look. It makes enough for a crowd and nicely rounds out a brunch.

    1 jar (10 ounces) maraschino cherries
    1 package (8 ounces) cream cheese, softened
    2 cups whipping cream, whipped
    1 can (20 ounces) pineapple tidbits, drained
    1 can (15-1/4 ounces) fruit cocktail, drained
    1 can (15 ounces) sliced peaches, drained and diced
    6 medium firm bananas, sliced
    3 cups pastel miniature marshmallows

Drain cherries, reserving 1/3 cup juice (save remaining juice for another use). Cut cherries in half; set aside. In a mixing bowl, beat cream cheese and reserved cherry juice until smooth. Fold in whipped cream. Fold in cherries, pineapple, fruit cocktail, peaches, bananas and marshmallows. Transfer to a serving bowl. Refrigerate for at least 1 hour. **Yield:** 18-22 servings.

HOMEMADE COFFEE MIX
Toye Spence, Baker City, Oregon

Starting with a basic recipe, I created several varieties of creamy coffee drinks. They're great to offer at a get-together or to give as gifts.

BASIC COFFEE MIX:
    1/3 cup sugar
    1/4 cup non-dairy creamer
    1/4 cup instant coffee granules
ADDITIONAL INGREDIENT FOR MOCHA COFFEE:
    2 teaspoons baking cocoa
FOR ORANGE CAPPUCCINO COFFEE:
    6 orange Lifesavers, finely crushed
FOR VIENNESE COFFEE:
    1/2 teaspoon ground cinnamon

Combine coffee mix ingredients; store in an airtight container. To prepare, combine mix with 8 cups boiling water (or use 2 tablespoons mix per cup); stir until dissolved. To prepare any of the flavored coffees, add the additional ingredient to the basic mix before adding water. **Yield:** 8 servings per batch.

CHEESY BACON MUFFINS
Marilyn Gail Sharpless, Bloomington, California

Savory cheese and bacon and a pinch of cayenne pepper give these slightly sweet goodies a flavorful punch. They're versatile—you can serve them for breakfast or brunch...or with soup for lunch or supper.

1-3/4 cups all-purpose flour
    1/2 cup shredded sharp cheddar cheese
    1/4 cup sugar
    2 teaspoons baking powder
    1/4 teaspoon salt

    1/8 to 1/4 teaspoon cayenne pepper
    1 egg
    3/4 cup milk
    1/3 cup vegetable oil
    6 bacon strips, cooked and crumbled

In a large bowl, combine the first six ingredients. In another bowl, combine the egg, milk and oil; stir into dry ingredients just until moistened. Fold in bacon. Fill greased muffin cups two-thirds full. Bake at 375° for 20-25 minutes or until muffins test done. **Yield:** 8 muffins.

ORANGE-CREAM FRENCH TOAST
Marilyn Lehman, Millersville, Pennsylvania

My citrus-flavored toast adds a refreshingly fruity twist to standard brunch fare. It's also a convenient make-ahead dish.

    6 eggs
    1/2 cup orange juice
    1/3 cup half-and-half cream
    3 tablespoons sugar
    1/2 teaspoon grated orange peel
    1/4 teaspoon vanilla extract
Pinch salt
    8 to 10 slices French bread (3/4 inch thick)
    1/4 cup butter *or* margarine
ORANGE BUTTER:
    1 cup butter *or* margarine, softened
    1/3 cup orange marmalade
    3 tablespoons chopped mandarin oranges

In a mixing bowl, beat eggs, orange juice, cream, sugar, orange peel, vanilla and salt. Dip the bread in egg mixture, coating each side. Place in a greased 13-in. x 9-in. x 2-in. baking dish. Pour remaining egg mixture over the bread. Cover and refrigerate overnight. In a large skillet, melt butter; add bread. Cook for 5 minutes on each side or until golden brown. Meanwhile, combine orange butter ingredients in a small mixing bowl; beat until blended. Serve with French toast. **Yield:** 4-5 servings.

TRADITIONAL ENGLISH MUFFINS
Loretta Kurtz, Allensville, Pennsylvania

Our neighbors love these yeast treats I make. They tell me my muffins taste so much better than store-bought ones!

    2 packages (1/4 ounce *each*) active dry yeast
    1 tablespoon sugar
    3 cups warm water (110° to 115°), *divided*
    2 eggs, beaten
2/3 cup honey
    1 teaspoon salt
    9 to 10 cups all-purpose flour

In a mixing bowl, dissolve yeast and sugar in 2 cups water. Beat in eggs, honey, salt, 2 cups flour and remaining water. Add enough remaining flour to form a soft dough. Turn onto a floured surface; knead until smooth and elastic, about 6-8 minutes. Place in a greased bowl, turning once to grease top. Cover and let rise in a warm place until doubled, about 1 hour. Punch dough down. On a floured surface, roll to 1/2-in. thickness. Cover and let stand for 5 minutes. Cut into 4-in. circles. Place 2 in. apart on greased baking sheets. Bake at 375° for 8 minutes or until bottom is browned. Turn and bake 7 minutes longer or until second side is browned. Cool on wire racks. To serve, split with a fork and toast. **Yield:** about 3 dozen.

HAM AND MUSHROOM TOAST
Winnie Hanzlicek, Great Bend, Kansas

Here's a fast, fun way to use up leftover Christmas ham. The creamy mushroom sauce takes only minutes to put together, and assembling the meat and toast points is easy.

```
    3 cups sliced fresh mushrooms
1/3 cup butter or margarine
    2 tablespoons all-purpose flour
1/4 teaspoon salt
1/8 teaspoon pepper
3/4 cup chicken broth
    2 cups (16 ounces) sour cream
    2 teaspoons snipped chives
1/4 to 1/2 teaspoon dill weed
    12 toast points
    6 slices fully cooked ham, halved
```

In a saucepan, saute mushrooms in butter until tender. Stir in flour, salt and pepper until blended. Gradually add broth. Bring to a boil; boil and stir for 2 minutes. Reduce heat to low. Stir in sour cream, chives and dill; heat through. Place two slices of ham on each toast point; top with mushroom sauce. **Yield:** 6 servings.

HOME-FOR-CHRISTMAS FRUIT BAKE
Bonnie Baumgardner, Sylva, North Carolina

Pop this special dish in the oven and mouths will water in anticipation—the cinnamony aroma is tantalizing! The fruit comes out tender and slightly tart while the pecan halves add a delightful crunch.

```
1 medium apple, peeled and thinly sliced
1 teaspoon lemon juice
1 can (20 ounces) pineapple chunks
1 can (29 ounces) peach halves, drained
1 can (29 ounces) pear halves, drained
1 jar (6 ounces) maraschino cherries, drained
1/2 cup pecan halves
1/3 cup packed brown sugar
1 tablespoon butter or margarine
1 teaspoon ground cinnamon
```

Toss apple slices with lemon juice. Arrange in a greased 2-1/2-qt. baking dish. Drain pineapple, reserving 1/4 cup juice. Combine pineapple, peaches and pears; spoon over apples. Top with cherries and pecans; set aside. In a small saucepan, combine brown sugar, butter, cinnamon and reserved pineapple juice. Cook and stir over low heat until sugar is dissolved and butter is melted. Pour over fruit. Bake, uncovered, at 325° for 45 minutes or until apples are tender. Serve warm. **Yield:** 12-14 servings.

JACK CHEESE OVEN OMELET
Laurel Roberts, Vancouver, Washington

Although it's easy, the omelet looks like you fussed. Sometimes I toss in mushrooms and cheddar cheese for a different flavor.

```
    8 bacon strips, diced
    4 green onions, sliced
    8 eggs
    1 cup milk
1/2 teaspoon seasoned salt
2-1/2 cups (10 ounces) shredded Monterey Jack
      cheese, divided
```

In a skillet, cook bacon until crisp. Drain, reserving 1 tablespoon drippings. Set bacon aside. Saute onions in drippings until tender; set aside. In a bowl, beat eggs. Add milk, seasoned salt, 2 cups cheese and sauteed onions. Transfer to a greased shallow 2-qt. baking dish. Bake, uncovered, at 350° for 35-40 minutes. Sprinkle with remaining cheese. **Yield:** 6 servings.

BLUEBERRY BLINTZ SOUFFLE
Toni Anselmo, Rancho Palos Verdes, California

This luscious recipe is one I serve for Christmas and on New Year's, too. The rich blueberry syrup is delicious and easy.

```
1/4 cup butter or margarine, softened
1/3 cup sugar
    6 eggs
1-1/2 cups (12 ounces) sour cream
1/2 cup orange juice
    1 cup all-purpose flour
    2 teaspoons baking powder
FILLING:
    2 cups (16 ounces) small-curd cottage cheese
    1 package (8 ounces) cream cheese, softened
    2 egg yolks
    1 tablespoon sugar
    1 teaspoon vanilla extract
BLUEBERRY SYRUP:
    1 can (15 ounces) blueberries
    1 tablespoon cornstarch
1/2 cup corn syrup
1/2 teaspoon lemon juice
Dash salt
Dash ground cinnamon
```

In a mixing bowl, cream butter and sugar. Add eggs, one at a time, beating well after each addition. Beat in sour cream and orange juice. Combine flour and baking powder; stir into egg mixture. Set aside. Combine filling ingredients in a small mixing bowl; beat until blended. Pour half of the batter into a greased 13-in. x 9-in. x 2-in. baking dish. Top with filling and remaining batter. Bake, uncovered, at 350° for 40-50 minutes or until a knife inserted near the center comes out clean. Meanwhile, for syrup, drain blueberries, reserving juice; set berries aside. In a saucepan, combine cornstarch, corn syrup, lemon juice, salt, cinnamon and reserved blueberry juice until smooth. Bring to a boil over medium heat; boil and stir for 2 minutes or until thickened. Add blueberries; heat through. Serve warm with the souffle. **Yield:** 12 servings.

Christmas Breads

GLAZED LEMON MUFFINS
Carol Stevison, Akron, Ohio

Offer these at Christmas—and watch folks come back for more! The topping and glaze complement the lemony muffin.

1-1/2 cups all-purpose flour
1-1/2 cups sugar
  1/4 cup cold butter *or* margarine
MUFFINS:
1-1/2 cups butter *or* margarine, softened
    3 cups sugar
    6 eggs
1-1/2 cups (12 ounces) sour cream
    3 tablespoons lemon juice
    2 tablespoons grated lemon peel
4-1/2 cups all-purpose flour
  1/2 teaspoon baking soda
  1/2 teaspoon salt
GLAZE:
  3/4 cup confectioners' sugar
  1/3 cup lemon juice

In a bowl, combine flour and sugar. Cut in butter until crumbly; set aside. For muffins, cream butter and sugar in a mixing bowl. Beat in eggs, sour cream, lemon juice and peel. Combine flour, baking soda and salt; stir into creamed mixture just until moistened. Fill greased or paper-lined muffin cups two-thirds full. Sprinkle with reserved crumb topping. Bake at 350° for 25-30 minutes or until muffins test done. Cool in pans for 5 minutes before removing to wire racks. Combine glaze ingredients; drizzle over muffins. **Yield:** about 2 dozen.

CARAMEL ORANGE RING
Marjorie Poindexter, Coldwater, Mississippi

It's tradition for me to set out this sugary ring at Christmas brunch. I'm glad to do it because it's so easy! The recipe relies on purchased marmalade, refrigerated biscuits and a few other simple ingredients.

  1/2 cup orange marmalade, warmed
  1/2 cup chopped pecans
    2 cups packed brown sugar
    2 teaspoons ground cinnamon
    2 tubes (12 ounces *each*) refrigerated buttermilk
      biscuits
  1/2 cup butter *or* margarine, melted

Spoon marmalade into a greased and floured 10-in. fluted tube pan. Sprinkle with pecans. In a small bowl, combine brown sugar and cinnamon; set aside. Separate biscuits into 20 pieces. Dip in butter, then roll in the brown sugar mixture. Arrange biscuits side by side with the narrow edge standing upright. Drizzle with remaining butter; sprinkle with remaining brown sugar mixture. Bake at 350° for 30-35 minutes or until lightly browned. Cool for 10 minutes; invert onto a serving platter. **Yield:** 10-14 servings.

PECAN PUMPKIN BISCUITS
Connie Bolton, San Antonio, Texas

Our two daughters love munching on these rich pecan-studded biscuits for breakfast. I make dozens and serve them piping-hot with butter and honey.

    2 cups all-purpose flour
  1/4 cup sugar
    4 teaspoons baking powder
  1/2 teaspoon salt
  1/2 teaspoon ground cinnamon
  1/2 teaspoon ground nutmeg
  1/2 cup cold butter *or* margarine
  1/3 cup chopped pecans, toasted
  2/3 cup cooked *or* canned pumpkin
  1/3 cup half-and-half cream

In a large bowl, combine the first six ingredients. Cut in butter until mixture resembles coarse crumbs. Stir in pecans. Combine pumpkin and cream; stir into dry ingredients. Turn onto a floured surface; knead four to six times. Roll to 1/2-in. thickness; cut with a 2-1/2-in. biscuit cutter. Place on a greased baking sheet. Bake at 400° for 12-15 minutes or until golden brown. Serve warm. **Yield:** 1 dozen.

CINNAMON SWIRL BREAD
Betty Lou Wellman, Silverton, Oregon

Here's a yummy recipe for yeast bread that doesn't require kneading! The cereal in it adds moisture and a slight crunch, and the swirled cinnamon filling looks and tastes good.

    2 packages (1/4 ounce *each*) active dry yeast
  1/2 cup warm water (110° to 115°)
    1 cup warm milk (110° to 115°)
  1/2 cup butter *or* margarine, softened
    1 egg
  1/2 cup uncooked Malt-O-Meal cereal
  1/3 cup sugar
    2 teaspoons salt
    4 to 4-1/2 cups all-purpose flour
FILLING:
    1 egg white, lightly beaten
  1/2 cup sugar
    1 tablespoon ground cinnamon

In a mixing bowl, dissolve yeast in water. Add milk, butter, egg, cereal, sugar, salt and 2 cups flour; mix until smooth. Stir in enough remaining flour to form a soft dough. Do not knead. Cover and let rise in a warm place until doubled, about 1-1/4 hours. Punch dough down; divide in half. Roll each portion into a 12-in. x 7-in. rectangle. Brush with egg white. Combine sugar and cinnamon; sprinkle over rectangles. Starting with a short side, roll up tightly and seal edges. Place each in a greased 8-in. x 4-in. x 2-in. loaf pan. Cover and let rise until doubled, about 30 minutes. Bake at 375° for 40-45 minutes or until golden brown. Remove from pans to cool on wire racks. **Yield:** 2 loaves.

HERBED YEAST BREAD
Lucille Proctor, Panguitch, Utah

One year I gave away these savory loaves instead of sweet treats. Our friends so enjoyed the change of pace that they were disappointed when they didn't receive this bread the next year. I haven't let them down since!

    2 tablespoons active dry yeast
    3 cups warm water (110° to 115°), *divided*
1/4 cup butter *or* margarine, softened
    4 eggs, beaten
    1 cup sugar
2/3 cup instant nonfat dry milk powder
    2 teaspoons salt
  11 to 12 cups all-purpose flour
HERB BUTTER:
1/4 cup butter *or* margarine, melted
    2 teaspoons garlic salt
    2 teaspoons dried parsley flakes
    1 teaspoon dill weed
1/4 teaspoon dried oregano

In a mixing bowl, dissolve yeast in 1 cup water. Add butter, eggs, sugar, milk powder, salt and remaining water; mix well. Beat in 8 cups flour until smooth. Stir in enough remaining flour to form a soft dough. Turn onto a floured surface; knead until smooth and elastic, about 6-8 minutes. Place in a greased bowl, turning once to grease top. Cover and let rise in a warm place until doubled, about 1 hour. Punch dough down. Roll to 1/2-in. thickness; cut with a 2-1/2-in. biscuit cutter. Combine herb butter ingredients; brush over circles. Fold in half with buttered sides out. Place circles with folded edge down in five greased 8-cup fluted tube pans or 8-in. x 4-in. x 2-in. loaf pans. Bake at 350° for 20-25 minutes or until golden brown. **Yield:** 5 loaves.

OLD-FASHIONED MOLASSES MUFFINS
Paula Spink, Gilford, New Hampshire

The spicy aroma of these muffins in the oven is truly mouth-watering! I've fixed batches for Christmas breakfast…frozen more to snack on later…and sent plenty to school with our youngsters.

1-1/4 cups all-purpose flour
  1/4 cup sugar
  1/2 teaspoon baking soda
  1/2 teaspoon *each* ground ginger, cinnamon and
        nutmeg
  1/4 teaspoon salt
    1 egg
  1/2 cup water
  1/4 cup vegetable oil
  1/4 cup molasses

In a large bowl, combine the dry ingredients. In another bowl, beat egg, water, oil and molasses. Stir into dry ingredients just until moistened. Fill greased or paper-lined muffin cups two-thirds full. Bake at 325° for 20-25 minutes or until muffins test done. Cool in pan for 5 minutes before removing to a wire rack to cool completely. **Yield:** 9 muffins.

CRANBERRY ALMOND SWEET ROLLS
Marian Platt, Sequim, Washington
(Pictured below)

Perfect for brunch or a festive luncheon, these delicious sweet rolls feature tangy cranberries, crunchy almonds and vanilla chips. I don't save them just for special occasions, though. They're fun to serve anytime!

    1 package (16 ounces) hot roll mix
    2 tablespoons sugar
  1/2 teaspoon ground cinnamon
  1/2 teaspoon ground ginger
  1/4 teaspoon ground nutmeg
    1 cup warm water (110° to 115°)
    2 tablespoons butter *or* margarine, softened
    1 egg, beaten
    1 cup finely chopped fresh *or* frozen cranberries
    1 package (11 ounces) vanilla chips, *divided*
    1 cup slivered almonds
  1/4 cup confectioners' sugar
  1/2 teaspoon lemon juice
    3 to 4 teaspoons milk

In a large bowl, combine the contents of hot roll mix, sugar, cinnamon, ginger and nutmeg; mix well. Stir in water, butter and egg to form a soft dough. Turn onto a floured surface; knead until smooth and elastic, about 6-8 minutes. Cover and let rest for 5 minutes. Roll into a 15-in. x 10-in. rectangle; sprinkle with cranberries. Set aside 1/2 cup vanilla chips for glaze. Sprinkle almonds and remaining chips over cranberries. Roll up, starting with a long side; pinch edge to seal. Cut into 12 slices; place in a greased 13-in. x 9-in. x 2-in. baking pan. Cover and let rise in a warm place until doubled, about 30 minutes. Bake at 375° for 18-20 minutes or until lightly browned. In a saucepan over low heat, melt reserved vanilla chips. Stir in confectioners' sugar, lemon juice and enough milk to achieve desired consistency. Drizzle over warm rolls. **Yield:** 1 dozen.

HOLIDAY BREADS. Shown clockwise from top right: Cloverleaf Rolls (p. 18), Crispy Almond Strips (p. 18), Holiday Tree Bread (p. 19), Orange-Chip Cranberry Bread (p. 18) and Butterscotch Crescents (p. 18).

ORANGE-CHIP CRANBERRY BREAD
Donna Smith, Victor, New York
(Pictured on page 16)

Tart berries, crunchy nuts and sweet chocolate are simply scrumptious when mixed together in this easy quick bread. Sometimes I'll top it off with an orange-flavored glaze.

2-1/2 cups all-purpose flour
    1 cup sugar
    1 teaspoon baking soda
    1 teaspoon baking powder
1/4 teaspoon salt
    2 eggs
3/4 cup vegetable oil
    2 teaspoons grated orange peel
    1 cup buttermilk
1-1/2 cups chopped fresh *or* frozen cranberries, thawed
    1 cup miniature semisweet chocolate chips
    1 cup chopped walnuts
3/4 cup confectioners' sugar, optional
    2 tablespoons orange juice, optional

In a mixing bowl, combine the first five ingredients. In another bowl, combine eggs, oil and orange peel; mix well. Add to dry ingredients alternately with buttermilk. Fold in cranberries, chocolate chips and walnuts. Pour into two greased 8-in. x 4-in. x 2-in. loaf pans. Bake at 350° for 55-65 minutes or until a toothpick inserted near the center comes out clean. Cool for 10 minutes before removing from pans to wire racks. If glaze is desired, combine confectioners' sugar and orange juice until smooth; spread over cooled loaves. **Yield:** 2 loaves.

CLOVERLEAF ROLLS
Pam Hays, Little Rock, Arkansas
(Pictured on page 17)

Tender and tasty, these rolls have been a favorite among our friends and family for more than 23 years. I'm the official holiday baker for our clan, so I bake dozens of these come Christmas.

    2 packages (1/4 ounce *each*) active dry yeast
1/2 cup warm water (110° to 115°)
1-1/2 cups warm milk (110° to 115°)
1/2 cup sugar
    1 egg
1/4 cup shortening
    2 teaspoons salt
5-1/2 to 6 cups all-purpose flour

In a mixing bowl, dissolve yeast in water. Beat in milk, sugar, egg, shortening and salt and 2 cups of flour until smooth. Stir in enough remaining flour to form a soft dough. Turn onto a floured surface; knead until smooth and elastic, about 6-8 minutes. Place in a greased bowl, turning once to grease top. Cover and let rise in a warm place until doubled, about 1 hour. Punch dough down. Roll into 90 balls; place three balls each in greased muffin cups. Cover and let rise until doubled, about 45 minutes. Bake at 375° for 12-14 minutes or until golden brown. Cool on wire racks. **Yield:** 2-1/2 dozen.

CRISPY ALMOND STRIPS
Darlene Markel, Roseburg, Oregon
(Pictured on page 17)

Remember sprinkling cinnamon and sugar on pieces of pastry dough and popping them in the oven along with the pie you just helped make? That's what these crisp strips taste like.

    1 cup cold butter (no substitutes)
    2 cups all-purpose flour
1/2 cup sour cream
2/3 cup sugar, *divided*
    1 cup ground almonds
    1 teaspoon ground cinnamon

In a bowl, cut butter into flour until mixture resembles coarse crumbs. With a fork, stir in sour cream until blended. Divide in half; shape each half into a ball and flatten. Wrap tightly and freeze for 20 minutes. Sprinkle 1/3 cup sugar on a lightly floured surface; roll each portion of dough into a 12-in. square. Combine almonds, cinnamon and remaining sugar; sprinkle over dough. Using a rolling pin, press nut mixture into dough. Cut into 1-in. strips; cut each strip widthwise into thirds. Place 1 in. apart on greased baking sheets. Bake at 400° for 12-14 minutes or until golden brown. **Yield:** 6 dozen.

BUTTERSCOTCH CRESCENTS
Phyllis Hofer, De Witt, Iowa
(Pictured on page 16)

When I was first married, I'd try all kinds of recipes to impress my husband. These crescents were such a hit I still make them!

    1 can (12 ounces) evaporated milk, *divided*
    1 package (3-1/2 ounces) cook-and-serve butterscotch pudding mix
1/2 cup butter *or* margarine
    1 package (1/4 ounce) active dry yeast
1/4 cup warm water (110° to 115°)
    2 eggs
    2 teaspoons salt
    5 to 5-1/2 cups all-purpose flour
FILLING:
2/3 cup packed brown sugar
2/3 cup flaked coconut
1/3 cup chopped pecans
1/4 cup butter *or* margarine, melted
    2 tablespoons all-purpose flour
FROSTING:
1/4 cup packed brown sugar
    2 tablespoons butter *or* margarine
    1 cup confectioners' sugar
    2 to 3 tablespoons hot water, optional

Set aside 2 tablespoons evaporated milk for frosting. In a saucepan, combine pudding mix and remaining evaporated milk until smooth. Bring to a boil over medium heat, stirring constantly. Remove from the heat; stir in butter until melted. Let stand until mixture cools to 110°-115°. Meanwhile, in a mixing bowl, dissolve yeast in water. Beat in eggs, salt, 2 cups flour and pudding mixture until smooth. Stir in enough remaining flour to form a soft dough. Turn onto a floured surface; knead until smooth and elastic, about 6-8 minutes. Place in a greased bowl, turning once to grease top. Cover and let rise in a warm place until doubled, about 1 hour. Punch dough down and divide into thirds. Roll each portion into a 15-in. circle. Combine filling ingredients; spread 1/2 cupful over each circle. Cut each into 12 wedges; roll each into a crescent shape, starting with the wide end. Place point side down on greased baking sheets. Cover and let rise until doubled, about 45 minutes. Bake at 375° for 12-15 minutes or until golden brown. Cool on wire racks. For frosting, combine brown sugar, butter and reserved evaporated milk in a saucepan. Cook and stir over low heat until smooth. Remove from the heat; stir in confectioners' sugar until smooth. Add water if needed to achieve desired consistency. Frost crescents. **Yield: 3 dozen.**

HOLIDAY TREE BREAD
Meredith Love, San Angelo, Texas
(Pictured on page 16)

This recipe's been a hit at parties—guests just gobble it up. I learned to make bread as a child and do it all the time now.

      1 package (1/4 ounce) active dry yeast
  2/3 cup warm water (110° to 115°)
      2 eggs, beaten
  1/3 cup butter *or* margarine, melted
  1/4 cup packed brown sugar
      1 teaspoon salt
      4 to 4-1/2 cups all-purpose flour
FILLING:
      5 teaspoons cold butter *or* margarine
      3 tablespoons brown sugar
  3/4 cup chopped nuts
      2 teaspoons beaten egg
  1/2 teaspoon ground cinnamon
  1/2 teaspoon vanilla extract
GLAZE:
      1 cup confectioners' sugar
  1/2 teaspoon vanilla extract
Pinch salt
      1 to 2 tablespoons milk
Candied red *and/or* green cherries

In a mixing bowl, dissolve yeast in water. Beat in eggs, butter, brown sugar, salt and 1-1/2 cups flour until smooth. Add enough remaining flour to form a soft dough. Turn onto a floured surface; knead until smooth and elastic, about 6-8 minutes. Place in a greased bowl, turning once to grease top. Cover and let rise in a warm place until doubled, about 1 hour. Meanwhile, in a bowl, cut butter into brown sugar until crumbly. Add nuts, egg, cinnamon and vanilla; stir well. Set aside. Punch dough down. Roll to 3/8-in. thickness; let stand for 5 minutes. Cut out 15 circles with a 3-in. round cutter. Place a heaping teaspoon of filling in the center of each circle. Shape dough around filling to form a ball; pinch to seal. Line a baking sheet with foil; grease the foil. To form a tree, place one ball seam side down in the center near the top of the baking sheet. Place two balls 1/4 in. apart in the second row. Repeat with remaining balls, adding one to each row until the tree has five rows. For trunk, shape dough scraps into a rectangle and center under the last row. Cover and let rise until doubled, about 45 minutes. Bake at 350° for 20-25 minutes or until

golden brown. Carefully remove from pan to a wire rack to cool. Combine confectioners' sugar, vanilla, salt and enough milk to achieve desired consistency; drizzle over tree, forming garland. Decorate with cherries. **Yield: 15 servings.**

SAVORY ONION CORN BREAD
Ruth Chastain, Bellflower, California

My corn bread is sweet and spicy, thanks to hot pepper sauce. Serve it with chili after caroling to warm everyone up!

      1 medium sweet onion, chopped
  1/4 cup butter *or* margarine
      1 egg
      1 cup cream-style corn
  1/3 cup milk
      2 drops hot pepper sauce
      1 package (8-1/2 ounces) corn bread/muffin mix
      1 cup (8 ounces) sour cream
      1 cup (4 ounces) shredded cheddar cheese, *divided*
  1/4 teaspoon salt
  1/4 teaspoon dill weed

In a skillet, saute onion in butter until tender; set aside. In a bowl, combine egg, corn, milk and hot pepper sauce; stir in muffin mix just until moistened. Pour into a greased 8-in. square baking pan. Combine sour cream, 1/2 cup cheese, salt, dill and sauteed onion; spoon over batter. Sprinkle with remaining cheese. Bake at 425° for 30-35 minutes or until a toothpick inserted near the center comes out clean. Cut into squares; serve warm. **Yield: 9 servings.**

STRAWBERRY NUT BREAD
Eunice Morton, Longview, Texas

I like to make sandwiches out of this quick bread by spreading the strawberry cream cheese between two slices.

      2 packages (10 ounces *each*) frozen sweetened
         sliced strawberries, thawed
      3 cups all-purpose flour
      2 cups sugar
      1 teaspoon baking soda
      1 teaspoon salt
      1 teaspoon ground cinnamon
      4 eggs
  1-1/4 cups vegetable oil
      1 teaspoon red food coloring, optional
  1-1/4 cups chopped pecans
      1 package (8 ounces) cream cheese, softened

Drain strawberries, reserving 1/2 cup juice. Set berries and juice aside. In a large bowl, combine flour, sugar, baking soda, salt and cinnamon. Combine eggs, oil, strawberries and food coloring if desired; stir into dry ingredients just until moistened. Stir in pecans. Pour into two greased 9-in. x 5-in. x 3-in. loaf pans. Bake at 350° for 55-60 minutes or until a toothpick inserted near the center comes out clean. Cool for 10 minutes; remove from pans to a wire rack. In a small mixing bowl, beat cream cheese and reserved strawberry juice until fluffy; refrigerate. Serve with the bread. **Yield: 2 loaves (2 cups spread).**

TEMPTING APPETIZERS. Clockwise from top right: Elegant Cheese Torte (p. 21), Pizza Poppers (p. 21), Sausage-Filled Stars (p. 21) and Homemade Smoked Almonds (p. 21).

Appetizers

PIZZA POPPERS
Denise Sargent, Pittsfield, New Hampshire
(Pictured on page 20)

Both my husband and I are big pizza fans, so we created these pizza rolls that we like to take to parties. I think they'd be fun to set out for Santa to enjoy, along with his milk and cookies!

   4 to 4-1/2 cups all-purpose flour
1/3 cup sugar
   1 package (1/4 ounce) active dry yeast
   1 teaspoon dried oregano
1/2 teaspoon salt
   1 cup water
   1 tablespoon shortening
   1 egg
   3 cups (12 ounces) shredded mozzarella cheese
1-1/3 cups minced pepperoni (about 5 ounces)
   2 cups pizza sauce, warmed

In a mixing bowl, combine 2 cups of flour, sugar, yeast, oregano and salt. Heat water and shortening to 120°-130°; add to flour mixture along with the egg. Beat on medium speed for 1 minute. Stir in cheese and pepperoni; mix well. Add enough remaining flour to form a soft dough. Turn onto a floured surface; knead until smooth and elastic, about 6-8 minutes. Place in a greased bowl, turning once to grease top. Cover and let rise in a warm place until doubled, about 1 hour. Punch dough down; divide into four portions. Cut each portion into eight pieces; roll each piece into a 12-in. rope. Tie into a loose knot, leaving two long ends. Fold top end under roll; bring bottom end up and press into center of roll. Place on greased baking sheets. Cover and let rise until doubled, about 30 minutes. Bake at 375° for 10-12 minutes or until golden brown. Serve warm with pizza sauce. **Yield: 32 appetizers.**

HOMEMADE SMOKED ALMONDS
Sheila Flodin, Farmington, Minnesota
(Pictured on page 20)

Mom passed this recipe on to me—much to my husband's delight! We like to take the flavorful nuts to all sorts of gatherings, from fancy holiday affairs to casual luncheons.

   1 egg white
   2 teaspoons garlic powder
   2 teaspoons celery salt
1/4 teaspoon salt
1/2 teaspoon liquid smoke
   3 cups whole unblanched almonds, toasted and cooled

In a bowl, whisk egg white until foamy. Add garlic powder, celery salt, salt and liquid smoke; stir until blended. Add almonds and stir until well coated. Evenly spread almonds in a 15-in. x 10-in. x 1-in. baking pan coated with nonstick cooking spray. Bake at 300° for 30 minutes, stirring every 10 minutes. Cool. Store in an airtight container. **Yield: 3 cups.**

SAUSAGE-FILLED STARS
Minnie Bell Millsaps, McCaysville, Georgia
(Pictured on page 20)

My family loves these snacks with a savory sausage-cheese filling. The star shape makes them perfect for Christmas.

   1 pound bulk sausage
1-1/2 cups (6 ounces) shredded cheddar cheese
1-1/2 cups (6 ounces) shredded Monterey Jack cheese
   1 medium sweet red pepper, diced
   1 medium green pepper, diced
   1 can (4 ounces) chopped green chilies, drained
   1 can (4-1/2 ounces) chopped ripe olives, drained
   1 envelope ranch salad dressing mix
  48 wonton wrappers
Vegetable oil

In a skillet, cook sausage until no longer pink; drain. Add cheeses, peppers, chilies, olives and dressing mix; mix well. Set aside. Brush both sides of wrappers with oil; press onto the bottom and up the sides of greased muffin cups. Bake at 350° for 5 minutes or until golden brown. Transfer to a baking sheet. Fill each with about 2 tablespoons of the sausage mixture. Bake for 5 minutes or until heated through. Serve warm. **Yield: 4 dozen.**

ELEGANT CHEESE TORTE
Donna Cline, Pensacola, Florida
(Pictured on page 20)

Rich and creamy, this eye-catching torte makes quite an impression. Every time I take it to a party, it receives rave reviews!

   4 packages (8 ounces *each*) cream cheese, softened
   1 cup butter *or* margarine, softened
   2 teaspoons coarsely ground pepper
   1 jar (5-3/4 ounces) stuffed olives, drained and chopped
   8 cups (32 ounces) shredded sharp cheddar cheese, room temperature
3/4 cup apple cider, room temperature
2-1/4 teaspoons paprika
   1 cup chopped pecans, toasted
Grapes and assorted crackers

In a mixing bowl, beat the cream cheese and butter until smooth. Remove 3-1/2 cups to a small bowl; stir in pepper and set aside. Fold olives into the remaining cream cheese mixture. Spread evenly over the bottom of a 9-in. springform pan; set aside. In a mixing bowl, beat cheddar cheese, cider and paprika on low speed for 1 minute. Beat on high until almost smooth. Spread half over olive layer. Top with peppered cheese mixture. Top with remaining cheddar mixture. Cover with plastic wrap; refrigerate for 6 hours or until firm. Place on serving plate and remove sides of pan. Press pecans into top; garnish with grapes. Serve with crackers. **Yield: 24-30 servings.**

FESTIVE CHEESE BITES
Patricia Kile, Greentown, Pennsylvania

Over the years, these buttery cheese treats have been a handy standby at our house. I often have some extra batches in the freezer that I can pop in the oven whenever company comes calling. Usually guests are reluctant to take the last one on a tray, but not these!

    1 unsliced loaf (1 pound) Italian bread
    1 block (8 ounces) cheddar cheese, cubed
    2 packages (3 ounces *each*) cream cheese, cubed
    1 cup butter *or* margarine, cubed
    4 egg whites

Cut bread into 1-in. cubes; set aside. In a saucepan over low heat, melt the cheeses and butter. In a mixing bowl, beat egg whites until stiff peaks form. Fold into cheese mixture. Dip bread cubes into cheese mixture. Place on greased baking sheets. Bake at 375° for 12-15 minutes or until golden brown. Serve warm. **Yield:** about 10 dozen. **Editor's Note:** Unbaked appetizers may be frozen for up to 4 months. Bake as directed (they do not need to be thawed first).

CREAMY SHRIMP DIP
Pam Clayton, Brownsboro, Texas

I first tasted this seafood dip at a family reunion and requested the recipe right away. It's since become a fixture at our Christmas Day celebration, partly because it's so easy—but mostly because it's so yummy!

    1 package (8 ounces) cream cheese, softened
    1/2 cup mayonnaise
    4 green onions, chopped
    1/2 teaspoon celery seed
    1/2 teaspoon garlic powder
    2 cans (6 ounces *each*) tiny shrimp, rinsed and drained
Potato chips *or* crackers

In a bowl, combine the first five ingredients; mix well. Stir in shrimp. Refrigerate until serving. Serve with chips or crackers. **Yield:** 2 cups.

BACON-WRAPPED SCALLOPS WITH CREAM SAUCE
Barb Horstmeier, Freeport, Illinois

Although the rich seafood tidbits look complicated, they're actually easy to assemble and cook. The dipping sauce, with its hints of mustard and maple syrup, complements the scallops nicely. It's a unique appetizer.

    10 bacon strips
    10 large sea scallops
    1 cup whipping cream
    2 tablespoons Dijon mustard
    2 tablespoons maple syrup
    1/8 teaspoon salt

Place bacon in an ungreased 15-in. x 10-in. x 1-in. baking pan. Bake at 350° for 7-10 minutes or until partially cooked and lightly browned. Drain on paper towels. Wrap each strip of bacon around a scallop; secure with toothpicks. In a saucepan, bring cream to a boil. Reduce heat; simmer, uncovered, until cream is reduced to 3/4 cup, about 8 minutes. Stir in the mustard, syrup and salt. Bring to a boil and boil for 2 minutes. Meanwhile, place the scallops on a greased baking sheet. Bake at 400° for 8-12 minutes or until firm and opaque. Serve with the cream sauce. **Yield:** 10 appetizers.

SPICY PINEAPPLE SPREAD
Mavis Diment, Marcus, Iowa

Want a sweet-and-spicy treat? Set out my spread! It features a delicious mixture of warm fruit preserves, zesty horseradish and mustard, which you pour over cream cheese and serve with crackers.

    1/4 cup apple jelly
    1/4 cup pineapple preserves
    4 to 5 teaspoons prepared horseradish
    4 to 5 teaspoons ground mustard
    1 package (8 ounces) cream cheese, softened
Assorted crackers

In a saucepan, combine jelly, preserves, horseradish and mustard. Cook and stir over medium-low heat until blended. Cover and refrigerate for 1 hour. Spoon over cream cheese. Serve with crackers. **Yield:** about 2/3 cup.

PIQUANT MEATBALLS
Jennifer Wunderl, San Angelo, Texas

These meatballs, baked in a well-seasoned sauce, are always on the menu for our family's informal Christmas Eve get-togethers. Leftovers—if there are any—are a cinch to reheat in a slow cooker.

    1 can (16 ounces) jellied cranberry sauce
    1 bottle (12 ounces) chili sauce
    1 tablespoon lemon juice
    2 eggs, lightly beaten
    1 cup crushed cornflakes
    1/3 cup ketchup
    1/3 cup dried parsley flakes
    3 tablespoons soy sauce
    2 tablespoons dried minced onion
    3/4 teaspoon salt
    1/2 teaspoon pepper
    1/4 teaspoon garlic powder
    2 pounds lean ground beef

In a saucepan, combine cranberry sauce, chili sauce and lemon juice. Bring to a boil over medium heat; cook and stir until smooth. Set aside. In a bowl, combine the next nine ingredients; add beef and mix well. Shape into 1-in. balls. Place in a greased 13-in. x 9-in. x 2-in. baking dish. Pour sauce over meatballs. Bake, uncovered, at 350° for 40-50 minutes or until the meatballs are no longer pink and sauce is bubbly. **Yield:** 4 dozen.

PINEAPPLE CRANBERRY PUNCH
Paula Zsiray, Logan, Utah

Combining refreshing pineapple flavor with the zing of cranberry juice is how I created an easy-to-fix sipper to take to holiday parties.

  1 bottle (64 ounces) cranberry juice, chilled, *divided*
  1 can (20 ounces) crushed pineapple, undrained
  1 can (46 ounces) pineapple juice, chilled
  1 liter ginger ale, chilled

Combine 2 cups cranberry juice and the crushed pineapple. Pour into a 6-cup ring mold; freeze. Just before serving, combine pineapple juice and remaining cranberry juice in a punch bowl; stir in ginger ale. Add the ice ring. **Yield:** about 3-1/2 quarts.

SESAME HAM PINWHEELS
Kathleen Lally, Columbus, Ohio

Rounding out a spread at our house is the task of these ham and cheese goodies rolled in sesame seeds. Not only are these appetizers delicious, they're pretty, too!

  1 tube (8 ounces) refrigerated crescent rolls
  1 cup (4 ounces) finely shredded cheddar *or* Swiss cheese
  4 thin slices fully cooked ham
  2 teaspoons prepared mustard
  1 egg white
1/4 cup sesame seeds

Unroll crescent rolls and divide into four rectangles; seal perforations. Sprinkle with cheese. Top with ham; spread mustard over ham. Roll up from a short side; pinch seam to seal. Cut each into five slices. In a shallow bowl, beat egg white. Roll dough edges of each slice in egg white, then in sesame seeds. Place on a greased baking sheet. Bake at 350° for 15 minutes or until bottoms are golden brown. **Yield:** 20 appetizers.

SAVORY MUSHROOM TARTLETS
Judi Vreeland, Alamo, California

About these robust morsels, my husband likes to say, "I bet you can't eat just one—they're that good!" And he's right. Folks always come back for more.

48 thin slices white bread, cut into 3-inch rounds
1/2 cup butter *or* margarine, softened, *divided*
  3 tablespoons finely chopped green onions
1/2 pound fresh mushrooms, finely chopped
  2 tablespoons all-purpose flour
  1 cup whipping cream
  2 tablespoons snipped chives
  1 tablespoon minced fresh parsley
1/2 teaspoon lemon juice
1/2 teaspoon salt
Dash cayenne pepper
  2 tablespoons Parmesan cheese, optional

Spread one side of bread rounds with 1/4 cup butter; place buttered side up in lightly greased miniature muffin cups. Bake at 400° for 10 minutes or until lightly browned. Cool for 2 minutes before removing to wire racks. In a saucepan, saute onions in the remaining butter for 3 minutes. Add mushrooms; saute for 10-12 minutes or until mushroom liquid has evaporated. Remove from the heat; stir in flour and cream until blended. Bring to a boil; boil and stir for 2 minutes or until thickened. Add chives, parsley, lemon juice, salt and cayenne; mix well. Cool slightly. Place bread cups on a baking sheet; fill with mushroom mixture. Sprinkle with Parmesan cheese if desired. Bake at 350° for 10 minutes. Broil 4 in. from the heat for 2 minutes or until lightly browned. **Yield:** 4 dozen.

OLIVE CHEESE NUGGETS
Lavonne Hartel, Williston, North Dakota

More than 20 years ago, I tried these olive-stuffed treats for a holiday party. Friends are still asking me to bring them to get-togethers.

  2 cups (8 ounces) shredded cheddar cheese
1-1/4 cups all-purpose flour
1/2 cup butter *or* margarine, melted
1/2 teaspoon paprika
 36 stuffed olives

In a small mixing bowl, beat cheese, flour, butter and paprika until blended. Pat olives dry; shape 1 teaspoon of cheese mixture around each. Place 2 in. apart on ungreased baking sheets. Bake at 400° for 12-15 minutes or until golden brown. **Yield:** 3 dozen.

CHOCOLATE-RASPBERRY FONDUE
Heather Maxwell, Fort Riley, Kansas

You don't need a fancy fondue pot to make this melt-in-your-mouth concoction. I serve the dip in my small slow cooker. Folks love the chocolate-raspberry combination.

  1 package (14 ounces) caramels
  2 cups (12 ounces) semisweet chocolate chips
  1 can (12 ounces) evaporated milk
1/2 cup butter (no substitutes)
1/2 cup seedless raspberry jam
Pound cake
Assorted fresh fruit

In a large saucepan, combine the first five ingredients. Cook over low heat until caramels, chips and butter are melted, about 15 minutes. Stir until smooth. Transfer to a small slow cooker or fondue pot. Serve warm with pound cake or fruit. **Yield:** 5 cups.

> ● An ice ring can add a festive touch to punch while keeping it cold. Fill a ring mold about half full with water or juice; freeze until slushy. Place fresh cranberries or other fruit and mint sprigs or lemon leaves around the ring. Add water or juice until the mold is full; freeze until solid.

Christmas Dinner

CHEESY ROSEMARY POTATOES
Jacqueline Thompson Graves, Lawrenceville, Georgia

Turning plain potatoes into spectacular spuds is what happens whenever I follow this recipe. The cheese and seasonings make them rich and flavorful.

> 1 medium onion, thinly sliced
> 3 to 4 garlic cloves, minced
> 1 tablespoon olive *or* vegetable oil
> 4 large potatoes, peeled and diced
> 1 teaspoon seasoned salt
> 1/8 teaspoon pepper
> 1/2 teaspoon grated lemon peel
> 2 cups (8 ounces) shredded cheddar cheese, *divided*
> 1/4 cup dry bread crumbs
> 1 tablespoon butter *or* margarine, melted
> 1/2 teaspoon dried rosemary, crushed

In a large skillet or saucepan, saute onion and garlic in oil until tender. Add potatoes, seasoned salt, pepper and lemon peel. Remove from the heat. Spoon half into a greased 1-1/2-qt. baking dish. Sprinkle with 1 cup cheese. Repeat layers. Combine bread crumbs, butter and rosemary; sprinkle over cheese. Cover and bake at 400° for 40 minutes. Uncover and bake 20 minutes longer or until potatoes are tender. **Yield:** 8-10 servings.

POTATO STUFFING
Lorraine Taylor, East Hartland, Connecticut

It wouldn't be Christmas in our family without this satisfying stuffing made from potatoes. My mother-in-law shared the recipe years ago, and I've since passed it on to our grown children.

> 8 cups riced cooked potatoes
> 4 cups fine soft bread crumbs
> 2 large onions, chopped
> 1 cup butter *or* margarine
> 4 eggs, beaten
> 1 to 2 tablespoons poultry seasoning
> 2 teaspoons salt
> 1/2 teaspoon pepper
> 1 turkey (10 to 12 pounds)

In a bowl, combine the potatoes and crumbs; set aside. In a skillet, saute onions in butter until tender; add to potato mixture. Stir in eggs, poultry seasoning, salt and pepper. Just before baking, stuff turkey. Skewer and fasten openings. Tie drumsticks together. Place with breast side up on a rack in a roasting pan. Cover and bake at 325° for 3 to 3-3/4 hours or until a meat thermometer reads 180° for the turkey and 165° for the stuffing. **Yield:** 8-10 servings. **Editor's Note:** Stuffing may also be baked in a greased 2-1/2-qt. baking dish. Cover and bake at 325° for 30 minutes. Uncover and bake 10-15 minutes longer or until heated through.

HERBED VEGETABLE SQUARES
Dorothy Pritchett, Wills Point, Texas

Flavorful veggies form the foundation for this side dish that I like to serve with beef and chicken. You could use this as an appetizer, too.

> 1 package (10 ounces) frozen chopped spinach, thawed and drained
> 2 tablespoons vegetable oil
> 1-1/2 cups chopped zucchini
> 1 package (10 ounces) frozen cut green beans, thawed
> 1 large onion, chopped
> 1/4 cup water
> 1 garlic clove, minced
> 1-1/2 teaspoons dried basil
> 1-1/2 teaspoons salt
> 1/8 teaspoon pepper
> 1/8 teaspoon ground nutmeg
> 4 eggs
> 1/4 cup grated Parmesan cheese
> Paprika

Squeeze spinach dry. In a skillet, saute spinach in oil for 2 minutes. Stir in zucchini, beans, onion, water, garlic, basil, salt, pepper and nutmeg. Cover and simmer for 10 minutes, stirring occasionally. Remove from the heat. In a bowl, beat eggs; gradually stir in 1-1/2 cups vegetable mixture. Return all to pan and mix well. Transfer to a greased 11-in. x 7-in. x 2-in. baking dish. Place in a 13-in. x 9-in. x 2-in. baking dish; fill the larger dish with hot water to a depth of 1 in. Bake at 350° for 25-30 minutes or until a knife inserted near the center comes out clean. Sprinkle with the Parmesan cheese and paprika. Let stand 10 minutes before cutting. **Yield:** 6-8 servings.

CARAMEL CUSTARD
Yvonne Wyble, Port Allen, Louisiana

Although my husband isn't a fan of egg-custard desserts, he finds this one irresistible. It's rich and velvety—a perfect dish to serve warm on a wintry day.

> 2 cups whipping cream
> 4 egg yolks
> 1 teaspoon vanilla extract
> 1/4 cup sugar
> 1/8 teaspoon salt
> Brown sugar

In a saucepan over medium-low heat, bring cream almost to a simmer. Remove from the heat. In a mixing bowl, beat egg yolks, vanilla, sugar and salt until thick and lemon-colored, about 3 minutes. Gradually beat in cream. Pour into an ungreased 1-qt. baking dish. Place baking dish into a 13-in. x 9-in. x 2-in. baking pan. Pour hot water into baking pan to a depth of 1 in. Bake at 350° for 55-60 minutes or until a knife inserted near the center comes out clean.

Cool on a wire rack for 15 minutes. Refrigerate until chilled. Remove from the refrigerator 30 minutes before serving. Sprinkle with enough brown sugar to cover the top. Broil 6 in. from the heat for 2 minutes or until sugar is melted. Serve immediately. **Yield: 6 servings.**

SAVORY WILD RICE CASSEROLE
Carol King, Onalaska, Wisconsin

Seasoned with sage and tasty pork sausage, this filling rice casserole is a hearty accompaniment to roast turkey, chicken or duck. I especially like the crunch that the sliced water chestnuts add.

    3 cups water
    1 cup uncooked wild rice
1/4 teaspoon salt
    1 pound bulk pork sausage
    1 medium onion, chopped
    1 can (14-1/2 ounces) chicken broth
    1 can (10-3/4 ounces) condensed cream of
      chicken soup, undiluted
    1 can (8 ounces) mushroom stems and pieces,
      drained
    1 can (8 ounces) sliced water chestnuts, drained
    1 teaspoon rubbed sage

In a saucepan, combine water, rice and salt; bring to a boil. Reduce heat; cover and simmer for 55-60 minutes or until rice is tender. Meanwhile, in a skillet, cook sausage and onion until meat is no longer pink; drain. Add broth, soup, mushrooms, water chestnuts, sage and rice. Transfer to a greased 3-qt. baking dish. Bake, uncovered, at 350° for 45-50 minutes or until heated through. **Yield: 8-10 servings.**

SNOW-WHITE SALAD
Sharon McClatchey, Muskogee, Oklahoma

I love to collect recipes for all kinds of occasions. This sweet gelatin salad is one I often make for Christmas, decorating it with halved red candied cherries for "holly berries" and green candied cherries cut into "leaves".

    2 envelopes unflavored gelatin
1/2 cup cold water
    1 can (20 ounces) crushed pineapple, undrained
1/4 cup sugar
    2 packages (8 ounces *each*) cream cheese,
      softened
    1 jar (7 ounces) marshmallow creme
    2 envelopes whipped topping mix
Red and green candied cherries, optional

In a small bowl, combine gelatin and water; set aside. In a saucepan, bring pineapple and sugar to a boil. Remove from the heat; stir in gelatin mixture until completely dissolved. In a mixing bowl, beat cream cheese. Add marshmallow creme and pineapple mixture. Refrigerate for 30 minutes. Prepare whipped topping according to package directions; fold into pineapple mixture. Pour into an ungreased 13-in. x 9-in. x 2-in. dish. Cover and refrigerate overnight. Decorate with cherries if desired. **Yield: 16 servings.**

AFTER-CHRISTMAS TURKEY POTPIE
Leona Luecking, West Burlington, Iowa
(Pictured above)

Need ways to use up leftover turkey? This is what I like to do. The cubed poultry, tender vegetables and herbs encased in a flaky crust is a favorite at our house.

    1 cup sliced carrots
    1 cup finely chopped onion
1/2 cup chopped celery
1/2 teaspoon dried thyme
1/8 teaspoon pepper
    3 tablespoons butter *or* margarine
    2 cups cubed cooked turkey
    1 tablespoon all-purpose flour
    1 can (10-3/4 ounces) condensed golden
      mushroom soup, undiluted
    1 cup frozen cut green beans, cooked and
      drained
Pastry for double-crust pie (9 inches)
    1 tablespoon milk

In a skillet, saute carrots, onion, celery, thyme and pepper in butter until vegetables are crisp-tender. In a large resealable plastic bag, combine turkey and flour; shake to coat. Add turkey, soup and green beans to the vegetable mixture; mix well. Line a 9-in. pie plate with bottom crust. Add turkey mixture. Roll out remaining pastry to fit top of pie; seal and flute edges. Cut slits in pastry. Brush with milk. Cover edges loosely with foil. Bake at 350° for 55-65 minutes or until golden brown. Serve warm. **Yield: 6 servings.**

A FINE FESTIVE FEAST. Shown clockwise from top right: Cranberry Dream Pie (p. 28), Citrus Carrots and Sprouts (p. 29), Flavorful Lamb Chops (p. 28), Herbed Rib Roast (p. 28) and Swiss Cheese Bread (p. 28).

CRANBERRY DREAM PIE
Lila Scheer, Ocean Park, Washington
(Pictured on page 27)

Plenty of cranberries are grown in this area, so the tart and tangy fruit finds its way into my cooking quite often. This luscious pie is one I regularly prepare for our many holiday get-togethers.

   3/4 cup sugar
     2 teaspoons cornstarch
  1/4 cup cold water
     2 cups fresh *or* frozen cranberries
     2 packages (3 ounces *each*) cream cheese, softened
     1 cup confectioners' sugar
     1 teaspoon vanilla extract
     1 cup whipping cream, whipped
     1 pastry shell, baked *or* graham cracker crust (9 inches)

In a saucepan, combine sugar, cornstarch and water until smooth. Add cranberries. Bring to a boil; boil and stir for 2 minutes. Reduce heat; cook until berries pop, about 5 minutes. Set aside. In a mixing bowl, beat cream cheese, confectioners' sugar and vanilla until fluffy. Fold in whipped cream. Spread evenly into pie shell. Top with the cranberry mixture. Chill for at least 4 hours. Store in the refrigerator. **Yield:** 6-8 servings.

SWISS CHEESE BREAD
Peggy Burdick, Burlington, Michigan
(Pictured on page 26)

Not only is this hearty whole wheat loaf filled with plenty of wonderful garlic and Swiss cheese flavor, the "holes" that appear when baking make it look just like a wedge of Swiss cheese!

     3 to 3-1/2 cups all-purpose flour, *divided*
     2 cups whole wheat flour, *divided*
  1/3 cup mashed potato flakes
     2 packages (1/4 ounce *each*) active dry yeast
1-1/2 teaspoons salt
     2 cups warm milk (120° to 130°)
  1/4 cup butter *or* margarine, melted
     2 eggs
     4 to 6 garlic cloves, minced
     1 block (6 ounces) Swiss cheese, cut into 1/4-inch cubes
     1 egg yolk
     1 tablespoon water

In a mixing bowl, combine 1 cup all-purpose flour, 1 cup whole wheat flour, potato flakes, yeast and salt. Add milk and butter; beat for 2 minutes. Add eggs and garlic; beat for 2 minutes. Stir in the remaining whole wheat flour and enough remaining all-purpose flour to form a soft dough. Turn onto a floured surface; knead for 4 minutes. Sprinkle with cheese; knead 2 minutes longer or until smooth and elastic. Place in a greased bowl, turning once to grease top. Cover and let rise in a warm place until doubled, about 1 hour. Punch dough down. Divide in half; shape each half into a ball. Place on greased baking sheets; flatten to 7-in.

diameter. With a sharp knife, make three parallel slashes about 1/2 in. deep on the top of each loaf. Cover and let rise in a warm place until doubled, about 30 minutes. Beat egg yolk and water; brush over loaves. Bake at 375° for 30-35 minutes or until golden brown. Cool on wire racks. **Yield:** 2 loaves.

HERBED RIB ROAST
Carol Jackson, South Berwick, Maine
(Pictured on page 26)

The pungent mixture of herbs and garlic turns this tender roast into a real treat. Our children and grandchildren look forward to feasting on it at Christmastime and other special family occasions.

     1 boneless rib roast (4 to 5 pounds)
     2 to 3 garlic cloves, thinly sliced
     1 teaspoon salt
  1/2 teaspoon pepper
  1/2 teaspoon dried basil
  1/2 teaspoon dried parsley flakes
  1/2 teaspoon dried marjoram

Cut 15-20 slits in the roast; insert garlic. Combine salt, pepper, basil, parsley and marjoram; rub over roast. Place fat side up on a rack in a roasting pan. Bake, uncovered, at 325° for 2 to 2-1/2 hours or until meat reaches the desired doneness (for rare, a meat thermometer should read 140; medium, 160°; well-done, 170°). **Yield:** 8-10 servings.

FLAVORFUL LAMB CHOPS
Margaret Pache, Mesa, Arizona
(Pictured on page 27)

These aren't your ordinary lamb chops. I flavor them with juice squeezed from oranges and limes we grow ourselves plus a generous dash of caraway. The chops always turn out nice and tender.

     2 tablespoons orange juice
     2 tablespoons lime juice
1-1/2 teaspoons caraway seeds
  1/2 teaspoon grated orange peel
     6 loin lamb chops (about 1-3/4 pounds)
     1 tablespoon vegetable oil
  1/2 teaspoon salt
  1/2 teaspoon pepper
  1/2 cup chicken broth
Fresh orange slices and parsley sprigs, optional

In a large resealable plastic bag or shallow glass container, combine the first four ingredients; add lamb chops. Seal or cover and refrigerate overnight, turning once. Drain, reserving marinade. In a nonstick skillet over medium-high heat, brown chops in oil. Season with salt and pepper. Remove chops and keep warm. Add broth and reserved marinade to the skillet; bring to a rolling boil. Return chops to pan; reduce heat. Cover and simmer for 20 minutes. Uncover and simmer 10 minutes longer. Serve chops with the pan juices. Garnish with oranges and parsley if desired. **Yield:** 6 servings.

CITRUS CARROTS AND SPROUTS
Sherri Gentry, Dallas, Oregon
(Pictured on page 27)

I love serving brussels sprouts this way. The carrots and orange peel sweeten them up just right, while the hot pepper sauce adds a bit of zip.

 1 pound fresh brussels sprouts, halved
 1 pound fresh baby carrots
 1/4 cup butter *or* margarine, melted
 1 tablespoon grated orange peel
 1 tablespoon minced fresh parsley
 1/2 teaspoon salt
 5 to 6 drops hot pepper sauce

Place brussels sprouts and carrots in a large saucepan with a small amount of water; cover and cook until tender, about 20 minutes. Meanwhile, combine the remaining ingredients. Drain vegetables; add butter mixture and toss to coat. **Yield:** 6-8 servings.

SWEDISH FRUIT SOUP
Dolores Bean, Baldwinsville, New York

Our children expect me to make this sweet soup for the holidays. It's a delicious dessert served with pound cake and whipped cream...or offer it as a fruit compote for brunch.

 4 cups cranberry-apple juice
 1/4 cup quick-cooking tapioca
 1 medium lemon, thinly sliced
 6 whole cloves
 1/4 teaspoon ground nutmeg
 1 can (20 ounces) pineapple chunks, drained
 1 can (11 ounces) mandarin oranges, drained
 1 package (10 ounces) frozen sweetened strawberries, thawed, undrained
 1/3 cup maraschino cherry juice *or* grenadine syrup, optional
 1/8 teaspoon salt

In a 3-qt. saucepan, combine the first five ingredients; let stand for 10 minutes. Bring to a boil over medium heat. Reduce heat; cook and stir for 15 minutes or until thickened and clear. Remove from the heat; discard lemon slices and cloves. Stir in remaining ingredients. Cover and refrigerate for at least 4 hours. **Yield:** 6-8 servings.

GREENS WITH CREAMY CELERY DRESSING
Bertille Cooper, St. Inigoes, Maryland

I love to top green salads with this slightly sweet, simple-to-fix dressing. My grandchildren request it all the time!

 1/2 cup mayonnaise *or* salad dressing
 1/2 cup sour cream
 2 tablespoons sugar
 1 tablespoon lemon juice
 1 tablespoon orange juice
 1 teaspoon celery seed
 6 cups torn salad greens
 3 green onions, sliced

In a bowl, whisk the first six ingredients. In a salad bowl, combine greens and onions. Drizzle with 1/3 cup dressing; toss to coat. Store leftover dressing in the refrigerator. **Yield:** 6 servings (1 cup dressing).

FESTIVE PEAS AND ONIONS
Carmella Robichaud, Richibucto, New Brunswick

The first time I tried this recipe, my friend finished half of it while my back was turned! That was over 30 years ago, but the dish is just as popular today.

 1 package (16 ounces) frozen pearl onions
 2 cups water
 1 package (10 ounces) frozen peas, thawed
 1 can (10-3/4 ounces) condensed cream of celery soup, undiluted
 1 jar (2 ounces) diced pimientos, *divided*
 1/3 cup shredded sharp cheddar cheese

In a covered saucepan, cook onions in water for 25 minutes or until tender. Drain, reserving 1/4 cup liquid. Combine onions, peas, soup, 2 tablespoons pimientos and reserved cooking liquid; stir to coat. Transfer to a greased 1-1/2-qt. baking dish. Bake, uncovered, at 350° for 35 minutes. Sprinkle with cheese and remaining pimientos. Bake 5 minutes longer or until the cheese is melted. **Yield:** 4-6 servings.

PERFECT SCALLOPED OYSTERS
Alice King, Nevada, Ohio

My family—husband, children and grandchildren—all look forward to this easy seafood side dish. It's one I've made for well over 30 years.

 2 cups crushed butter-flavored crackers (about 54)
 1/2 cup butter *or* margarine, melted
 1/2 teaspoon salt
Dash pepper
 1 pint shucked oysters *or* 2 cans (8 ounces *each*) whole oysters
 1 cup whipping cream
 1/4 teaspoon Worcestershire sauce

Combine cracker crumbs, butter, salt and pepper; sprinkle a third into a greased 1-1/2-qt. baking dish. Arrange half of the oysters over crumbs. Top with another third of the crumb mixture and the remaining oysters. Combine cream and Worcestershire sauce; pour over oysters. Top with remaining crumb mixture. Bake, uncovered, at 350° for 30-40 minutes or until top is golden brown. **Yield:** 8 servings.

> ● Citrus fruit peel contains flavorful oils that enhance foods. To easily grate the peel, use the small holes on a hand grater, being careful not to cut into any of the white pith.

Holiday Cookies

MOCHA TRUFFLE COOKIES
Sherrie Pickle, Kent, Washington

Cocoa and coffee come together deliciously in these treats preferred by my husband. I like to make extras to tuck in gift baskets for friends and family.

      1/2 cup butter *or* margarine
1-1/2 cups (9 ounces) semisweet chocolate chips,
      divided
      2 to 3 teaspoons instant coffee granules
      2 eggs
      3/4 cup sugar
      3/4 cup packed brown sugar
      2 teaspoons vanilla extract
      2 cups all-purpose flour
      1/3 cup baking cocoa
      1/2 teaspoon baking powder
      1/4 teaspoon salt

In a saucepan over low heat, melt butter and 1/2 cup chocolate chips. Remove from the heat; stir until smooth. Stir in coffee granules; cool for 5 minutes. Stir in eggs, sugars and vanilla. Combine flour, cocoa, baking powder and salt; fold into the chocolate mixture. Add the remaining chocolate chips. Drop by rounded teaspoonfuls 2 in. apart onto greased baking sheets. Bake at 350° for 9-11 minutes or until tops appear slightly dry and cracked. Cool for 1 minute before removing to wire racks. **Yield:** about 5-1/2 dozen.

MINTY CHOCOLATE CRACKLES
Pat Habiger, Spearville, Kansas

Each December, I whip up big batches of these chewy mint morsels, then watch them disappear in a flash! Everyone I know enjoys them.

      1 cup (6 ounces) semisweet chocolate chips
1/2 cup plus 4-1/2 teaspoons shortening
      3/4 cup sugar
      1 egg
1/4 cup light corn syrup
      1 teaspoon peppermint extract
      1 teaspoon vanilla extract
      2 cups all-purpose flour
1/2 teaspoon baking soda
1/4 teaspoon salt
1/4 cup crushed peppermint candy
Additional sugar

In a microwave or double boiler, melt chocolate chips; cool slightly. In a mixing bowl, cream shortening and sugar. Beat in egg, corn syrup, extracts and melted chocolate. Combine flour, baking soda and salt; gradually add to the creamed mixture. Fold in candy. Roll into 1-in. balls; roll in sugar. Place 2 in. apart on ungreased baking sheets. Bake at 350° for 12-14 minutes or until edges are firm and surface cracks (center will be soft). Cool for 5 minutes before removing to wire racks. **Yield:** about 4 dozen.

CARAMEL DATE PINWHEELS
Doris Barb, El Dorado, Kansas

When I want to make a cookie with fruit in it, this recipe is my first choice. It turns out well each time and has earned plenty of praise, including ribbons at our state fair.

      2/3 cup butter *or* margarine, softened
      1 cup packed brown sugar
      1 egg
      1 teaspoon vanilla extract
1-3/4 cups all-purpose flour
      1/2 teaspoon baking soda
      1/4 teaspoon salt
FILLING:
      1 package (8 ounces) chopped dates
      1/3 cup sugar
      1/2 cup water
      1/2 cup finely chopped walnuts
      2 tablespoons chopped red candied cherries

In a mixing bowl, cream butter and brown sugar. Beat in egg and vanilla. Combine flour, baking soda and salt; gradually add to the creamed mixture. Refrigerate for at least 2 hours. Meanwhile, in a saucepan, combine dates, sugar and water. Cook and stir over medium heat until thickened, about 5 minutes. Stir in walnuts and cherries. Cool completely. Divide dough in half; roll one portion between two sheets of waxed paper into a 12-in. x 10-in. rectangle. Spread with half of the filling. Roll up into a tight jelly roll, starting with a long side; wrap in waxed paper. Repeat with remaining dough and filling. Cover and refrigerate for 2 hours or until firm. Cut into 3/8-in. slices with a sharp knife; place 1 in. apart on greased baking sheets. Bake at 375° for 8-10 minutes or until lightly browned. Remove to wire racks to cool. **Yield:** 7-8 dozen.

COCONUT RASPBERRY BARS
Amanda Denton, Barre, Vermont

While mixing a batch of plain bars, I was inspired to add raspberry preserves and flaked coconut to the dough...and wound up with these yummy treats, now a family favorite.

      3/4 cup butter *or* margarine, softened
      1 cup sugar
      1 egg
1/2 teaspoon vanilla extract
      2 cups all-purpose flour
1/4 teaspoon baking powder
      2 cups flaked coconut, *divided*
1/2 cup chopped walnuts
      1 jar (12 ounces) raspberry preserves
      1 cup vanilla chips

In a mixing bowl, cream butter and sugar. Beat in egg and vanilla. Combine flour and baking powder; gradually add to the creamed mixture. Stir in 1-1/4 cups coconut and the walnuts. Press three-fourths of the dough into a greased

13-in. x 9-in. x 2-in. baking pan. Spread with preserves. Sprinkle with chips and remaining coconut. Crumble remaining dough over the top; press lightly. Bake at 350° for 30-35 minutes or until golden brown. Cool on a wire rack. Cut into squares. **Yield:** 3 dozen.

LIME SPRITZ COOKIES
Lori Daniels, Elkins, West Virginia

The refreshing citrus flavor in these pressed cookies comes from lime gelatin. They're easy, festive and delightfully different— always a big hit at potlucks and luncheons.

1-1/2 cups butter (no substitutes), softened
    1 cup sugar
    1 package (3 ounces) lime gelatin
    1 egg
    1 teaspoon vanilla extract
    4 cups all-purpose flour
    1 teaspoon baking powder
Red and green colored sugar, optional

In a mixing bowl, cream butter, sugar and gelatin. Beat in egg and vanilla. Combine flour and baking powder; gradually add to the creamed mixture. Using a cookie press fitted with the disk of your choice, press dough into desired shapes 2 in. apart onto ungreased baking sheets. Sprinkle with colored sugar if desired. Bake at 350° for 8-10 minutes or until set. Remove to wire racks to cool. **Yield:** 14 dozen.

BLACK FOREST OATMEAL CRISPS
Paula Smith, Naperville, Illinois

Although the recipe for my hearty chocolate-cherry novelties is sized right for a bake sale or cookie exchange, it can be cut in half for smaller gatherings.

    1 cup butter-flavored shortening
    1 cup sugar
    1 cup packed brown sugar
    2 eggs
    2 tablespoons milk
    1 teaspoon almond extract
1-2/3 cups all-purpose flour
    1 teaspoon baking soda
    3/4 teaspoon salt
    1/2 teaspoon baking powder
2-1/2 cups quick-cooking oats
    6 squares (1 ounce *each*) white baking chocolate, chopped *or* 1 cup vanilla chips
1-1/2 cups chopped red candied cherries
    1 cup (6 ounces) semisweet chocolate chips
    3/4 cup slivered almonds

In a mixing bowl, cream shortening and sugars. Add the eggs, one at a time, beating well after each addition. Beat in milk and extract. Combine flour, baking soda, salt and baking powder; gradually add to the creamed mixture. Stir in the remaining ingredients. Drop by heaping teaspoonfuls 2 in. apart onto ungreased baking sheets. Bake at 375° for 8-10 minutes or until golden brown. Remove to wire racks to cool. **Yield:** about 14 dozen.

SPUMONI SLICES
Mary Chupp, Chattanooga, Tennessee
(Pictured below)

My sweet rectangles get their name from the old-fashioned tri-colored ice cream. Our whole family prefers them.

    1 cup butter *or* margarine, softened
1-1/2 cups confectioners' sugar
    1 egg
    1 teaspoon vanilla extract
2-1/2 cups all-purpose flour
    2 squares (1 ounce *each*) semisweet chocolate, melted
    1/2 cup chopped pecans
    3 to 5 drops green food coloring
    1/4 cup finely chopped candied red cherries
    1/2 teaspoon almond extract
    3 to 5 drops red food coloring

In a mixing bowl, cream butter and sugar. Beat in egg and vanilla. Gradually add flour and mix well. Divide dough into three portions. Stir chocolate into one portion; mix well. Add pecans and green food coloring to the second portion. Add cherries, almond extract and red food coloring to the third. Roll each portion between two pieces of waxed paper into an 8-in. x 6-in. rectangle. Remove waxed paper. Place chocolate rectangle on a piece of plastic wrap. Top with the green and pink rectangles; press together lightly. Wrap with plastic wrap and chill overnight. Cut chilled dough in half lengthwise. Return one rectangle to the refrigerator. Cut remaining rectangle into 1/8-in. slices. Place 1 in. apart on ungreased baking sheets. Bake at 375° for 5-7 minutes or until set. Cool for 2 minutes before removing to wire racks. Repeat with remaining dough. **Yield:** about 7 dozen.

CHRISTMAS COOKIE COLLECTION. Clockwise from top right: Chocolate Fruit 'n' Nut Cookies (p. 35), Frosted Spice Cutouts (p. 34), Gingerbread Rings (p. 35), Chewy Pecan Drops (p. 34), Rich Chocolate Cream Bars (p. 34) and Cardamom Almond Biscotti (p. 34).

FROSTED SPICE CUTOUTS
Pamela Drake, Ventura, California
(Pictured on page 33)

The spicy taste of these cutouts is a festive change of pace from ordinary sugar cookies. Everyone in our house favors them.

> 1/2 cup butter (no substitutes), softened
> 1 cup vegetable oil
> 3/4 cup sugar
> 4 cups all-purpose flour
> 2 teaspoons baking powder
> 1 teaspoon ground cinnamon
> 1/2 teaspoon ground cloves
> 1/2 teaspoon ground nutmeg
> 1/3 cup milk
> **FROSTING:**
> 2 cups confectioners' sugar
> 2 tablespoons plus 2 teaspoons water
> Red and green paste food coloring, optional

In a mixing bowl, cream butter, oil and sugar. Combine flour, baking powder, cinnamon, cloves and nutmeg; gradually add to the creamed mixture. Beat in milk. Divide dough in half. Cover and refrigerate for 8 hours or overnight (dough will be soft). On a lightly floured surface, roll out one portion at a time to 1/4-in. thickness. Cut into desired shapes. Place 2 in. apart on ungreased baking sheets. Bake at 350° for 12-15 minutes or until edges begin to brown. Remove to wire racks. For frosting, beat confectioners' sugar and water in a mixing bowl. Add food coloring if desired. Frost cooled cookies. **Yield:** about 4 dozen.

RICH CHOCOLATE CREAM BARS
Michele Paul, Fort Collins, Colorado
(Pictured on page 32)

Thick and fudgy, these treats only look fussy. The truth is, they're layered bars that don't require any baking time at all! My grandmother concocted the recipe years ago.

> 1/2 cup butter (no substitutes)
> 5 tablespoons baking cocoa
> 1/4 cup sugar
> 1 egg, beaten
> 1 teaspoon vanilla extract
> 1-1/2 cups graham cracker crumbs (about 24 squares)
> 1 cup flaked coconut
> 1/2 cup chopped walnuts
> **FILLING:**
> 1/4 cup butter (no substitutes), softened
> 3 tablespoons milk
> 2 tablespoons instant vanilla pudding mix
> 2 cups confectioners' sugar
> 1 teaspoon vanilla extract
> **GLAZE:**
> 4 squares (1 ounce *each*) semisweet chocolate
> 1 tablespoon butter (no substitutes)

In the top of a double boiler, combine butter, cocoa, sugar, egg and vanilla. Cook and stir over simmering water until mixture reaches 160° and is thickened. In a large bowl, combine graham cracker crumbs, coconut and walnuts. Stir in cocoa mixture; blend well. Press into a greased 9-in.

square baking pan; set aside. For filling, combine butter, milk and pudding mix in a mixing bowl. Gradually beat in confectioners' sugar and vanilla until smooth; spread over crust. For glaze, melt chocolate and butter; spread over filling. Cover and refrigerate until set. Cut into bars. **Yield:** about 3 dozen.

CARDAMOM ALMOND BISCOTTI
Verna Eberhart, Watertown, South Dakota
(Pictured on page 32)

These crunchy slices are requested often during the holidays, particularly by my husband. He likes to dunk them in coffee.

> 1 cup butter (no substitutes), softened
> 1-3/4 cups sugar
> 2 eggs
> 2 teaspoons almond extract
> 5-1/4 cups all-purpose flour
> 1 teaspoon salt
> 1 teaspoon baking soda
> 1 teaspoon ground cardamom
> 1 cup (8 ounces) sour cream
> 1 cup chopped almonds

In a mixing bowl, cream butter and sugar. Add eggs, one at a time, beating well after each addition. Beat in extract. Combine flour, salt, baking soda and cardamom; add to the creamed mixture alternately with sour cream. Fold in almonds. Divide dough into fourths; shape each portion into a ball. On two greased baking sheets, roll each ball into a 15-in. log (two logs per pan). Bake at 350° for 30 minutes or until lightly browned and firm to the touch. Transfer to a cutting board; cut diagonally with a sharp knife into 1/2-in. slices. Place with cut side down on greased baking sheets. Bake for 10-12 minutes or until lightly browned. Remove to wire racks to cool. Store in airtight containers. **Yield:** about 7 dozen.

CHEWY PECAN DROPS
Violet Klause, Onoway, Alberta
(Pictured on page 32)

The cherry center gives a festive look to my nutty cookies. They're easy to make and take to holiday gatherings.

> 2 cups ground pecans
> 1/2 cup all-purpose flour
> 1-1/4 cups sugar, *divided*
> 4 egg whites
> 1/2 teaspoon vanilla extract
> 5 to 6 maraschino cherries, coarsely chopped

In a large bowl, combine pecans, flour and 1 cup sugar; set aside. In a small mixing bowl, beat egg whites until foamy. Gradually add remaining sugar, beating until stiff peaks form. Fold in vanilla and half of the flour mixture. Fold in remaining flour mixture. Drop by rounded teaspoonfuls 2 in. apart onto ungreased foil-lined baking sheets. Top each with a cherry piece. Bake at 325° for 20-25 minutes or until edges are lightly browned. Cool completely before removing from pans. **Yield:** about 5 dozen.

CHOCOLATE FRUIT 'N' NUT COOKIES
Valerie Putsey, Winamac, Indiana
(Pictured on page 33)

Filled with fruit, nuts, chocolate and loads of flavor, these traditional Italian treats hit the spot. We enjoy them at Christmas with a hot beverage.

>   6 tablespoons butter *or* margarine
> 1/3 cup milk
> 1/4 cup sugar
>   2 tablespoons honey
>   1 cup sliced almonds
> 1/2 cup mixed candied fruit, finely chopped
> 1/4 cup all-purpose flour
> 3/4 cup semisweet chocolate chips
>   2 tablespoons shortening

In a saucepan, combine butter, milk, sugar and honey. Bring to a full boil. Remove from the heat; stir in almonds and fruit. Stir in flour until blended. Drop by tablespoonfuls 3 in. apart onto greased and floured baking sheets. Spread batter with a spoon to form 2-1/2-in. circles. Bake at 350° for 6-9 minutes or until edges are lightly browned. Cool on pans for 1 minute before carefully removing to waxed paper to cool completely. For coating, combine chocolate chips and shortening in a small saucepan. Cook over low heat until melted. Spread 1 teaspoonful over the bottom of each cookie. When chocolate is almost set, draw wavy lines with a fork or cake decorating comb. Store in the refrigerator. **Yield:** about 2 dozen.

GINGERBREAD RINGS
Donna Hinton, Lincoln, Nebraska
(Pictured on page 32)

Baking batches of cookies in early December always puts me in the mood for Christmas. This particular recipe yields quite a bit, so I end up with plenty for my family and can still give some away to friends, too.

>   1 cup shortening
>   2 cups sugar
>   2 egg yolks
>   1 cup water
>   1 cup light molasses
>   8 cups all-purpose flour
>   2 teaspoons baking soda
> 1-1/2 teaspoons ground ginger
>   1 teaspoon ground cinnamon
>   1 teaspoon ground allspice
> 3/4 teaspoon salt
> FROSTING:
> 2-1/2 cups sugar
> 1/2 cup water
> 1/2 teaspoon light corn syrup
>   2 egg whites
>   1 teaspoon vanilla extract
> Red and green decorating gel, optional

In a mixing bowl, cream shortening and sugar. Beat in egg yolks, water and molasses. Combine dry ingredients; gradually add to the creamed mixture. Cover and refriger-ate for 2 hours or until easy to handle. On a lightly floured surface, roll out to 1/4-in. thickness. Cut with a 2-3/4-in. doughnut cutter. Remove and discard centers. Place 2 in. apart on ungreased baking sheets. Bake at 350° for 10 minutes or until set. Remove to wire racks. In a heavy saucepan, combine the sugar, water and corn syrup. Bring to a boil; cook until a candy thermometer reads 238° (soft-ball stage), about 5 minutes. Remove from the heat. In a mixing bowl, beat egg whites and vanilla until soft peaks form. Gradually add sugar mixture, beating on high for 7-8 minutes or until thickened. Frost cookies. Decorate if desired. **Yield:** about 5 dozen.

ALMOND CRESCENTS
Sandi Murray, Bismarck, North Dakota

To me, it isn't Christmas until my kitchen is filled with these almond cookies baking by the dozens. My husband, children and grandchildren all heartily agree!

>   1 cup butter (no substitutes), softened
> 1/3 cup sugar
> 1-2/3 cups all-purpose flour
> 3/4 cup finely ground almonds
> 1/4 teaspoon salt
> 1/2 cup confectioners' sugar
>   1 teaspoon ground cinnamon

In a mixing bowl, cream butter and sugar. Combine flour, almonds and salt; gradually add to the creamed mixture. Cover and refrigerate for 1 hour or until easy to handle. Divide dough into fourths. Roll out each portion into a long rope, about 1/4 in. in diameter. Cut into 2-in. lengths. Place 2 in. apart on lightly greased baking sheets; form each into a crescent. Bake at 325° for 14-16 minutes or until set. Cool for 2 minutes. Combine confectioners' sugar and cinnamon; dip warm cookies in sugar mixture. Place on wire racks to cool. **Yield:** about 10 dozen.

RASPBERRY KISSES
Ruth Vanderberg, Liberty, Missouri

These light and airy drops, bursting with bits of chocolate, have long been a holiday favorite at our house. I often make them for luncheons and teas.

>   3 egg whites
> 1/8 teaspoon salt
> 3/4 cup sugar
>   3 tablespoons plus 2 teaspoons raspberry gelatin powder
>   1 tablespoon vinegar
>   1 cup miniature chocolate chips

In a mixing bowl, beat egg whites and salt until foamy. Combine sugar and gelatin powder; gradually add to egg whites, beating until stiff peaks form and sugar is dissolved. Beat in vinegar. Fold in the chocolate chips. Drop by teaspoonfuls 2 in. apart onto parchment paper-lined baking sheets. Bake at 250° for 25 minutes. Turn oven off, leaving kisses in the oven 20 minutes longer. Remove to wire racks to cool. **Yield:** about 6 dozen.

CHEERY CONFECTIONS. Shown clockwise from the top: Chocolate Toffee Crunchies (p. 37), Dandy Caramel Candies (p. 37), Cinnamon Hard Candy (p. 37) and Sugary Orange Peel (p. 37).

Seasonal Sweets

DANDY CARAMEL CANDIES
Marlene Pierce, Welch, Texas
(Pictured on page 36)

I've made these morsels almost every Christmas for the past 35 years. Everyone enjoys the chewy treats.

    1 cup sugar
    1 cup packed brown sugar
    1 cup dark corn syrup
    1 cup butter (no substitutes)
    2 cups whipping cream
3-3/4 cups chopped pecans (about 1 pound)
    1 teaspoon vanilla extract
Dark *or* milk chocolate confectionery coating,* melted

In a heavy saucepan, combine sugars, corn syrup, butter and cream. Bring to a boil over medium-high heat, stirring constantly. Cook over medium heat until a candy thermometer reads 248° (firm-ball stage). Remove from the heat; stir in pecans and vanilla. Quickly spread into a buttered 13-in. x 9-in. x 2-in. baking pan. Cool. Cut into 1-in. squares. Place squares on waxed paper-lined baking sheets; chill thoroughly. Dip each candy into melted confectionery coating. Return to refrigerator to harden. **Yield:** about 8 dozen. ***Editor's Note:** Confectionery coating is found in the baking section of most grocery stores. It is sometimes labeled "candy coating" and is often sold in bulk packages of 1 to 1-1/2 pounds.

CINNAMON HARD CANDY
Mary Ellen Geigley, Willcox, Arizona
(Pictured on page 36)

My Amish aunt made dozens of these spicy red squares for holiday gatherings when I was a tot. I'd always look for them glowing among the other candies she'd carry in! Nowadays, I stir up her recipe for my family.

    2 cups sugar
    1 cup water
1/2 cup light corn syrup
1/4 to 1/2 teaspoon cinnamon oil*
1/2 teaspoon red food coloring

In a large heavy saucepan, combine sugar, water and corn syrup. Bring to a boil over medium heat, stirring occasionally. Cover and cook for 3 minutes. Uncover and cook over medium-high heat, without stirring, until a candy thermometer reads 310° (hard-crack stage). Remove from the heat; stir in oil and food coloring, keeping face away from the mixture as the odor will be very strong. Immediately pour onto a greased baking sheet. Quickly spread into a 13-in. x 9-in. rectangle. Using a sharp knife, score into 1-in. squares. Recut rectangle along scored lines until candy is cut into squares. Let stand at room temperature until dry. Separate into squares, using a knife if necessary. **Yield:** 1 pound. ***Editor's Note:** Cinnamon oil can be found in some pharmacies or at kitchen and cake decorating supply stores.

SUGARY ORANGE PEEL
Alice Schmidlin, Banks, Oregon
(Pictured on page 36)

These sugar-coated citrus strips attract lots of compliments whenever I set them out at parties.

    4 medium navel oranges
2 to 3 cups sugar, *divided*
    1 cup water
1/2 teaspoon salt
1/2 cup semisweet chocolate chips, optional
    2 teaspoons shortening, optional

With a knife, score the peel from each orange into quarters. With fingers, remove peel with white pith attached. Place peel in a saucepan; cover with water. Bring to a boil. Boil, uncovered, for 30 minutes. Drain and repeat twice. Meanwhile, in another saucepan, combine 1 cup of sugar, water and salt. Bring to a boil; boil and stir for 2 minutes or until sugar is dissolved. Drain peel and add to syrup. Bring to a boil; reduce heat. Simmer, uncovered, for 50-60 minutes or until syrup is almost all absorbed, stirring occasionally. (Watch carefully to prevent scorching.) Drain any remaining syrup. Cool orange peel in a single layer on a foil-lined baking sheet for 1 hour. Cut into 1/8-in. to 1/4-in. strips. Sprinkle remaining sugar on an ungreased 15-in. x 10-in. x 1-in. baking pan. Sprinkle strips over sugar; toss to coat. Let stand for 8 hours or overnight, tossing occasionally. If desired, melt chocolate chips and shortening. Dip one end of each orange strip into chocolate; let stand on waxed paper until chocolate hardens. Store in an airtight container for up to 3 weeks. **Yield:** 5 cups.

CHOCOLATE TOFFEE CRUNCHIES
Joni Crans, Woodhull, New York
(Pictured on page 36)

From the buttery crust to the golden toffee, melted chocolate and chopped pecans, these bars are filled with Noel flavor.

    2 cups vanilla wafer crumbs
1/4 cup packed brown sugar
1/2 cup butter (no substitutes), melted
TOPPING:
1/2 cup butter (no substitutes)
1/2 cup packed brown sugar
    1 cup (6 ounces) semisweet chocolate chips
1/2 cup finely chopped pecans

Combine crumbs, brown sugar and butter. Press into an ungreased 13-in. x 9-in. x 2-in. baking pan. Bake at 350° for 8-10 minutes or until lightly browned. In a saucepan, bring butter and brown sugar to a boil over medium heat; boil and stir for 1 minute. Pour evenly over crust. Bake at 350° for 10 minutes. Remove from oven; let stand for 2 minutes. Sprinkle with chocolate chips; let stand until chocolate is melted. Spread evenly over top; sprinkle with pecans. Cool completely before cutting. **Yield:** 4 dozen.

DIPPED PEANUT BUTTER LOGS
Paddy Schwemlein, Sandwich, Illinois

Nibbling on my nutty confections has long been a Christmas tradition. Even after our seven children moved away, they'd still ask me to send batches to them each December.

   1 cup butter (no substitutes), melted
  1/2 cup chunky peanut butter
  3-3/4 cups confectioners' sugar
  3-3/4 cups (10 ounces) flaked coconut
   1 cup chopped pecans
  1/2 cup graham cracker crumbs (about 8 squares)
   2 teaspoons vanilla extract
   2 cups (12 ounces) semisweet chocolate chips
   2 tablespoons shortening

In a mixing bowl, combine the first seven ingredients; mix well. Chill for 1 hour or until firm enough to shape. Shape into 2-in. logs; place on a waxed paper-lined baking sheet. In a microwave or double boiler, melt chocolate chips and shortening. Dip one end of each log into chocolate or drizzle chocolate over logs. Return to waxed paper-lined sheet; chill until chocolate is set. **Yield:** about 4 dozen.

BUTTERMILK PRALINES
Dorothy Purdy, Fontanelle, Iowa

Years ago, I received this candy recipe from a dear friend in Texas. The creamy texture and sumptuous sweetness has earned me rave reviews each time I've made it.

   2 cups sugar
   1 cup buttermilk
   1 teaspoon baking soda
   1 tablespoon butter (no substitutes)
 1-1/2 cups pecan halves
   1 teaspoon vanilla extract

In a heavy 3-qt. saucepan, combine sugar, buttermilk and baking soda. Cook and stir over medium heat until a candy thermometer reads 210°. Stir in butter and pecans; cook until thermometer reads 230°. Remove from the heat; add vanilla. Beat with a wooden spoon until mixture loses its gloss and begins to set, about 8 minutes. Quickly drop by teaspoonfuls onto foil-lined baking sheets. Cool. **Yield:** 1-1/2 pounds.

FESTIVE POPCORN BARS
Ella Scheller, Odessa, Washington

For a popcorn ball taste but with less fuss, try these bars. Adding peanut butter and M&M's makes them fun. They're a hit with all ages.

   4 cups popped popcorn
   3 cups puffed rice cereal
   2 cups peanut M&M's
   1 cup light corn syrup
   1 cup sugar
  1/4 cup butter (no substitutes)
  3/4 cup peanut butter

In a large greased bowl, combine the popcorn, cereal and M&M's; set aside. In a heavy saucepan, combine the corn syrup, sugar and butter. Cook and stir over low heat until sugar is dissolved. Add peanut butter; stir until blended. Pour over popcorn mixture; toss gently to coat. Spread into a greased 15-in. x 10-in. x 1-in. baking pan. Cool before cutting. **Yield:** about 3 dozen.

RASPBERRY TRUFFLES
J. Hill, Sacramento, California

Although they look fussy, these melt-in-your-mouth delights are actually a cinch to make. What's more, they're a hit everywhere I take them.

  1/2 cup evaporated milk
  1/4 cup sugar
   1 package (11-1/2 ounces) milk chocolate chips
  1/4 cup seedless raspberry preserves
  1/2 teaspoon instant coffee granules
  3/4 cup finely chopped almonds, toasted

In a heavy saucepan, combine milk and sugar. Bring to a rolling boil over medium heat; boil and stir for 3 minutes. Remove from the heat; stir in chocolate chips, preserves and coffee until mixture is smooth. Chill for 1 hour. Roll into 1-in. balls; roll in almonds. Place on waxed paper-lined baking sheets. Chill until firm. Cover and store in the refrigerator. **Yield:** 2-1/2 dozen.

PEANUT BUTTER MALLOW CANDY
Rita Goshaw, South Milwaukee, Wisconsin

My children loved these treats when they were growing up. I still like to make them since they're so easy.

   2 packages (10 ounces *each*) peanut butter
    or butterscotch chips
  3/4 cup butter (no substitutes)
  1/2 cup peanut butter
   1 package (10-1/2 ounces) miniature
    marshmallows
  3/4 cup chopped peanuts
  3/4 cup flaked coconut

In a microwave or double boiler, heat chips, butter and peanut butter until melted. Add remaining ingredients and mix well. Spread into a lightly greased 15-in. x 10-in. x 1-in. baking pan. Refrigerate until firm. Cut into squares. **Yield:** about 5 dozen.

CHOCOLATE CARAMEL WAFERS
Susan Laubach, Vida, Montana

To keep my holiday cooking quick, I've come to rely on fast recipes like this one. The crunchy-chewy tidbits are our youngsters' favorite.

   1 package (14 ounces) caramels
  1/4 cup evaporated milk

1 package (12 ounces) vanilla wafers
8 plain milk chocolate candy bars (1.55 ounces *each*), broken into squares
Chopped pecans, optional

Place caramels and milk in a microwave-safe bowl; microwave, uncovered, on high for 3 minutes or until melted. Stir until smooth. Spread over vanilla wafers; place on ungreased baking sheets. Top each with a square of chocolate. Place in a 225° oven for 1-2 minutes or until chocolate is melted. Spread with an icing knife. Top with pecans if desired. **Yield:** about 7 dozen. **Editor's Note:** This recipe was tested in an 850-watt microwave.

SPEEDY OVEN FUDGE
Beverly Bernholtz, Lake City, Iowa

This rich fudge is a holiday favorite for me and my family. The recipe yields plenty of old-fashioned flavor with no-fuss preparation.

1/2 cup milk
1 cup butter (no substitutes)
2/3 cup baking cocoa
2 pounds confectioners' sugar
2 teaspoons vanilla extract
1 cup chopped nuts

Place the first four ingredients in the order listed in a 3-qt. baking dish (do not stir). Place in a 350° oven for 15 minutes or until butter is melted. Carefully transfer to a mixing bowl. Add vanilla; beat on high for 2 minutes. Stir in nuts. Pour into a buttered 11-in. x 7-in. x 2-in. baking pan. Cool before cutting. **Yield:** 3 pounds.

NUTTY SANDWICH TREATS
Kim Rehfeldt, Bellingham, Washington

The ingredients in my layered snacks provide plenty of texture and flavor. Plus, kids can help out by spreading the filling on the graham crackers.

2/3 cup chunky peanut butter
2 tablespoons butter (no substitutes)
1 cup miniature marshmallows
1/2 cup chopped pecans
8 whole graham crackers (4-3/4 inches x 2-1/2 inches)
6 ounces white confectionery coating,* melted

In a saucepan over low heat, cook and stir peanut butter and butter until blended. Stir in marshmallows until melted. Remove from the heat; fold in pecans. Break or cut each graham cracker into four pieces. Spread with peanut butter mixture; top with remaining crackers. Spread confectionary coating over both sides. Line a baking sheet with lightly greased waxed paper; place crackers on waxed paper and chill until firm. **Yield:** 16 treats. ***Editor's Note:** Confectionery coating is found in the baking section of most grocery stores. It is sometimes labeled "almond bark" or "candy coating" and is often sold in bulk packages of 1 to 1-1/2 pounds.

SUGARPLUMS
Suzanne McKinley, Lyons, Georgia

When our kids read about sugarplums in a holiday tale, they were intrigued…and so was I! In short order, I figured out a no-bake way to make the sweets from dried fruits and nuts.

1 package (15 ounces) raisins
1 package (12 ounces) pitted prunes
1 package (8 ounces) dried mixed fruit
1-1/2 cups chopped pecans
Sugar

In a food processor, coarsely chop raisins, prunes, mixed fruit and pecans. Transfer to a bowl; mix well. Roll into 1-in. balls, then roll in sugar. Place on waxed paper and let stand at room temperature for 4 hours. Store in an airtight container. Roll in additional sugar before serving if desired. **Yield:** about 8 dozen.

COCONUT SURPRISE CANDY
Irene Smith, Lidgerwood, North Dakota

What's the secret ingredient in these dipped balls? Mashed potatoes! The spuds create the creamy texture, while coconut and chocolate chips figure big in the flavor.

2-1/2 cups flaked coconut
2-1/2 cups confectioners' sugar
1/3 cup mashed potatoes (prepared without milk and butter)
1 cup (6 ounces) semisweet chocolate chips
1 tablespoon shortening
Chopped walnuts, optional

In a large bowl, combine coconut, sugar and mashed potatoes; mix well. Roll into 1-in. balls; place on waxed paper-lined baking sheets. In a microwave or double boiler, melt chocolate chips and shortening; stir until smooth. Dip the balls into chocolate and then walnuts if desired. Return to waxed paper until chocolate is set. **Yield:** about 4 dozen.

ORANGE-SUGARED PECANS
Nancy Johnson, Laverne, Oklahoma

I regularly cook up these candied pecans for Christmas gift-giving and family munching. The citrusy-sweet flavor is different and delicious.

1-1/2 cups sugar
1/4 cup water
3 tablespoons orange juice concentrate
2 cups pecan halves
1/2 teaspoon grated orange peel

In a heavy saucepan, combine sugar, water and orange juice concentrate. Cook over medium-high heat, without stirring, until a candy thermometer reads 238° (soft-ball stage). Remove from the heat; stir in pecans and orange peel. Beat with a spoon until mixture thickens and loses its gloss, about 2 minutes. Drop by teaspoonfuls onto waxed paper to harden. Store in an airtight container. **Yield:** 2-1/2 dozen.

DELIGHTFUL DESSERTS! Clockwise from top: White Christmas Cake (p. 41), Coffee Cream Pie (p. 41) and Almond Fruit Squares (p. 41).

ALMOND FRUIT SQUARES
Iola Egle, McCook, Nebraska
(Pictured on page 40)

These sweet squares are easy to fix, thanks to the refrigerated crescent roll dough that serves as the crust!

  2 tubes (8 ounces *each*) refrigerated crescent rolls
  3 tablespoons sugar, *divided*
  1 package (8 ounces) cream cheese, softened
1/3 cup almond paste
1/2 teaspoon almond extract
  2 cups halved fresh strawberries
  1 can (11 ounces) mandarin oranges, drained
  1 cup fresh raspberries
  1 cup halved green grapes
  2 kiwifruit, peeled, quartered and sliced
1/2 cup apricot preserves, warmed
1/2 cup slivered almonds, toasted

Unroll crescent dough and separate into eight rectangles. Place in an ungreased 15-in. x 10-in. x 1-in. baking pan. Press onto bottom and up sides; seal seams and perforations. Sprinkle with 1 tablespoon sugar. Bake at 375° for 14-16 minutes or until golden brown. Cool. In a mixing bowl, beat cream cheese, almond paste, extract and remaining sugar until smooth. Spread over crust. Top with fruit. Brush with preserves; sprinkle with almonds. **Yield:** 16 servings.

WHITE CHRISTMAS CAKE
Sue Ross, Casa Grande, Arizona
(Pictured on page 40)

Garnished with red and green gumdrops, this moist cake makes a holiday statement! The white chocolate, almond and coconut flavors taste even better a day after baking.

  1 cup butter *or* margarine, softened
  2 cups sugar
  4 eggs
  4 ounces white confectionery coating, melted
  1 teaspoon almond extract
  1 teaspoon vanilla extract
2-1/2 cups cake flour
  1 teaspoon baking powder
  1 cup buttermilk
  1 cup flaked coconut
White frosting

In a mixing bowl, cream butter and sugar. Add eggs, one at a time, beating well after each addition. Add confectionery coating and extracts; beat well. Combine the flour and baking powder; add to creamed mixture alternately with buttermilk. Stir in coconut. Pour into two greased 9-in. round baking pans. Bake at 350° for 30 minutes or until a toothpick inserted near the center comes out clean. Cool for 10 minutes before removing from pans to wire racks to cool completely. Frost between layers; frost top and sides of cake. **Yield:** 12 servings.

COFFEE CREAM PIE
Letha DeMoss, Ames, Iowa
(Pictured on page 40)

I created this sweet coffee-flavored recipe as an entry for our state fair, adding the toffee topping to "dress it up". I'm glad I did—the pie won first place and is now a family holiday favorite!

2/3 cup sugar
1/2 cup all-purpose flour
1/2 teaspoon salt
  2 cups milk
  3 tablespoons instant coffee granules, crushed
  3 egg yolks, lightly beaten
  2 tablespoons butter *or* margarine
  2 teaspoons vanilla extract
  1 chocolate crumb crust (8 *or* 9 inches)
TOPPING:
  1 teaspoon instant coffee granules
  1 cup whipping cream
  2 tablespoons confectioners' sugar
1/2 teaspoon vanilla extract
  1 Heath candy bar (1.4 ounces), crushed*

In the top of a double boiler, combine the sugar, flour and salt; gradually stir in milk until smooth. Cook and stir over boiling water until thickened, about 10 minutes. Stir in coffee granules. Gradually stir a small amount into egg yolks; return all to pan. Cook and stir for 3 minutes. Remove from the heat; add butter and vanilla. Cool for 30 minutes. Pour into crust; chill. In a mixing bowl, dissolve coffee granules in a small amount of cream. Add sugar, vanilla and remaining cream. Whip until stiff peaks form. Spread over filling; sprinkle with crushed candy bar. Chill. **Yield:** 6-8 servings. ***Editor's Note:** Candy bar crushes easily if frozen.

HOLIDAY CRANBERRY COBBLER
Helen Weissinger, Caribou, Maine

For a change of pace from pumpkin pie, I prepare this merry berry cobbler at Christmas. Our children, grandchildren and great-grandchild all enjoy it.

  1 can (21 ounces) peach pie filling
  1 can (16 ounces) whole-berry cranberry sauce
  1 package (18-1/4 ounces) yellow cake mix
  1 teaspoon ground cinnamon
1/4 teaspoon ground nutmeg
  1 cup cold butter *or* margarine
  1 cup chopped nuts
Vanilla ice cream *or* whipped cream

Combine pie filling and cranberry sauce. Spread in an ungreased 13-in. x 9-in. x 2-in. baking dish. In a bowl, combine dry cake mix, cinnamon and nutmeg; cut in butter until crumbly. Stir in nuts; sprinkle over fruit. Bake at 350° for 35-40 minutes or until a toothpick inserted near the center of cake comes out clean. Serve warm with ice cream or whipped cream. **Yield:** 12-15 servings.

SPICE CAKE BARS
Dena Hayden, Vassar, Michigan

Whenever I went to Grandmother's, she served these flavorful bars, topped with creamy frosting. Today, I do the same for our grandchildren, who like the little treats just as much.

- 1 cup butter *or* margarine, softened
- 1 cup sugar
- 1 cup molasses
- 1 cup hot water
- 1 egg
- 3 cups all-purpose flour
- 2 teaspoons ground ginger
- 2 teaspoons ground allspice
- 1 teaspoon baking soda
- 1 teaspoon ground cloves

FROSTING:
- 1/2 cup shortening
- 1/2 cup butter *or* margarine, softened
- 2 to 3 teaspoons lemon juice
- 4 cups confectioners' sugar

In a mixing bowl, cream butter and sugar. Beat in molasses, water and egg. Combine flour, ginger, allspice, baking soda and cloves; gradually add to the creamed mixture. Pour into a greased 15-in. x 10-in. x 1-in. baking pan. Bake at 375° for 18-22 minutes or until a toothpick inserted near the center comes out clean. Cool on wire rack. In a mixing bowl, cream shortening, butter and lemon juice. Beat in sugar until fluffy. Frost bars. **Yield:** about 2 dozen.

NUTCRACKER SWEET
Patty Webb, Calgary, Alberta

My mother baked this chocolate-almond dessert for family gatherings and her bridge club meetings when I was growing up. Continuing the tradition, I take the cake to potlucks, neighborhood parties and Christmas celebrations.

- 1 cup graham cracker crumbs (about 16 squares)
- 1 cup finely chopped almonds
- 1 square (1 ounce) unsweetened chocolate, grated
- 6 eggs, *separated*
- 1 cup sugar, *divided*
- 1/4 cup all-purpose flour
- 1-1/4 teaspoons baking powder
- 1-1/4 teaspoons ground cinnamon
- 1/4 teaspoon ground cloves
- 2 tablespoons vegetable oil
- 1 teaspoon almond extract

ALMOND CREAM:
- 2 cups whipping cream
- 1/2 cup confectioners' sugar
- 1/2 teaspoon almond extract
- Grated semisweet chocolate, optional

Combine the crumbs, almonds and chocolate; set aside. In a small mixing bowl, beat egg whites until foamy. Gradually beat in 1/2 cup sugar until stiff peaks form; set aside. In a large mixing bowl, combine the flour, baking powder, cinnamon, cloves and remaining sugar. In another bowl, beat egg yolks, oil and extract. Add to dry ingredients; beat on medium speed for 1 minute. Stir in crumb mixture. Fold in egg whites. Pour into two greased 9-in. round baking pans lined with greased waxed paper. Bake at 350° for 30-35 minutes or until a toothpick inserted near the center comes out clean. Cool for 10 minutes; remove from pans to wire racks. Carefully remove waxed paper; cool completely. In a mixing bowl, beat cream and confectioners' sugar until soft peaks form. Add extract; beat until stiff peaks form. Split cake layers in half horizontally; spread almond cream over each layer. Stack on a serving plate. (Do not frost sides of cake.) Garnish with grated semisweet chocolate if desired. Cover and refrigerate overnight. **Yield:** 12-16 servings.

SNOWFLAKE PUDDING
Patricia Stratton, Muskegon, Michigan

Flakes of coconut give my pudding it's snow-like texture— and plenty of taste besides! The crimson currant-raspberry sauce is delicious and pretty, too.

- 1 envelope unflavored gelatin
- 1-1/4 cups milk, *divided*
- 1/2 cup sugar
- 1/2 teaspoon salt
- 1 teaspoon vanilla extract
- 1-1/3 cups flaked coconut, toasted
- 1 cup whipping cream, whipped

SAUCE:
- 1 package (10 ounces) frozen sweetened raspberries, thawed
- 1-1/2 teaspoons cornstarch
- 1/2 cup red currant jelly

In a small bowl, combine gelatin and 1/4 cup milk; let stand for 1 minute. In a saucepan, combine sugar, salt and remaining milk; heat just until sugar is dissolved. Remove from the heat; stir in gelatin mixture and vanilla. Refrigerate until partially set. Fold in coconut and whipped cream. Pour into dessert dishes or small bowls; refrigerate for at least 2 hours. Meanwhile, strain raspberries to remove seeds. Combine cornstarch, raspberry pulp and currant jelly in a saucepan; stir until smooth. Bring to a boil; boil and stir for 2 minutes. Chill for at least 1 hour. Pour sauce over pudding just before serving. **Yield:** 6 servings.

MINCEMEAT TRIFLE
Mary Pilgrim, Oromocto, New Brunswick

Instead of fixing a traditional pie, I gussied up mincemeat by creating this fancy trifle. The recipe's a time-saver, since it can be prepared a day ahead.

- 6 egg yolks
- 2 cups milk
- 2/3 cup sugar
- 4 teaspoons grated lemon peel
- 1/4 teaspoon salt
- 2 teaspoons vanilla extract
- 2 cups prepared mincemeat
- 1/3 cup lemon juice
- 1 prepared angel food cake (10 inches)

1 cup whipping cream
3 tablespoons confectioners' sugar
Red and green candied cherries, optional

In a saucepan, combine egg yolks, milk, sugar, lemon peel and salt until blended. Cook over medium-low heat until mixture reaches 160°, about 12-15 minutes. Remove from the heat; stir in vanilla. Cover and refrigerate for 1 hour. Meanwhile, combine mincemeat and lemon juice. Tear cake into 1-in. cubes; place a third of the cake in a trifle bowl or 2-qt. serving bowl. Top with a third of the custard and half of the mincemeat. Repeat layers. Top with remaining custard. In a mixing bowl, beat cream and confectioners' sugar until soft peaks form; spread over custard. Garnish with cherries if desired. Cover and chill for at least 2 hours. **Yield:** 8-10 servings.

WALNUT APPLE CAKE
Dorothy Anderson, Ottawa, Kansas

Loaded with tart apples and crunchy walnuts, this cake is fun to take to potlucks or family gatherings. The sweet buttery sauce tops off pieces just right.

    1/2 cup butter *or* margarine, softened
    2 cups sugar
    2 eggs
    2 cups all-purpose flour
    1 teaspoon baking powder
    3/4 teaspoon baking soda
    1/2 teaspoon salt
    1/2 teaspoon ground cinnamon
    1/2 teaspoon ground nutmeg
    3 cups chopped peeled tart apples (about 3)
1-1/2 cups chopped walnuts
SAUCE:
    1 cup sugar
    1/2 cup butter *or* margarine
    1/2 cup half-and-half cream
    1/2 teaspoon rum extract

In a mixing bowl, cream butter and sugar. Add eggs, one at a time, beating well after each addition. Combine flour, baking powder, baking soda, salt, cinnamon and nutmeg; gradually add to the creamed mixture. Stir in apples and walnuts. Spoon into a greased 13-in. x 9-in. x 2-in. baking pan. Bake at 325° for 45-50 minutes or until a toothpick inserted near the center comes out clean. In a saucepan, combine sugar, butter and cream; mix well. Cook over low heat until heated through. Remove from the heat; stir in extract. Serve warm with the cake. **Yield:** 12-16 servings.

PUMPKIN MOUSSE CHEESECAKE
Dawn Oswald, Kailua, Hawaii

Fresh from the vine comes my merry after-dinner delight! The scrumptious pumpkin filling makes this cheesecake different from most, and the glaze adds a nice touch. It's a big hit among my family and friends.

    1 cup graham cracker crumbs (about 16 squares)
    3 tablespoons sugar

    1/4 cup butter *or* margarine, melted
FILLING:
    3 packages (8 ounces *each*) cream cheese, softened
    1 cup sugar
    1 cup cooked *or* canned pumpkin
    3 tablespoons all-purpose flour
    1 teaspoon ground cinnamon
    1/4 teaspoon ground nutmeg
    4 eggs
GLAZE:
    1/2 cup vanilla chips
    1 tablespoon shortening

Combine crumbs, sugar and butter. Press into a greased 9-in. springform pan. Bake at 325° for 8 minutes. Cool on a wire rack. Meanwhile, in a mixing bowl, beat cream cheese and sugar until smooth. Add pumpkin, flour, cinnamon and nutmeg. Add eggs; beat on low speed just until combined. Pour into crust. Bake for 50 minutes or until center is almost set. Cool on a wire rack for 10 minutes. Carefully run a knife around edge of pan to loosen; cool 1 hour longer. Refrigerate overnight. In a saucepan over low heat, melt chips and shortening; stir until smooth. Drizzle over cheesecake. Refrigerate until firm, about 30 minutes. **Yield:** 12-14 servings.

MARBLED PEPPERMINT ANGEL CAKE
Kathy Kittell, Lenexa, Kansas

Although it doesn't puff up as much as other angel food cakes during baking, the refreshing minty flavor and festive red swirls raise this version above ordinary desserts!

1-1/2 cups egg whites (about 12)
1-1/2 teaspoons cream of tartar
1-1/2 teaspoons vanilla extract
    1 teaspoon peppermint extract
    1/4 teaspoon salt
1-1/2 cups sugar, *divided*
    3/4 cup all-purpose flour
    6 drops red food coloring, optional
GLAZE:
    2 cups confectioners' sugar
    1/4 cup milk
    1/4 teaspoon peppermint extract
    6 drops red food coloring, optional
    1/4 cup crushed peppermint candies

In a mixing bowl, beat egg whites, cream of tartar, extracts and salt on high speed. Gradually add 3/4 cup of sugar, beating until stiff peaks form and sugar is dissolved. Combine flour and remaining sugar; gradually fold into the batter, 1/4 cup at a time. Divide batter in half; tint half with red food coloring. Alternately spoon plain and pink batters into an ungreased 10-in. tube pan. Cut through the batter with a knife to remove air pockets. Bake at 350° for 30-40 minutes or until cake springs back when lightly touched. Immediately invert pan; cool completely. Run a knife around sides of cake and remove from the pan. For glaze, combine confectioners' sugar, milk, extract and food coloring if desired. Drizzle over cake. Sprinkle with crushed candies. **Yield:** 12-16 servings.

TASTEFUL CHRISTMAS GIFTS. Clockwise from top left: Nutmeg Logs (p. 45), Golden Fruitcake (p. 45) and Gift-Wrapped Brownies (p. 45).

Gifts from the Kitchen

GOLDEN FRUITCAKE
Ruth Hempstead, Royal Oak, Michigan
(Pictured on page 44)

Fruitcake has been favored by my family ever since my sister shared this light version. It's moist and filled with goodies.

2 packages (15 ounces *each*) golden raisins
1-1/2 cups shortening
2-1/4 cups sugar
8 eggs
1 teaspoon vanilla extract
4 cups all-purpose flour
1 teaspoon cream of tartar
1 teaspoon salt
1/2 teaspoon baking soda
1/2 cup milk
2-1/2 cups chopped walnuts
1-1/3 cups diced candied pineapple (about 8 ounces)
1 cup chopped candied cherries (about 8 ounces)
1 cup flaked coconut

Place raisins in a bowl; cover with boiling water and let stand for 5 minutes. Drain well and set aside. In a mixing bowl, cream shortening and sugar. Add eggs, one at a time, beating well after each addition. Beat in vanilla. Combine dry ingredients; add to the creamed mixture alternately with milk. Stir in the walnuts, pineapple, cherries, coconut and raisins. Spoon into nine greased 5-3/4-in. x 3-in. x 2-in. loaf pans. Bake at 300° for 65-75 minutes or until a toothpick inserted near the center comes out clean. Cool for 10 minutes before removing from pans to wire racks. **Yield:** 9 loaves. **Editor's Note:** Fruitcakes can be baked in two batches. Refrigerate batter until baking.

NUTMEG LOGS
Marjorie Gegelmann, Bismarck, North Dakota
(Pictured on page 44)

The crispy-tender texture and mildly spicy flavor of these cookies will tempt all ages. My whole family enjoys them.

1 cup butter (no substitutes), softened
3/4 cup sugar
1 egg
2 teaspoons vanilla extract
3 cups all-purpose flour
1-1/2 teaspoons ground nutmeg
1/4 teaspoon salt
Additional sugar

In a mixing bowl, cream butter and sugar. Beat in egg and vanilla. Combine flour, nutmeg and salt; gradually add to the creamed mixture. Cover and chill for 1 hour or until firm. On a sugared surface, shape 1/2 cupfuls of dough into 1/2-in.-thick logs. Cut logs into 2- to 2-1/2-in. pieces. Place 2 in. apart on ungreased baking sheets. Bake at 350° for 12-14 minutes or until lightly browned. Remove to wire racks to cool. **Yield:** about 5 dozen.

GIFT-WRAPPED BROWNIES
Doris Roots, Big Timber, Montana
(Pictured on page 44)

With bright green and red frosting "ribbon" piped on top, these chocolaty "packages" are a pretty addition to any holiday gathering. They'll make a sweet gift for everyone on your Christmas list!

1/2 cup shortening
4 squares (1 ounce *each*) semisweet baking chocolate
3 eggs
1 cup sugar
2 teaspoons vanilla extract, *divided*
1/2 cup all-purpose flour
1/2 cup chopped nuts
1/2 teaspoon salt
1/2 teaspoon baking powder
2 cups confectioners' sugar
1/4 cup whipping cream
Red and green food coloring

In a small saucepan over low heat, melt shortening and chocolate; set aside. In a mixing bowl, beat eggs, sugar and 1 teaspoon vanilla. Add the flour, nuts, salt, baking powder and chocolate mixture; mix well. Pour into a greased 8-in. square baking pan. Bake at 350° for 20-25 minutes or until a toothpick inserted near the center comes out clean. Cool on a wire rack. Cut into 2-in. x 1-in. rectangles; remove from pan. In a bowl, combine confectioners' sugar, cream and remaining vanilla; set half aside. Spread remaining frosting over top of brownies. Tint half of the reserved frosting red and half green. Cut a small hole in the corner of two plastic or pastry bags; fill one bag with red frosting and one with green. Insert pastry tip if desired. To decorate brownies, pipe ribbon and bows as shown in photo (at left) or create designs of your choice. **Yield:** 2-1/2 dozen.

ROSY CIDER JELLY
Regina Stock, Topeka, Kansas

For an easy-to-prepare present, try this jelly made with cider and cranberry juice. I got the recipe, now a family favorite, from our local county Extension office.

3 cups apple cider
1 cup cranberry juice
1 teaspoon lemon juice
1 package (1-3/4 ounces) powdered fruit pectin
5 cups sugar

In a large kettle, combine the first four ingredients. Bring to a rolling boil over high heat, stirring constantly. Stir in sugar. Return to a full rolling boil; boil for 1 minute, stirring constantly. Remove from the heat; skim off any foam. Pour hot liquid into hot jars, leaving 1/4-in. headspace. Adjust caps. Process for 5 minutes in a boiling-water bath. **Yield:** 6 half-pints.

CONFETTI BEAN SOUP MIX
Rebecca Lambert, Staunton, Virginia

With its colorful variety of beans and delicious flavor, this soup is tempting. I like to give it to friends each Christmas.

   1 pound *each* dry navy beans, great northern
      beans, red kidney beans, pinto beans and green
      split peas
SEASONING MIX:
   12 beef bouillon cubes
   3/4 cup dried minced chives
   6 teaspoons salt
   4 teaspoons dried savory
   2 teaspoons ground cumin
   2 teaspoons coarsely ground pepper
   4 bay leaves
ADDITIONAL INGREDIENTS FOR SOUP:
   12 cups water, *divided*
   1 can (14-1/2 ounces) stewed tomatoes
   1/4 teaspoon hot pepper sauce, optional

Combine beans and peas; place 3-1/4 cups each in four large resealable plastic bags. Set aside. In four snack-size resealable plastic bags or on four squares of plastic wrap, place 3 bouillon cubes, 3 tablespoons chives, 1-1/2 teaspoons salt, 1 teaspoon savory, 1/2 teaspoon cumin, 1/2 teaspoon pepper and 1 bay leaf. Seal bags or tie plastic wrap with ribbon if desired. **To prepare soup:** Place the contents of one bag of beans in a Dutch oven; add 7 cups water. Bring to a boil; boil for 2 minutes. Remove from the heat; cover and let stand for 1 hour. Drain beans and discard liquid. Add remaining water and contents of one seasoning bag. Bring to a boil. Reduce heat; cover and simmer for 1 hour or until beans are tender, stirring occasionally. Add tomatoes and hot pepper sauce if desired. Simmer, uncovered, for 20 minutes. Discard bay leaf before serving. **Yield:** 4 batches, 9 servings (2-1/4 quarts) per batch.

PRETZEL WREATHS
Roberta Spieker, Duncan, South Carolina

Youngsters love to lend a hand with this recipe. Our two girls help me measure, pour, stir, shape…and, of course, eat the chewy pretzel rounds when they're done!

   1 package (1/4 ounce) active dry yeast
1-1/2 cups warm water (110° to 115°)
   4 cups all-purpose flour
   1 tablespoon sugar
   1 teaspoon salt
   1 egg white, lightly beaten
Coarse salt *or* colored sugar

In a mixing bowl, dissolve yeast in water; let stand for 5 minutes. Add 2 cups flour, sugar and salt; beat until smooth. Stir in enough remaining flour to form a soft dough. Turn onto a floured surface; knead until smooth and elastic, about 6 minutes. Cover and let rest for 15 minutes. Divide dough into 16 portions. Roll each portion into a 15-in. rope. Fold each rope in half and twist two or three times; shape into a circle and pinch ends together. Place on greased baking sheets. Brush with egg white; sprinkle with salt or sugar. Bake at 425° for 12-15 minutes. **Yield:** 16 pretzels.

NUTTY CARAMEL POPCORN
Sharon Buchinski, Endeavour, Saskatchewan

Folks who've tasted my snack are quick to remind me to make it again for them the following Christmas! The sugary combination of popcorn and crunchy nuts really hits the spot.

   4 quarts popped popcorn
1-1/3 cups pecan halves, toasted
   2/3 cup whole unblanched almonds, toasted
1-1/3 cups sugar
   1 cup butter (no substitutes)
   1/2 cup light corn syrup
   2 teaspoons vanilla extract

Place popcorn in a large greased bowl. Sprinkle pecans and almonds over top; set aside. In a heavy saucepan, combine the sugar, butter and corn syrup; cook and stir over medium heat until a candy thermometer reads 300°-310° (hard-crack stage). Remove from the heat; stir in vanilla. Immediately pour over popcorn mixture; toss gently. Spread on greased baking sheets. When cool, break into small pieces. Store in airtight containers. **Yield:** about 20 cups.

CURRIED RICE MIX
Pat Kelly, Worthington, West Virginia

Giving containers filled with homemade goodies is my merry habit. This zesty rice side dish is a particular favorite.

   2 cups uncooked long grain rice
   1 cup chopped dried mixed fruit
   1 cup slivered almonds
   1/2 cup golden raisins
   2 tablespoons dried minced onion
   4 teaspoons beef bouillon granules
   4 teaspoons curry powder
   1 teaspoon salt
ADDITIONAL INGREDIENTS FOR RICE:
2-1/2 cups water
   2 tablespoons butter *or* margarine

In a large bowl, combine the first eight ingredients. Store in an airtight container. **To prepare rice:** Combine water and butter in a saucepan; bring to a boil. Add 2 cups rice mix; reduce heat. Cover and simmer for 20 minutes or until liquid is absorbed. **Yield:** 2 batches, 4-6 servings per batch.

FUDGY WALNUT SAUCE
Dorothy Bateman, Carver, Massachusetts

This rich sauce will satisfy any sweet tooth. It tastes great poured over pound cake or drizzled on scoops of ice cream.

   1 cup sugar
   1/2 cup half-and-half cream
   2 squares (1 ounce *each*) unsweetened chocolate
   2 squares (1 ounce *each*) semisweet chocolate
   1/2 cup butter (no substitutes)
   2 egg yolks
   1 teaspoon vanilla extract
   1 cup coarsely chopped walnuts

In a saucepan, combine sugar and cream. Bring to boil over medium heat, stirring occasionally. Add chocolate and butter; stir until melted. Remove from the heat. In a small bowl, beat egg yolks. Whisk a small amount of the chocolate mixture into yolks. Return all to the pan; whisk until smooth. Bring to a gentle boil; cook and stir for 2 minutes. Remove from the heat; stir in vanilla and walnuts. Pour into jars; cool. Cover and store in the refrigerator. To serve, reheat in a double boiler or microwave. **Yield:** 2 cups.

PLUM-APPLE BUTTER
Nancy Michel, Lakeland, Florida

I look forward to cooking up this fruity spread each December, using the plums I picked and froze during summer.

    2 pounds tart apples, peeled and quartered
    2 pounds plums, pitted and quartered
    1 cup water
    3 cups sugar
1-1/2 teaspoons ground cinnamon
    1 teaspoon ground nutmeg
1/4 teaspoon ground allspice

Place apples, plums and water in a large kettle; cover and simmer until tender, about 15 minutes. Cool. Puree in batches in a food processor or blender; return all to the kettle. Add sugar and spices. Simmer, uncovered, for 20-30 minutes or until thickened, stirring frequently. Cool completely. Pour into jars. Cover and store in the refrigerator for up to 3 weeks. **Yield:** 5 cups.

CINNAMON GRANOLA
Linda Agresta, Colorado Springs, Colorado

Although it's meant for breakfast, my family eats this crunchy cereal by the handful all day long.

    2 cups old-fashioned oats
3/4 cup whole unsalted nuts
2/3 cup flaked coconut
1/2 cup sunflower kernels
1/3 cup sesame seeds
1/3 cup wheat germ
1/4 cup oat bran
    2 tablespoons cornmeal
    2 tablespoons whole wheat flour
    1 tablespoon ground cinnamon
1/2 cup honey
    2 tablespoons vegetable oil
    2 tablespoons vanilla extract
1/4 teaspoon salt
    1 cup golden raisins

In a large bowl, combine the first 10 ingredients; mix well. In a saucepan over medium heat, cook honey and oil for 4-5 minutes. Remove from the heat; stir in vanilla and salt. Pour over oat mixture and toss to coat. Transfer to a greased 15-in. x 10-in. x 1-in. baking pan. Bake at 275° for 45-50 minutes or until golden brown, stirring every 15 minutes. Cool, stirring occasionally. Stir in raisins. Store in an airtight container. **Yield:** 7 cups.

DANISH COFFEE CAKE
Marjorie Hanson, Rose Valley, Saskatchewan

Filled with almond paste, sugar and butter, this pastry will melt in your mouth. It's a must for me to make each holiday.

    1 package (1/4 ounce) active dry yeast
    2 tablespoons plus 1 teaspoon sugar, *divided*
1/4 cup warm water (110° to 115°)
2-1/2 cups all-purpose flour
1/2 teaspoon salt
1/2 cup cold butter *or* margarine
    1 egg
1/2 cup whipping cream
FILLING:
    1 can (8 ounces) almond paste, cubed
1/4 cup packed brown sugar
1/4 cup butter *or* margarine, softened
    1 egg
    1 teaspoon water
GLAZE:
    1 cup confectioners' sugar
1/4 teaspoon almond extract
    2 to 3 tablespoons milk
Sliced almonds

In a small bowl, dissolve yeast and 1 teaspoon sugar in water; set aside. Combine flour, salt and remaining sugar in a large bowl; cut in butter until the mixture resembles coarse crumbs. Add egg and cream to yeast mixture. Add to flour mixture; stir to form a stiff dough. Divide in half; cover and refrigerate for 3 hours. In a mixing bowl, beat almond paste, brown sugar and butter until smooth. On a lightly floured surface, roll each portion of dough into a 15-in. x 6-in. rectangle. Spread filling down center third of dough to within 1/2 in. of edges. Beat egg and water; brush over edges of dough. Fold sides over filling; seal seam and edges. Place seam side down on greased baking sheets. Cut five to six small slits in top. Cover and let rise in a warm place for 30 minutes. Bake at 375° for 20-25 minutes or until golden brown. Cool completely. For glaze, combine confectioners' sugar, extract and enough milk to achieve desired consistency; drizzle over coffee cakes. Sprinkle with almonds. **Yield:** 2 coffee cakes (10-12 servings each).

HONEY-MUSTARD SALAD DRESSING
Jean Keffer, Bend, Oregon

This zippy recipe is one a friend shared years ago. I like to give the dressing to others in jelly jars trimmed with baling twine.

    3 cups mayonnaise
1/2 cup sugar
1/2 cup honey
1/4 cup prepared mustard
1/4 cup vinegar
1/4 cup chopped onion
    1 cup vegetable oil
1/4 cup minced fresh parsley

In a blender or food processor, combine the first six ingredients. Slowly add oil; process until smooth. Stir in parsley. Cover and chill for at least 1 hour. Can be refrigerated for up to 1 week. **Yield:** about 5 cups.

Tasteful Sleigh Will Make Spirits Bright!

HOP ABOARD this sugar cookie sleigh—it comes complete with Santa, a team of sweet reindeer (including Rudolph, of course) and a wintry wonderland scene!

Our *CW* kitchen staff reined in the idea for this dashing accent for a buffet table or a mantel. It's fun to fix…so you can deliver one to your decor in merry fashion.

SUGAR COOKIE SLEIGH

        1 cup butter (no substitutes), softened
        2 cups sugar
        2 eggs
    1/2 teaspoon almond extract
    1/2 teaspoon vanilla extract
        5 cups all-purpose flour
    1-1/2 teaspoons baking powder
        1 teaspoon baking soda
    1/2 teaspoon salt
    1/4 cup milk
    Green colored sugar
    Cookie cutters—4-inch and 5-1/4-inch Christmas
        trees, 4-1/2-inch Santa and 3-inch reindeer

In a mixing bowl, cream butter and sugar. Add eggs, one at a time, beating well after each addition. Beat in extracts. Combine flour, baking powder, baking soda and salt; add to creamed mixture alternately with milk. Cover and refrigerate for 15-30 minutes or until easy to handle.

Trace patterns on page 50 onto waxed paper, tagboard or thin cardboard; cut out. Divide dough in half. Using a lightly floured rolling pin, roll out each portion of dough onto a greased baking sheet to 1/4-in. thickness. Position patterns on dough 2 in. apart. Using a sharp knife, cut out a sleigh front, back, base and two sides. Remove patterns. Remove dough scraps; cover and refrigerate.

Generously sprinkle one side of sleigh front, back and side pieces that will face out with green colored sugar.

Leave base plain. Bake at 350° for 10 minutes or until edges begin to brown. Remove to wire racks to cool.

Roll out dough scraps. Using cookie cutters, cut out three 5-1/4-in. trees, one 4-in. tree, five reindeer and one Santa. Place on greased baking sheets. Bake at 350° for 8-10 minutes or until edges begin to brown. Remove to wire racks to cool.

ICING AND ASSEMBLY:
        4 egg whites
    7-1/2 cups confectioners' sugar
        6 teaspoons hot water
    22-inch x 16-inch display base (heavy-duty cardboard,
        cutting board or piece of plywood, covered with
        foil wrapping paper or aluminum foil)
    Serrated knife *or* emery board
    Pastry bags *or* heavy-duty resealable plastic bags
    Pastry tips—#3 round, #67 leaf and #27 star
    Canned goods and small spice bottles for propping
        4 peppermint candy canes
    Green, brown and red paste food coloring
        4 brown plus 7 red candy-coated milk chocolate
        balls, such as Hershey's
    Chocolate and colored sprinkles
        13 vanilla wafers
    Red colored sugar
    Flaked coconut
        1 package (16 ounces) Starburst candies,
        unwrapped
        4 pieces red shoestring licorice (10 to 12 inches)

In a mixing bowl, beat egg whites until foamy. Gradually add sugar and a few teaspoons of hot water; beat for 12-15 minutes. If too stiff, add more hot water; if too thin, add more sugar. Place a damp cloth over the bowl and cover tightly between uses. **Editor's Note:** This icing is for *decorative purposes only*. If the decoration will be eaten, substitute a royal icing recipe using meringue powder.

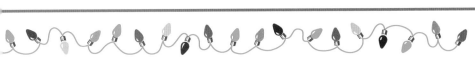

To assemble sleigh: Test sleigh pieces to make sure they fit together snugly. If necessary, file carefully with a serrated knife or emery board to make them fit.

Insert #3 tip into pastry bag; fill two-thirds full with icing. Pipe a wide strip of icing along the outside edges of the sleigh base. Position and press the sleigh sides, sugar side out, against the icing. Prop with cans.

Pipe icing on the sides of the front and back sleigh pieces. Position front and back pieces, sugar side out, between the sides and touching the icing on the base. Prop with cans. (See Photo 1.) Pipe icing along the inside edges of the front, back and side pieces. Set aside to dry completely, about 4 hours.

To decorate sleigh: For runners, cut 3-1/2 in. from the straight end of two candy canes; set aside. Gently turn sleigh over. Ice along the bottom edges of the sides. Position candy canes, curved ends down, so the curved edges nearly touch the sleigh front. Press into icing. Place one piece of reserved cut peppermint stick on each side to complete the runners. (See Photo 2.) Set aside to dry completely, about 4 hours.

Turn sleigh right side up. Tint 2/3 cup icing with green food coloring. Use #67 tip to make a wreath on each side of sleigh. Set aside remaining green icing for the trees. Gently press three red candy-coated milk chocolate balls into each wreath for berries.

To decorate deer: With brown food coloring, tint 2 tablespoons icing tan and 1 cup icing brown. Frost one side of deer brown; frost antlers tan. With a dab of brown icing, attach one brown candy-coated milk chocolate ball on each of four deer for the nose and one red candy-coated ball for Rudolph's nose. Using white icing, place a dot on each deer for eyes. Place one chocolate sprinkle in the center of each dot. Set aside to dry completely, about 1 hour. Set remaining brown icing aside for Santa and trees.

Place a dab of white icing on four vanilla wafers. Press the back and front legs of two deer into icing on each wafer. Prop with cans; set aside.

Place a dab of white icing on two more wafers; press back legs of two deer into icing. Cut another wafer in half and one into quarters. Place one halved wafer, cut edge down, on work surface. Prop up halved piece with a

quartered piece on one or both sides; join pieces with icing. With a dab of icing, attach the front legs of the two deer to the wafer stands; prop with spice bottles. (See Photo 3.)

For Rudolph, place a mound of icing in center of one wafer. Attach Rudolph's back legs to icing; rest the front legs on a small spice bottle so they are suspended 2 in. above the base. (See Photo 4.) Allow to harden.

To decorate Santa: Tint 3 tablespoons icing with red food coloring. Frost hat, jacket, pants and sack; sprinkle red colored sugar over sack. Insert #27 tip into pastry bag; fill with white icing. Pipe a star at the tip of Santa's hat. Make a zigzag design on the hat brim and jacket bottom. Frost beard; cover with coconut. Pipe a thin line down the front of jacket. Place a small dot of icing for eyes and insert a chocolate sprinkle in the center of each. With some of the reserved brown icing, frost Santa's boots. Pipe a belt and buttons with white icing and #3 tip. Place on waxed paper to harden.

To decorate gifts: Using white icing and #3 tip, pipe a ribbon and bow on each Starburst candy. Place on waxed paper to harden.

To decorate trees: Using reserved brown icing, frost the trunk of each cookie tree. Using reserved green icing, frost cookies; sprinkle with decorating sprinkles. Place on waxed paper to harden. Attach each tree to a vanilla wafer with a dab of icing (as in deer decorating instructions). Prop with cans, placing a Starburst between tree and can.

To assemble entire table decoration: Working from one corner toward the center, spread a thin layer of white icing on one-third of the display board. Position sleigh in the corner of frosted board with curved runners facing the opposite corner. Sprinkle coconut over icing and press down.

Using white icing, completely frost the remaining board. Lay wet paper towels over frosting if it begins to dry. Immediately position the two deer on flat wafers about 2 in. from the sleigh front and 2 in. from each other. Place the two deer on stands 2 in. from the first deer and 2 in. apart.

Center Rudolph 2 in. in front of second pair of deer. Return spice bottle under Rudolph's front legs until displaying. Attach trees to display board. Carefully sprinkle coconut over icing

(Instructions continue on next page)

Photo 1. Position sleigh pieces, attaching each with piped-on icing, then prop sleigh with cans until icing is dry, about 4 hours.

Photo 2. Attach candy canes, curved ends down, to sleigh bottom so curves touch sleigh front. Add cut canes to complete runners.

Photo 3. After attaching vanilla wafer stands to legs of reindeer, prop deer with spice bottles until icing is completely dry.

Photo 4. Place icing on wafer; press Rudolph's back legs into icing. Rest front legs on bottle so legs are 2 in. above work surface.

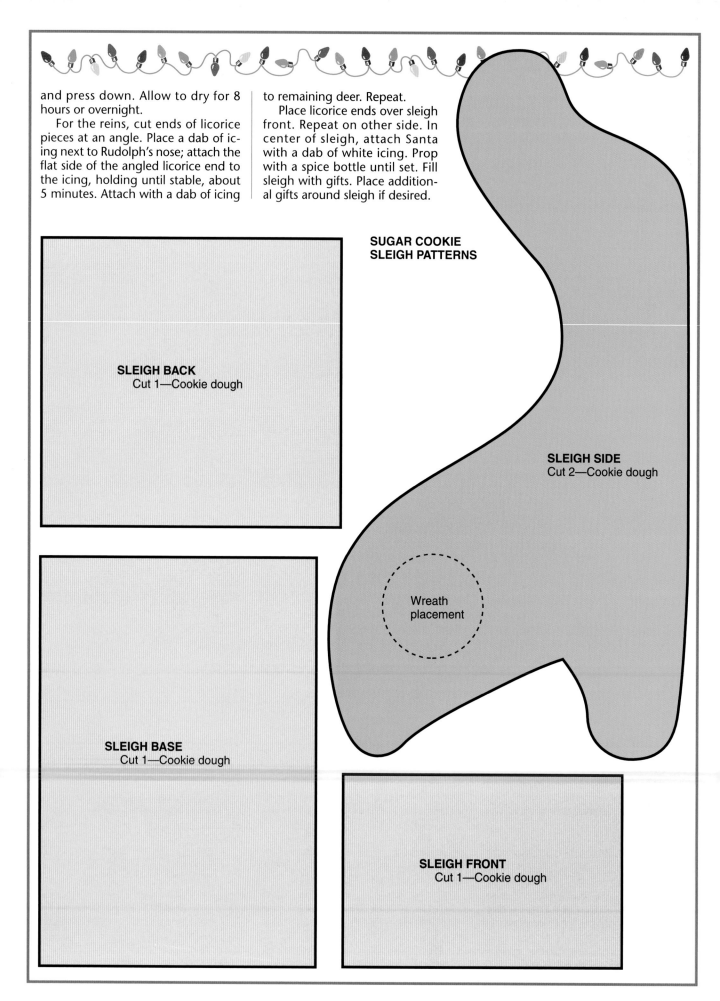

and press down. Allow to dry for 8 hours or overnight.

For the reins, cut ends of licorice pieces at an angle. Place a dab of icing next to Rudolph's nose; attach the flat side of the angled licorice end to the icing, holding until stable, about 5 minutes. Attach with a dab of icing

to remaining deer. Repeat.

Place licorice ends over sleigh front. Repeat on other side. In center of sleigh, attach Santa with a dab of white icing. Prop with a spice bottle until set. Fill sleigh with gifts. Place additional gifts around sleigh if desired.

SUGAR COOKIE
SLEIGH PATTERNS

SLEIGH BACK
Cut 1—Cookie dough

SLEIGH SIDE
Cut 2—Cookie dough

Wreath placement

SLEIGH BASE
Cut 1—Cookie dough

SLEIGH FRONT
Cut 1—Cookie dough

Her Holiday Paper Work Makes Sweet Impression

LIKE most country women, Peggy Dunder gives her cookie molds quite a workout during December. But the batches she bakes with those old-fashioned ceramic pieces are for eyeing instead of eating.

"The 'dough' I make is actually the fixings for homemade paper," she details from her Hermitage, Pennsylvania kitchen. "I fill molds with the mix and pop out shaped sheets I turn into gift tags, cards and ornaments. They're treats that stay fresh forever!"

Peggy's handiwork *did* have a sugary start. The first time she tried a mold, she used traditional cookie dough—with less than successful results.

"What a failure that was," she grinningly admits. "The cookies came out of the oven looking like big blobs, not the pretty shapes I had intended. I almost tossed the mold out."

Instead, Peggy tucked it away...until the mold finally made a worthwhile impression. "I'd discovered paper-mak-

ing but wanted to create something more than just flat pieces," she recalls. "So I gave that mold another chance—and was pleased with the outcome!"

The festive designs Peggy stamps out these days range from chubby cherubs to festive wreaths and Yuletide trees, as well as motifs for other occasions. "Anytime I find a fun mold, I put it into production," she describes.

Stirring Up Fun

Fiber—in paper form—is the main ingredient in the recipe this former newspaper editor follows.

"I combine plain newsprint, torn-up tissue paper and cotton linter, a by-product of cotton processing, in my blender," she details. "The measurements aren't exact. Instead, I use my grandmother's method—a handful of this and a pinch of that."

Warm water is last to go in before the blending begins. With a few whirls, the mixture, called "slurry", is just right. "I pour it into a strainer to drain before packing it into molds coated with cooking spray," Peggy says. "Then I press a towel on top to soak up excess water.

"The molds are microwaved for several minutes to speed up drying. After they cool, I gently remove the damp imprinted papers and place them between old magazines overnight."

Once they're completely dry, Peggy pulls out paints,

CASTING GLANCES at tree trims Peggy Dunder shapes from paper is niece Mary Louise (above). Other accents Peggy cooks up in her old-fashioned cookie molds include painted package tags, greeting cards.

glitter, ribbons and other accents to adorn the designs. As the last step, she chooses what to use each for—a card or a tree trim perhaps.

By working assembly-line fashion, Peggy is able to roll out reams of paper pieces. "I can create several dozen in one evening," she reports.

"Close to Christmas, the pace picks up quite a bit. Thankfully, my husband, Rick, doesn't mind when meals are late ...or sometimes skipped altogether!"

After all, he understands that even if what's cookin' in the kitchen isn't flavorful...it certainly is noteworthy.

Editor's Note: *Peggy offers her shaped paper crafts through the mail. For more information, send a self-addressed stamped envelope to her at Papier Impressions, 1442 Monticello Ave., Hermitage PA 16150. Or call 1-724/ 962-1332.*

Country Decorating...

Old-Time Signs of the Season Color Her Cabin

By Kathy Wilbanks of Lyman, South Carolina

TONING UP home for Christmas is a cinch for Kathy Wilbanks (at lower left), thanks to furnishings already featuring holiday hues. To accent, she adds tree, boughs, Santas, more.

THE FRAMEWORK for the festive look I create each year in the log cabin husband Billy and I built comes from our favorite pastime...collecting old-fashioned treasures of all kinds!

In fact, many of the venerable furnishings we've brought home or constructed ourselves sport holiday tones, making it that much easier to enhance every room during December in the traditional reds and greens we favor.

Take, for example, the white Hoosier cabinet near the living room with its handy crimson counter. Already bearing suitable shades, it needs little more than a bucket bursting with poinsettias, a tin

or two of cookies and a basket filled with bread to dress it up.

Another Yule-hued example is the green step-back cupboard Billy crafted. Not only is the paint job appropriate, so are the pints of ripe tomatoes and other preserved produce I annually pack onto the shelves.

Bow-bundled boughs plus a wooden "Merry Christmas" and fabric "Joy" sign are the only extras needed.

Then there's the gleaming white tinware and canned goods sporting eye-catching red and yellow labels that I've been collecting for ages.

Both permanently pretty up a hutch we created from old lumber, along with other spots around the combination kitchen/dining/living room on the first floor. These bits of yesteryear add holiday cheer to our home all year.

Of course, I enhance that everyday decor with festive trimmings, in the form of rich evergreen garlands, velvety ribbons and other Noel niceties.

One of my favorites is the fresh-cut fir we place near the sofa, then adorn with a string of cutout Kris Kringles, assorted old ornaments and a gingham treetop bow. Dolls dating back several decades line up below the branches.

The nostalgic cardboard Claus standing near the kitchen cookstove has a fun secret—he isn't nearly as old as he

looks! A friend found the figure a few years back at a local market and brought it over, knowing how well this classic depiction would fit into our decor.

Plenty of other ageless amenities deck the halls and walls, too. The mantel above the cast-iron stove that serves as a fireplace sprouts swags of spruce, plus Santas of all sizes. Enlivening the brick hearth is a cheery chorister and pots of vibrant poinsettias.

Marching up the simple staircase is a trio of snow-white teddy bears, all gussied up in North Pole knitwear. Above them hang some flouncy calico wreaths I sewed one year.

More handmades grace the dining table in the form of a fabricated swan centerpiece, surrounded by matching place mats. When I add my fine pine china for meals we make for our three children and five grandchildren, the area gleams with holiday greetings.

That welcoming look extends beyond the sturdy walls. Billy and I tie bunches of greenery and crimson ribbons to the front door and on the arbor to the garden, as well as to the sheds we've constructed around our acreage.

Inside this cozy Carolina cabin and out, Christmas fits right into our bygone style. Thanks for stopping in!

Heart-Melting Holiday Lay Over Fields, Through Woods

By Gaye Hughes of Mount Vernon, Ohio

WHENEVER December snow starts falling, I'm reminded of a white Christmas in the early 1930's—one that taught me the magic of rural ingenuity *and* the meaning of "family".

By the time that day dawned, drifts had piled high. My new foster parents, who ended up raising me, knew the roads would be nearly impassable.

Still, Mom and Dad hadn't missed a Yuletide dinner at Mom's parents' in years, and I had not yet met my new grandparents.

What's more, Mom and I had already baked all sorts of goodies to bring. The last thing we wanted was to set carefully made plans aside because of a few icy flakes!

Unfortunately, Dad's 1929 Model A Ford wasn't up to making the trip over slick lanes. Nor did we have a sleigh that his horses, "Maudie" and "Charlie", could pull. For a short while, it looked like this first Christmas with my new family would be a homebound one.

Old-Time "Mud Boat" Led Way

Then Dad snapped his fingers and hurried to the barn. In no time, he returned—leading the team hitched to a simple heavy mud boat. On top, he'd attached the spring seat from a wagon. A strip of rusty bells jingle-jangled festively from the sled's hames.

With big grins and nimble steps, Mom and I loaded up our "chariot" with spicy pumpkin pies, a moist hickory-nut cake, rolls and a date pudding.

That done, we climbed aboard. Dad tucked a huge cowhide robe around our legs to protect us from below-zero temperatures, then clicked "giddyap" to the two draft horses—and we were off!

It wasn't over the river, but it was through the woods and fields to Grandmother's house we went. Piercing cold and pellets of wind-driven snow made my eyes water and skin smart. I turned my head away and into the soft fur collar on my mother's winter coat.

Soon, we approached the last gate leading into Grandpa's barnyard. He was standing beside it, waving to us, an immense smile lighting up his face.

After we slid to a stop, Grandpa stepped forward and peered at me through squinted eyes, exclaiming, "Oh my, she's a keeper. She's got blue eyes, just like me!"

"Spotty", his English bulldog, ran frantically around and around the horses in greeting, a corncob from the granary clenched between his teeth. As we reached the porch, the stout pooch laid the cob down at our feet and wagged his stump of a tail, eager to be petted.

While Dad and Grandpa put the team away, Mom and I unloaded our sweet cargo into the aroma-filled kitchen and Grandma's waiting arms.

After putting everything in its place, Grandma removed my cap, brushed back a strand of hair, then hugged me oh-so-tight. I couldn't have felt more welcome!

Hearty Christmas Fare

Soon, we all sat at a table piled high with tasty dishes—succulent turkey, savory dressing, tart cranberry sauce, fluffy mashed potatoes with a golden pat of butter gleaming in the center, candied sweet potatoes, warm gravy and assorted cooked vegetables.

I perched atop a thick Sears catalog so I could reach the table. How I enjoyed each morsel on my plate, particularly the luscious pudding and cake I'd helped make.

After dinner, we gathered in the formal parlor made cozy by a crackling fire in the big wood-burning stove. There, we each opened a present. All were simple handmades—except one. Mine was a store-bought teddy bear, a gift unlike any I'd ever received.

Before I knew it, the day was over. We bundled up and retraced our almost-covered tracks through the fields and woods toward home.

Clutching my precious teddy, I was snug on my mother's lap as our makeshift sleigh whisked us along. It had been the best Christmas of my life!

Grandma's 'Brag' Page

WRAPPED UP in Yule cheer is Jean Urquhart's nephew Joshua. "He was so thrilled to get our gift, he jumped on top of it, did jig," she jots from Gondola Point, New Brunswick.

HEAVEN-SENT is adorable granddaughter Amanda, according to Jean Moore of Rancho Palos Verdes, California. "She must be an angel," beaming Grandma alleges. "Amanda sprouted wings right in front of the Christmas tree!"

WHAT A CHARACTER! Earnest little elf Cecelia Marie Otto finds first Christmas to be serious business. Grandma Sue Hall, Madison, Wisconsin, shares precious picture.

HAPPY HAUL. Lexi Kruse (at left) finds joy aboard miniature tractor. "Since she loves to watch Daddy and Grandpa ride theirs, we knew she'd like her own," reveals doting Grandmother Sandy from Harmon, Illinois.

MAKING MERRY for Jeanne Lesselyoung, Faulkton, South Dakota, is her grandson Cole Baloun (right). "He laughs all of the time," she tells.

STOCKING UP on holiday cheer is easy for Grandma Gwen Wassilak, River Grove, Illinois. "I craft Christmas goodies for our grandsons Nicholas and Clayton," she presents. Below, they enjoy her homemade socks.

Crafter's Jolly Designs Carve Out Noel Niche

HEWN FOR HOLIDAYS. The merry models Ilona Steelhammer (top left) carves fill her studio (below left), home with cheer all year.

GO, FIGURE—that's exactly what Ilona Steelhammer does in a colorful Yuletide way every day!

When she's done with chores, this Centralia, Washington farm wife whittles away the hours creating delightful North Pole personalities by the dozens.

"Carving is my favorite way to spend time," she affirms. "I chisel accents for other occasions, too, such as Halloween ghosts and funny Easter bunnies. The ones I like best, though, are those we look for in December—Santas, reindeer, angels and the like.

"In fact, no matter what the season, it's likely to look like Christmas in my workroom—and around the house!"

For inspiration, Ilona doesn't have to go far afield. She relies on the rural scenes right outside the kitchen window, adapting them to fit festive themes.

"Our country life dictates what I do. Many times, my Santas are pulling sleighs or toting gift-filled sacks," she details. "Critters often wander into my designs, too. I've perched songbirds on a snowman's shoulder and shaped geese and sheep gathered around a Nativity.

"Activities my husband, Norman, our three grown children and I've enjoyed together also inspire. Based on our outings, I've created ice-skating angels, a Santa hauling a Christmas tree, sledding St. Nicks and more."

Paints Pointed the Way

Ingrained in Ilona is the need to keep her characters colorful, which she does with some clever brushwork. "That comes from my other favorite activity," she confides.

"I've been picturing country folks for years by creating oil paintings and greeting cards. The carvings came about when I wanted to try something new."

A self-taught woodworker, Ilona sticks to sculpting simple forms from balsa blocks. "I'm no master carver," she admits.

"Besides, I keep the cutting rough for a rustic look. The real beauty comes in the finishing."

After she's chipped out a Noel fellow, Ilona applies bright coats of acrylic. Employing clever patterns, such as zigzags and checkered edgings, makes her designs even more eye-catching. The final step, sanding and applying stain, gives each piece an old-fashioned look.

The appeal of Ilona's carvings are just as long-lasting. "People often tell me how they display my pieces well beyond Christmas," she beams. "Hearing that makes my character-building efforts all worth it!"

Editor's Note: *Ilona's holiday carvings are available at retail stores nationwide. Contact Midwest of Cannon Falls, 32057-64th Ave., Cannon Falls MN 55009 for shops near you. For more on her paintings and greeting cards, send a self-addressed stamped envelope to Common Folk Co., 125 E. High St., Centralia WA 98531.* ⬤

IN CHARACTER. Drawing on life as a farm wife first provided fodder for paintings like Claus at top right. Now it yields whittle ideas including Santas, angels, more. "I still enjoy brushing on colors," Ilona confides.

Craft Section...

Holidays Are Highlighted By Brightly Hued Garland

YOU'LL want to turn the light on this pleasing seasonal project! Helen Rafson shares the festive garland she developed in her Louisville, Kentucky home.

"I used easy-to-cut art foam I found at a local discount store to create all the shapes," she recounts. "The best part is that the bulbs on my garland *never* burn out."

Materials Needed:
Patterns on this page
Tracing paper and pencil
Scrap of lightweight cardboard
Plastic art foam—one sheet each or scraps of gray for light base and blue, green, orange, red and yellow or colors of choice for light bulbs (art foam sheets are available at most craft stores)
White acrylic craft paint
Small flat paintbrush
Black permanent markers—fine-line and medium
2 yards of 1/4-inch-wide white grosgrain ribbon
Craft glue
Scissors

Finished Size: The garland measures about 64 inches long x 3-1/2 inches high. Each light bulb measures about 1-3/4 inches across x 3-1/2 inches high.

Directions:
Trace patterns onto tracing paper and cut out. Trace around patterns onto lightweight cardboard and cut out. Place cardboard patterns on art foam and trace around patterns onto colors as directed on patterns. Cut out shapes.

Referring to pattern for placement, use medium marker to draw five lines lengthwise across each base.

Using fine-line marker, add a very thin line around the outside edges of each base. Add a broken line to the curved edge of each bulb as shown on the pattern.

Using flat brush, add white highlights to each bulb as shown on pattern. Let dry.

Glue a base to each colored bulb with straight edges meeting and bulb centered along bottom of base as shown in photo. Do not overlap edges. Let dry.

Mark center of ribbon and place ribbon on a flat surface. Place one light bulb right side up at center of ribbon. Place remaining light bulbs about 3 in. apart along length of ribbon, alternating colors as desired. Glue base of each bulb to ribbon as shown in photo.

For hanging loop, glue one end of ribbon to center back of first light at same

BRIGHT LIGHTS GARLAND PATTERNS
Trace 1 each—tracing paper
Cut 1 each—lightweight cardboard

BASE
Cut 15—gray plastic art foam

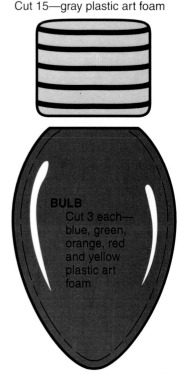

BULB
Cut 3 each—blue, green, orange, red and yellow plastic art foam

end of garland. Make another hanging loop at other end of garland in the same way.

Fun Is Afoot with Red-Nosed Rudolph!

STEP in a dashing decorating direction by adding this "endeering" doll to your Yuletide array. Mary Ayres of Boyce, Virginia constructed the critter from an unusual supply. "I used a pair of my husband's old socks," she grins.

Materials Needed:
One pair of men's brown terry knit socks
20-inch x 3-1/2-inch piece of red plaid fabric for scarf
Two tan pipe cleaners (chenille stems) for antlers
Two 1/4-inch black shank buttons or beads for eyes
1-inch red pom-pom
Polyester stuffing
Brown all-purpose thread
Standard sewing supplies
Candy cane

Finished Size: Sock reindeer is about 20 inches long x 6 inches across.

Directions:
Turn both of the socks inside out. Use the looped side of each sock as the right side throughout the project.

Cut down the middle of one sock through both layers, from the open end of the cuff to the heel, making a cut about 9 in. long. The cut area will form the legs. The remainder of the sock, from the heel to the toe, will form the body and the head of the reindeer.

To make an antler, bend a pipe cleaner in half and twist the ends around each other, forming a 1-in. loop as shown in Fig. 1a. Using the ends of the pipe cleaner, form a similar loop on each side of the first loop as shown in Fig. 1b. Wrap the ends around the base of the first loop and then twist ends together. Repeat for the other antler.

Insert the twisted ends of the antlers into the toe of the cut sock, placing them about 3 in. apart as shown in the photo at left. Hand-stitch ends of antlers to sock to secure them.

Stuff reindeer head and body with polyester stuffing. Turn the cut edges of legs and underside of body 1/2 in. to the wrong side and hand-stitch seams, concealing raw edges. Hand-stitch ends of legs closed.

Cut a 2-in. section from the toe of the remaining sock and cut toe section in half for ears as shown in Fig. 2. Turn 1/4 in. of cut edges on each ear to the wrong side and hand-stitch together, concealing the raw edges. Fold each ear in half lengthwise and stitch one to each side of the head below the antlers as shown in photo.

Hand-stitch the button or bead eyes 2-1/2 in. down from the top of the head, spacing them about 1/2 in. apart as shown in the photo.

Hand-stitch the pom-pom centered 1 in. below the eyes.

Wrap the length of red plaid fabric for scarf around the reindeer's neck just below the pom-pom nose and tie the ends in an overhand knot as shown in photo. Pull threads from the short ends of the scarf to make fringe.

To make the arms, cut a 14-1/2-in. x 3-in. section from remaining sock piece as shown in Fig. 2. Turn 1/2 in. along long edges to the wrong side and hand-stitch the long edges together, creating a tube. Tie a loose overhand knot in the center of the tube for the hands. Turn raw edges at each end to the wrong side and hand-stitch the ends together.

Slip the arms over and around the sock reindeer, placing the hands in front and the ends in back. Hand-stitch the ends to the center back of the reindeer below the scarf.

Insert a candy cane through knot of hands as shown in the photo. Then place the reindeer on a mantel or tuck it in a stocking for extra holiday cheer. ◑

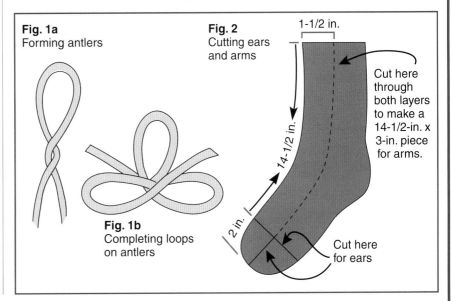

Fig. 1a
Forming antlers

Fig. 1b
Completing loops on antlers

Fig. 2
Cutting ears and arms

1-1/2 in.

14-1/2 in.

2 in.

Cut here through both layers to make a 14-1/2-in. x 3-in. piece for arms.

Cut here for ears

Her Snowy Scene Spreads Miles of Smiles at Meals

THERE'S no better way to brighten dining—or keep messes to a minimum—than to top the table with a festive cloth. This one's shared by Dorothy Boehne of Lockwood, Missouri.

"The appliques I created are on the easy side," she notes, "especially for anyone familiar with the technique."

Materials Needed:
Patterns on next page
Tracing paper and pencil
44-inch-wide 100% cotton or cotton-blend fabrics—2-1/4 yards of light Christmas print for center and corners of tablecloth and for large tree appliques; 1-3/4 yards of green solid for borders; 1/3 yard each or scraps of a coordinating Christmas print for small and medium tree appliques; and 1/8 yard each or scraps of white metallic for snowmen, red check for hats and scarves and gold solid for stars
1-1/2 yards of paper-backed fusible web
7-1/2 yards of 1/2-inch-wide white lace
Gold six-strand embroidery floss
Embroidery needle
Black fine-line permanent marker
All-purpose thread—green, red and white
Standard sewing supplies

Finished Size: Tablecloth measures 60 inches x 70 inches.

Directions:
Pre-wash fabrics without fabric softeners, washing colors separately. If the water from any fabric is discolored, wash again until rinse water runs clear. Dry and press fabrics.

Stitch all seams with right sides together and a 1/4-in. seam. Press seams toward darker fabric.

CUTTING: From the light Christmas print, cut a 54-in. x 44-in. rectangle for tablecloth center and four 9-in. squares for corners.

From green solid, cut two lengthwise 54-in. x 9-in. strips and two 44-in. x 9-in. strips for borders.

Overcast edges of all pieces with a narrow zigzag stitch.

APPLIQUES: Trace tree patterns onto folded tracing paper. Cut out and open for complete patterns.

Trace trees and all remaining patterns onto paper side of fusible web as directed on patterns, leaving 1/2 in. between shapes. Cut shapes apart.

Following manufacturer's directions, fuse shapes to wrong side of fabrics as directed on patterns. Cut out shapes on traced lines and remove paper backing.

Following Assembly Diagram at far right, fuse trees and snowmen onto green border strips as shown. Fuse a gold star onto the top of each large tree. Fold bottom edge of each hat under and then up as shown on pattern. Fuse a hat and scarf to each snowman where shown on pattern.

Using white and a medium-width satin stitch, applique around each tree and the body of each snowman. With red, applique around each scarf and hat, leaving folds of hats unstitched.

Separate gold six-strand floss and use three strands to stitch a lazy daisy stitch over each point on each star. See Fig. 1 for stitch illustration.

Using black marker, add eyes, nose, mouth and buttons to each snowman as shown on pattern.

ASSEMBLY: Referring to Assembly Diagram, stitch the top edge of one 44-in.-long green border strip to one matching edge of center (Step 1). Repeat, stitching top edge of remaining 44-in.-long green border strip to other matching edge of center.

Stitch a corner square to each 9-in.

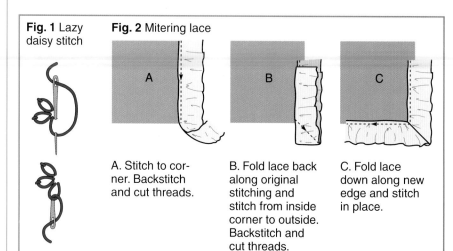

Fig. 1 Lazy daisy stitch

Fig. 2 Mitering lace

A. Stitch to corner. Backstitch and cut threads.

B. Fold lace back along original stitching and stitch from inside corner to outside. Backstitch and cut threads.

C. Fold lace down along new edge and stitch in place.

edge of a 54-in.-long green border strip, making a 71-in.-long pieced border (Step 2). Repeat, using remaining 9-in. squares and border strip. Then stitch the top edges of the pieced borders to matching edges of the tablecloth (Step 3).

FINISHING: Stitch lace over each corner border seam with the straight edge of lace along seamline and lace extending over green border fabric. In the same way, attach lace to seams around center of tablecloth, mitering each corner as shown in Fig. 2.

Press 1/4 in. along the outside edges of tablecloth to wrong side, trimming to round corners if desired. Fold 1/4 in. to wrong side again and stitch close to first fold for hem. ●

APPLIQUE KEY
—— Outline/stitching line
----- Placement line
—— Inside design line

ASSEMBLY DIAGRAM

Step 1
Add the 44-in. appliqued borders first.

Step 2
Add 9-in. square to each end of each 54-in. appliqued border to create two 71-in. borders.

Step 3
Add the 71-in. pieced borders.

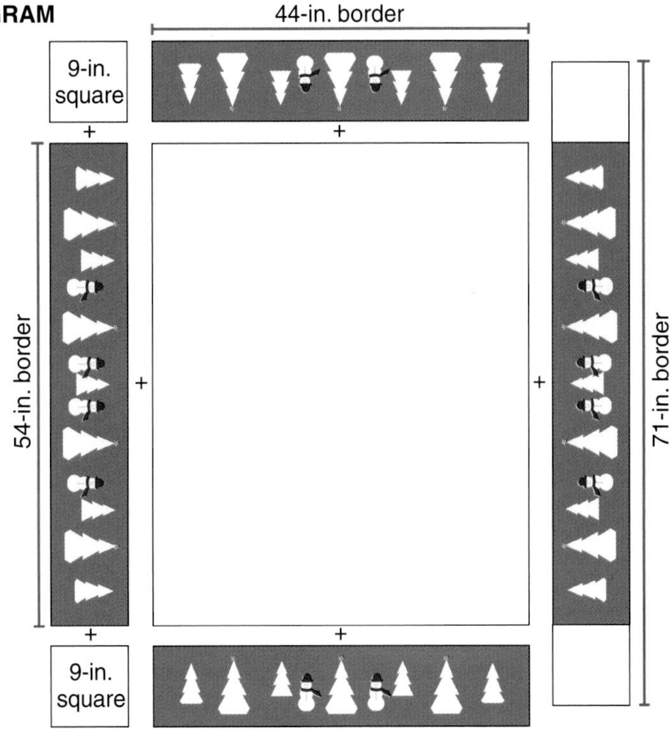

9-in. square

44-in. border

9-in. square

54-in. border

71-in. border

9-in. square

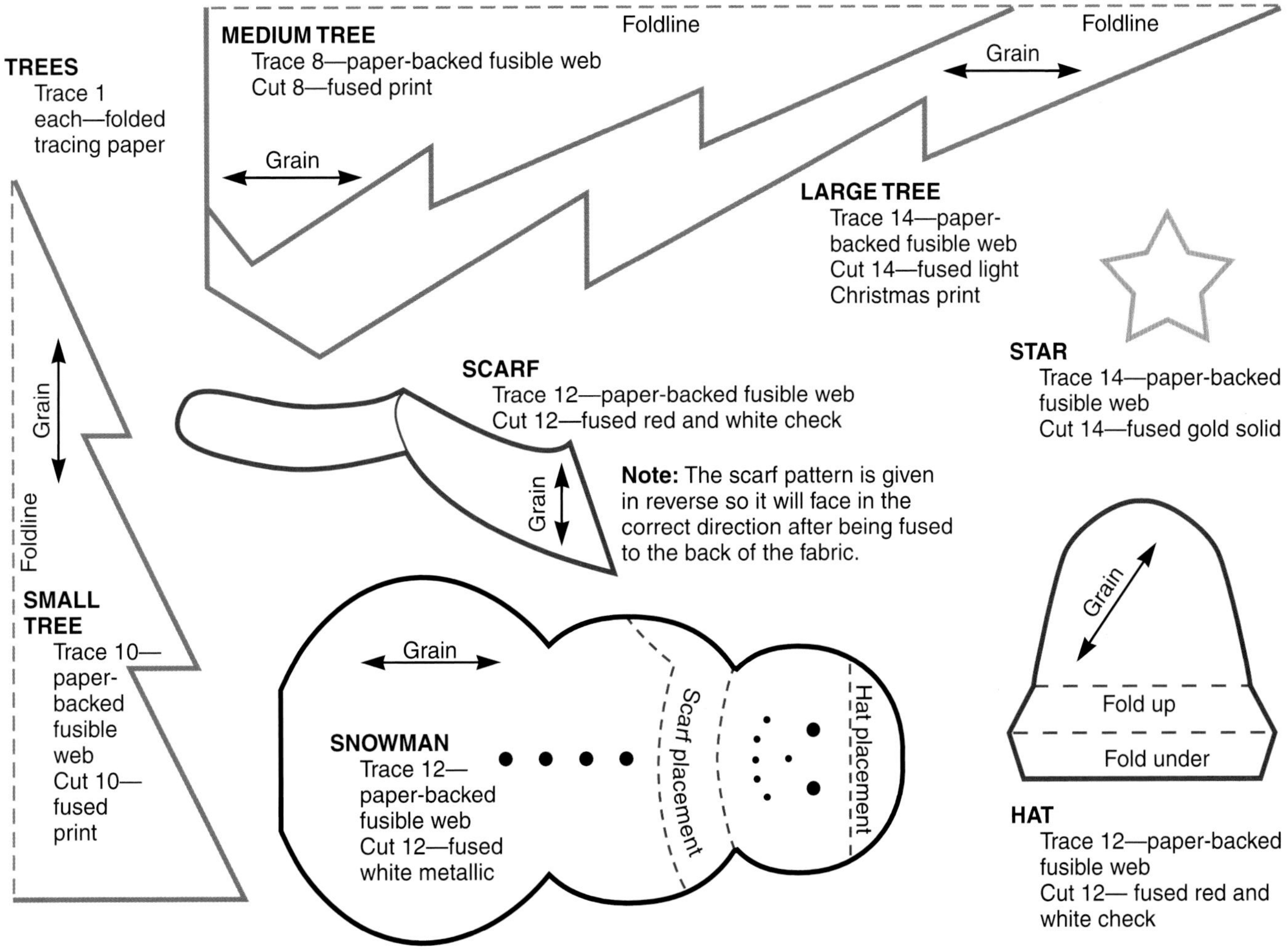

9-in. square

TREES
Trace 1 each—folded tracing paper

MEDIUM TREE
Trace 8—paper-backed fusible web
Cut 8—fused print

Foldline

Grain

Foldline

Grain

LARGE TREE
Trace 14—paper-backed fusible web
Cut 14—fused light Christmas print

STAR
Trace 14—paper-backed fusible web
Cut 14—fused gold solid

SCARF
Trace 12—paper-backed fusible web
Cut 12—fused red and white check

Grain

Note: The scarf pattern is given in reverse so it will face in the correct direction after being fused to the back of the fabric.

Grain

Foldline

SMALL TREE
Trace 10— paper-backed fusible web
Cut 10— fused print

Grain

SNOWMAN
Trace 12— paper-backed fusible web
Cut 12—fused white metallic

Scarf placement

Hat placement

Grain

Fold up

Fold under

HAT
Trace 12—paper-backed fusible web
Cut 12— fused red and white check

Merry Mugs Are Filled with Christmas Cheer

WHAT A PAIR! These cups, sporting Santa and his missus, are sure to flavor your family get-togethers festively.

Mary Cosgrove of Rockville, Connecticut stitched the Christmas couple on pieces of plastic canvas. Then she inserted the pieces into mugs she found at a craft store. "It was quick and easy to do," Mary reports.

Materials Needed (for both):
Charts on next page
One sheet of clear 7-count plastic canvas
Worsted-weight or plastic canvas yarn—2 yards of black, 5 yards of camel, 17 yards of green, 2 yards of pink, 19 yards of red and 4 yards of white
6 yards of heavy black braid
6 yards of gold metallic cord
Size 16 tapestry needle
Sharp craft scissors
Two plastic snap-together craft mugs— one with a red insert for Santa and one with a green insert for Mrs. Claus

Finished Size: Santa and Mrs. Claus designs are each 66 bars long x 24 bars high. Each mug is 4 inches high x 3-1/4 inches across.

Directions:
CUTTING: Remembering to count bars and not holes, cut two pieces of plastic canvas 66 bars long x 24 bars high.

STITCHING: Working with 18-in. to 20-in. lengths of yarn, follow charts on next page and instructions that follow to stitch Santa and Mrs. Claus. See Fig. 1 for stitch illustrations.

Do not knot yarn on back of work. Instead, leave a 1-in. tail on the back of the plastic canvas and work the next few stitches over it. To end a strand, run yarn on back of canvas under completed stitches of the same color and clip yarn close to work.

Referring to the charts, position Santa and Mrs. Claus between the bars as indicated.

Santa: Using Continental stitch and yarn, stitch face pink; suit red; beard, mustache and fur trim white; mittens and boots black; and chair camel.

Straight-stitch mouth with red yarn, eyes with black yarn and buckle with gold metallic cord.

Add red French knot for nose.

Use black braid to backstitch Santa where shown on chart.

Mrs. Claus: Using Continental stitch and yarn, stitch face and hands pink, dress green, hair and feet white, knitting red and chair camel.

Straight-stitch knitting needles with gold metallic cord, and ball of yarn and collar with red yarn. Straight-stitch blouse with white yarn, following direction of stitches shown on chart.

Stitch French-knot eyes with black braid.

Use black braid to backstitch Mrs. Claus where shown on the chart.

Background (for both): Fill in remaining canvas with slanted Gobelin stitches as shown on charts, using green yarn for Santa and red yarn for Mrs. Claus and leaving the outside edges unstitched. Add gold metallic backstitching to each as shown on chart.

Overcast outside edges of each with red or green yarn as indicated on charts.

FINISHING: Place the completed Santa in the mug with the right side facing toward the outside of the mug as shown in the photo above left. Snap the red insert into place.

Place the completed Mrs. Claus in the remaining mug in the same way and add the green insert. ●

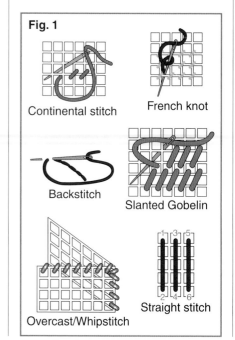

Fig. 1

Continental stitch

French knot

Backstitch

Slanted Gobelin

Overcast/Whipstitch

Straight stitch

SANTA

Bar 16   Bar 50

MRS. CLAUS

Bar 19   Bar 47

SANTA AND MRS. CLAUS MUGS COLOR KEY	NEEDLOFT
✎ Black	00
✎ Red	02
✎ Pink	07
✎ Green	28
✎ White	41
✎ Camel	43
STRAIGHT STITCH	
— Black	00
— Red	02
— White	41
FRENCH KNOT	
● Red	02
OVERCAST	
— Red	02
— Green	28
	KREINIK
STRAIGHT STITCH	
— Gold Metallic Cord	01
BACKSTITCH	
— Gold Metallic Cord	01
— Black Heavy Braid	32
FRENCH KNOT	
● Black Heavy Braid	32

Simple Accent Enhances Branches Naturally

PINING for a pleasing way to liven up the Christmas tree? This bird-bedecked adornment will suit—and then some!

Lisa Reese of Greenwood, Indiana went right to the source for supplies. "I first picked up a large pinecone, then added sprigs of greenery and some flowers, then finally perched a feathered friend on top," she describes.

Materials Needed:

Large pinecone—fully opened and dry
1-1/2 yards of 1/8-inch-wide red satin ribbon
Sprig of artificial wired pine bough
Three artificial holly picks
Baby's breath
2-inch bird or size appropriate for pinecone
Glue gun and glue sticks
Scissors

Finished Size: Ornament pictured is 6 inches long x 4 inches across without ribbon hanger. Finished size will vary depending on size of pinecone used.

Directions:

Cut three 12-in. pieces of ribbon. Form each length of ribbon into three loops. Glue each set of loops around pinecone about 1 in. from the base as shown in photo at right.

Form pine bough into a circle and glue it to pinecone base above ribbon loops. Add holly and baby's breath as shown in photo, leaving room in center for bird.

Glue bird to base of pinecone as shown in photo.

Cut a 4-in. piece of ribbon and glue center of ribbon to bird's beak. Glue ends of remaining ribbon to opposite sides of pinecone for hanger. 🌸

Door Decor Delivers Sweet Welcome

GOOD TASTE abounds when you flavor your entryway for the holidays with this crafty confection.

Not only do the fun fabric candy canes stir cheer into festive events, they're a cinch to cook up, affirms Lu Ella Reimer of Hillsboro, Kansas.

"I kept both the supplies and sewing on the simple side," reveals the country crafter. "The entire craft can be finished in just a few hours."

Materials Needed:

Patterns on this page and next page
Tracing paper and pencil
44-inch-wide 100% cotton or cotton-blend fabrics—1/3 yard each of red and white stripe and green solid
Matching all-purpose thread
Polyester stuffing for candy canes
Scrap of lightweight batting for bow and ribbon
Four 10mm gold jingle bells
Small plastic ring for hanger
Standard sewing supplies

Finished Size: Candy canes measure 9-1/2 inches high x 9-1/2 inches wide.

Directions:

Trace candy cane pattern on next page onto tracing paper and cut out. Cut candy canes from striped fabric as directed on pattern.

Pin two candy cane pieces with right sides together and raw edges matching. Sew the two pieces together with a 1/4-in. seam, leaving an opening for turning as indicated on the pattern. Turn candy cane right side out through the opening. Repeat with remaining candy cane pieces.

Stuff each candy cane firmly. Turn edges of openings in and hand-stitch openings closed. Hand-stitch the two candy canes together along the seams of the openings, positioning them as shown in photo below.

Trace bow and ribbon patterns onto tracing paper as directed on patterns. Cut out patterns, leaving a 1-in. margin around each.

Place the green solid fabric on a flat surface and fold it in half with right sides together. Place the batting on top of the fabric. Place the bow and ribbon patterns on top of the batting, matching grain on each pattern to grain of fabric. Pin all layers together.

Using matching thread and a straight stitch, sew through all layers on traced lines of outside edges of patterns only, leaving openings between dots for turning. Remove patterns. Trim through all layers 1/4 in. outside stitching. Trim corners diagonally.

Turn ribbon right side out through opening so batting is on the inside and fabric is on the outside. Turn edges of opening in and hand-stitch opening closed. Repeat for bow.

Fold ribbon in half over center of bow as shown in photo and hand-stitch ribbon to bow. Hand-stitch bow to front of candy canes and bells to tips of ribbon as shown in photo.

Hand-stitch plastic ring to the center back of candy canes for hanger. ●

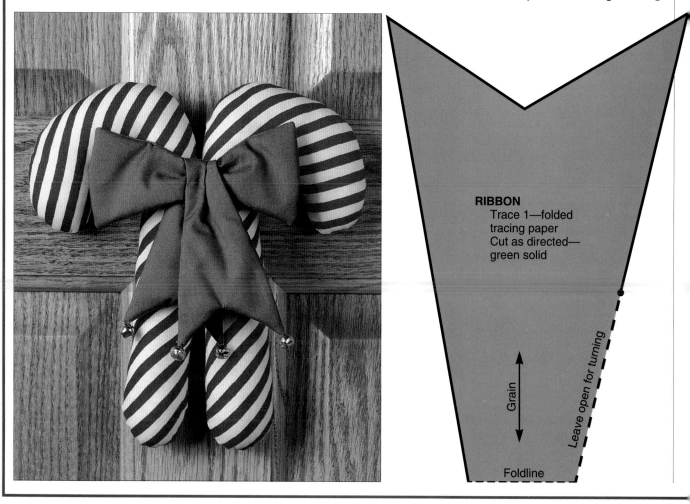

RIBBON
Trace 1—folded tracing paper
Cut as directed—green solid

Grain

Leave open for turning

Foldline

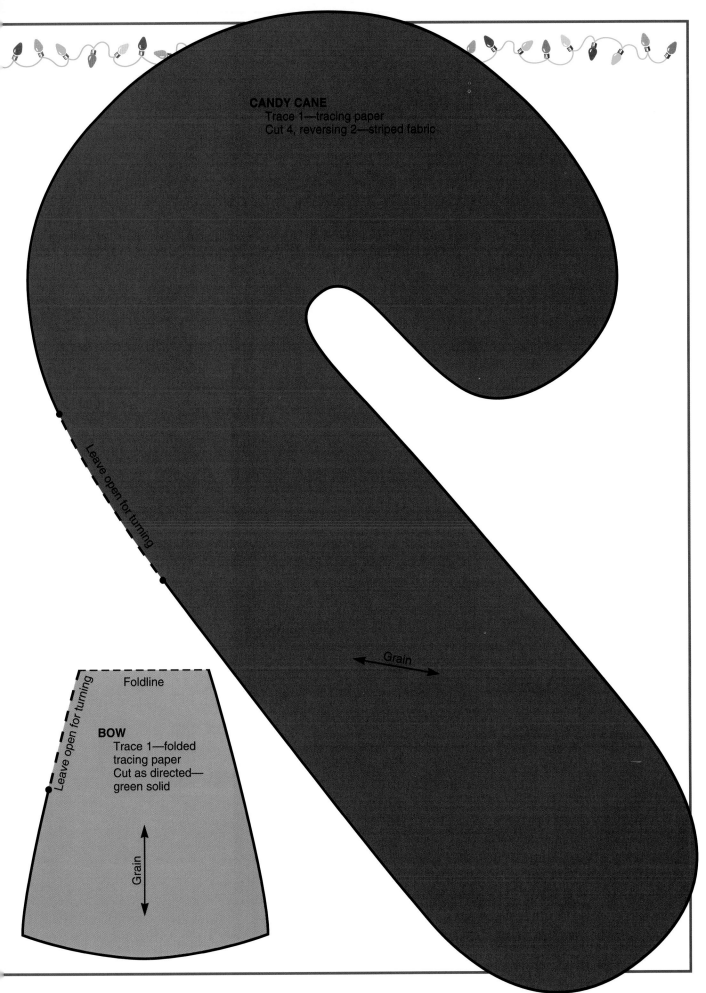

CANDY CANE
Trace 1—tracing paper
Cut 4, reversing 2—striped fabric

Leave open for turning

Grain

Foldline

Leave open for turning

BOW
Trace 1—folded
tracing paper
Cut as directed—
green solid

Grain

Busy Santa Claus Arrives Just in the Nick of Time

THE VISION Renee Dent of Conrad, Montana has of the days before Christmas is a last-minute one—as the busy St. Nick in her cross-stitch trim illustrates! "I'm always in a rush prior to December 25," she confirms. "I imagine Santa must be, too. So I cross-stitched him working right up to his 'deadline'."

Materials Needed:

Chart on this page
Bell pattern on next page
Tracing paper and pencil
6-inch square of ivory 18-count Aida cloth
DMC six-strand embroidery floss in colors listed on color key
Two 6-inch squares of lightweight cardboard
6-inch square of polyester fleece fabric for padding
6-inch square of Christmas print for backing
1/2 yard of 1/2-inch-wide pre-gathered ivory eyelet lace
1/2 yard of 1/8-inch-wide red satin ribbon
White (tacky) glue
Size 26 tapestry needle
Scissors

Finished Size: Santa trim is 5 inches high x 5 inches across. Design area is 54 stitches wide x 54 stitches high.

Directions:

Zigzag or overcast edges of Aida cloth to prevent fraying. Fold cloth in half lengthwise, then fold in half crosswise to determine center and mark this point. To find center of chart, draw lines across chart connecting arrows. Begin stitching at this point so design will be centered.

Working with 18-in. lengths of six-strand floss, separate strands and use two strands for cross-stitching and one strand for backstitching, straight stitches and French knots. See Fig. 1 for stitch illustrations.

Each square on the chart equals one stitch worked over a set of fabric threads. Use colors indicated on color key to complete all cross-stitching, then backstitching, straight stitches and French knots.

Do not knot floss on back of work. Instead, leave a short tail of floss on back of work and hold it in place while working the first few stitches over it. To end a strand, run needle under a few neighboring stitches in back before cutting floss close to work.

FINISHING: Trace bell pattern onto folded tracing paper. Cut out and open for a complete pattern. Trace around pattern onto fleece and cardboard as directed on pattern and cut out.

With edges matching, glue fleece to one piece of cardboard. Center completed cross-stitch right side up over padded side of cardboard. Trim away excess fabric to about 1 in. from outside edge of cardboard. Glue edges of Aida cloth to back of cardboard, carefully smoothing front and clipping curves to reduce bulk. In the same way, cover remaining cardboard with backing fabric, omitting fleece.

Glue gathered edge of eyelet lace to back of padded cross-stitch piece so lace extends beyond outside edges.

Fig. 1

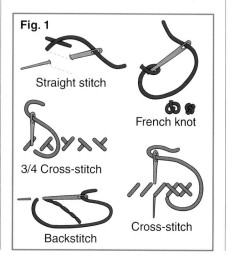

Straight stitch

French knot

3/4 Cross-stitch

Backstitch

Cross-stitch

SANTA TRIM COLOR KEY	DMC
▫ White	000
◣ Black	310
▨ Christmas Red	321
✳ Pearl Gray	415
◪ Light Antique Blue	432
■ Dark Christmas Red	498
✴ Dark Christmas Green	699
▤ Medium Christmas Green	701
▣ Medium Pink	776
▦ Medium Antique Blue	931
▱ Light Pink Beige	951
▥ Black Brown	3371
✕ Dark Rose Brown	3772
△ Dark Straw	3820

STRAIGHT STITCH
— Dark Christmas Green—pine needles on calendar 699

BACKSTITCH
— Pewter Gray—Santa's boots 317
— Christmas Red—trim on sled 321
— Medium Antique Blue—paint can handle 931
— Black Brown—everything else 3371
— Dark Straw—design on sled 3820

FRENCH KNOTS
● Christmas Red—berries on calendar 321

SANTA TRIM CHART

Overlap ends of lace at top of bell and glue to secure.

Cut a 6-in. piece of ribbon and glue ends of ribbon to top center back of stitched piece to form hanging loop. Tie remaining piece of ribbon into a bow and glue bow to top of bell as shown in photo at left.

With wrong sides together and edges of cardboard matching, glue stitched design to covered back. ●

BELL PATTERN
Trace 1—folded
tracing paper
Cut 1—fleece
Cut 2—cardboard

Foldline

Candy-Striped Santas Add Lively Flavor to the Season

THE SECRET INGREDIENT in this deliciously easy design from Christine Cathcart of Spotswood, New Jersey is fun. She confirms, "The Santas produce grins whether I use them on the tree, in a garland or even as pins."

Materials Needed (for one):
Pattern on this page
Tracing paper and pencil
6-inch square of red and white striped
*   fabric*
Small amount of polyester stuffing
Two 4mm black seed beads for eyes
6 inches of 1-inch-wide pre-gathered
*   white eyelet lace*
7mm pink pom-pom
2 inches of 1/4-inch-wide white satin
*   ribbon*
6 inches of 1/8-inch-wide white satin
*   ribbon*
Tiny artificial holly leaf
1/2-inch white button
12 inches of red crochet cotton or
*   six-strand embroidery floss*
All-purpose thread—black and white
Gold metallic thread for hanger
Standard sewing supplies
White (tacky) glue

Finished Size: Candy cane trim is about 3-1/2 inches tall x 1-3/4 inches across.

Directions:
Trace pattern onto tracing paper.

Fold striped fabric in half with right sides together. Pin candy cane pattern on top of fabric, matching grain on pattern with stripes as desired. Using matching thread and a straight stitch, sew through all layers on traced line of pattern, leaving opening as indicated for turning. Remove pattern.

Cut out candy cane 1/4 in. outside stitching. Clip curves.

Turn candy cane right side out through opening. Stuff firmly with polyester stuffing. Turn raw edges of opening in and hand-stitch opening closed.

Use red crochet cotton or six-strand embroidery floss to tie button to tip of candy cane. Trim ends.

Wrap 1/4-in.-wide ribbon around the candy cane to create a hatband as shown in the photo at right. Trim excess and glue ends in place. Tuck holly leaf behind ribbon as shown in photo and glue to secure.

With black thread, hand-stitch beads about 1/4 in. below hatband for eyes.

For beard, hand-stitch eyelet lace to candy cane as follows: Fold raw edge of one end a scant 1/4 in. to wrong side. Using white thread, stitch this fold to a side seam with bottom edge of eyelet lace even with bottom of candy cane. Hand-stitch along top edge of eyelet lace to other side seam.

Fold eyelet lace back across candy cane, allowing about 1/4 in. of first row to show. Stitch along top edge to other side seam. Continue in this way, covering about 2 in. of the candy cane. Fold raw edge of end a scant 1/4 in. to wrong side and stitch fold to side seam.

Cut 1/8-in.-wide ribbon into two 3-in. pieces. Layer the two pieces and tie an overhand knot in the center. Trim ends at an angle. Glue knot centered over the top edge of eyelet for Santa's mustache.

Glue pom-pom to knot of ribbon mustache for nose.

Stitch a piece of gold metallic thread through center top and tie ends in an overhand knot at desired length for hanger. ●

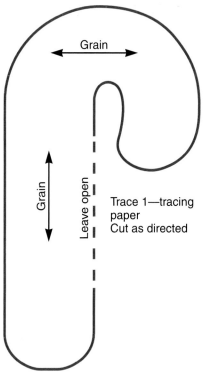

CANDY CANE SANTA TRIM

Grain

Grain

Leave open

Trace 1—tracing paper
Cut as directed

Rising Star Is Just Right For Setting Yuletide Table

CHRISTMAS COLORS will sparkle at your holiday table with this crocheted place mat and napkin ring set.

The bright design of the star is based on a quilting pattern, explains Marion Cornett of Fowlerville, Michigan. It's a wonderful way to catch the high points of the holidays!

Materials Needed (for one set):
4-ply worsted-weight yarn—two 3-1/2-ounce skeins each of red and green (Marion used Coats and Clark Red Heart Classic yarn No. 902 Jockey Red and No. 686 Paddy Green)
Size K/10-1/2 (6.50mm) crochet hook or size needed to obtain correct gauge
Tapestry needle

Gauge: Using two strands of yarn and working in sc, 7 sts and 8 rows = 3 inches.

Finished Size: Place mat is about 17 inches long x 13 inches high. Napkin ring measures 1-1/2 inches across x 3 inches high.

SPECIAL TECHNIQUES: Chain Color Change: Yarn over with the new color and draw the yarn through the last loop on the hk. Leave a short tail of yarn on the back to be woven in later.

Single Crochet Color Change: Colors are changed while completing the last stitch made with the previous color. Work last sc before color change indicated on chart until there are two loops on the hk. Drop the first color and yarn over with new color; draw the new color through the last two loops of the sc.

Star Chart: Each square on chart represents a sc st. Read chart from right to left on odd-numbered rows and from left to right on even-numbered rows. Work evenly on 30 sts throughout, following chart and color key for color changes. Attach new colors as needed. When a color is no longer used, break off yarn, leaving an end to weave in.

Directions:
Using two strands of yarn as one, wind two balls of red and one ball of green with approximately 20 yds. on each. Attach balls of yarn when needed for color changes.

Use two strands of yarn held together as one throughout.

PLACE MAT: Row 1: Ch 5 with red; ch 20 with green; ch 6 with red. Sc in second ch from hk and in each remaining ch across row, following Row 1 of chart for color changes: 30 scs.

Rows 2-10: Ch 1, turn; sc in each sc across row, following Rows 2-10 of chart for color changes.

Rows 11-34: Ch 1, turn; sc in each sc across row with red, using yarn from skeins.

Rows 35-44: Ch 1, turn; turn chart and sc in each sc across row, following Rows 35-44 for color changes.

Fasten off all yarns at end of Row 44. Use tapestry needle to weave in ends.

NAPKIN RING: Row 1: With two strands of green, ch 7; sc in second ch from hk and in each remaining ch across row: 6 scs.

Row 2: Ch 1, turn; work 1 sc in each sc across row: 6 scs.

Repeat Row 2 until piece measures approximately 5 in.

Fold piece with right sides together so first and last rows meet, forming a ring. Work 1 row of sc, picking up sts from first and last rows for seam. Fasten off yarns. Use tapestry needle to weave in ends. Turn right side out. ●

ABBREVIATIONS

ch(s)	chains
hk	hook
sc(s)	single crochet(s)
st(s)	stitch(es)

CROCHET PLACE MAT STAR COLOR KEY
- ■ Red
- ■ Green

STAR CHART

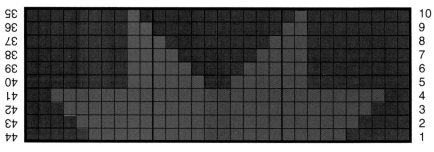

Twinkling Trimmer'll Shine on Pine

THIS STARRY DELIGHT will brighten up boughs for the holidays. Mina Dyck of Boissevain, Manitoba dreamed up the design using plastic canvas embroidery and quick-to-finish crochet edging.

Materials Needed:
Chart on this page
5-inch star shape in 7-count plastic canvas
10 yards of gold metallic cord
One ball of gold metallic crochet cotton (Mina used Knit-Cro-Sheen Thread)
Size 5 steel crochet hook
30 inches of 1/4-inch-wide gold metallic ribbon
Glue gun and glue sticks
3/4-inch gold metallic ball button with shank or gold metallic bead
Scissors

Finished Size: Star measures about 5-3/4 inches across.

Directions:
Cut five 55-in. lengths of gold cord. Apply a bit of glue to one end of each length of cord to stiffen it and prevent fraying, making it easier to use without a needle.

Following chart and leaving a 1-1/2-in. tail at back of work, thread one 55-in. length through holes of one section of the plastic canvas star. When section is completed (at number 46 on chart), cut excess cord, leaving a 1-1/2-in. tail of cord on back. Glue starting and ending tails to back of work, being careful not to get glue in holes along outer edges of star. Repeat for remaining sections of star.

EDGING: With gold metallic crochet cotton, crochet around outside edges of completed star as follows:

Round 1: Starting at first hole to the side of the plastic hanger, * sc in each hole around edge to next point of star; work 2 scs in the hole at point of star; repeat from * three more times; sc in each hole to hanger; ch 1, turn.

Round 2: * Sc in each sc to next point of star; work 2 scs in each of the two scs at point of star; repeat from * three more times; sc in each sc to end; ch 3, turn.

Round 3: * Sl st in each of next two scs, ch 3; repeat from * around, ending with sl st in last two scs. Fasten off.

FINISHING: From gold ribbon, make a small bow as shown in photo below. Trim ends at an angle. Glue bow to top of star over hanger. Glue button or bead to center of star.

STAR TREE TRIM CHART

Start with cord from back at 1 and insert from front to back at 2. Continue in the same way, following numbering sequence as shown and inserting cord through holes from back to front on all odd numbers and from front to back on all even numbers. Stitch each section of star in the same way.

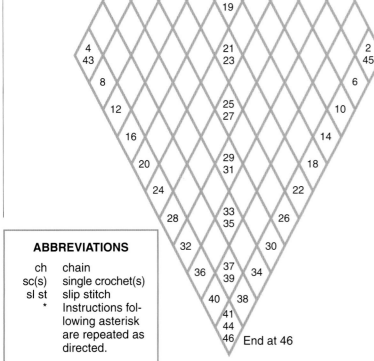

Start at 1

End at 46

ABBREVIATIONS

ch	chain
sc(s)	single crochet(s)
sl st	slip stitch
*	Instructions following asterisk are repeated as directed.

Stitched-on Snowman Fashions Frosty Fun!

BREAKING THE ICE is what Avon Mackay's smiley snowman applique does best. She reports from her Waukesha, Wisconsin home that the design brings out grins from her youngest grandchild on up.

"All ages find the snowman appealing," Avon attests. "Crafters are especially fond of him, though—he's a breeze to build."

Materials Needed:
Patterns on next page
Green sweatshirt (either make one yourself from a commercial pattern or purchase one)
100% cotton or cotton-blend fabrics—
1/4 yard each or scraps of red plaid, black solid, gold solid, green solid, red solid and white solid
1/2 yard of paper-backed fusible web
1/2 yard of tear-away stabilizer or typing paper
All-purpose thread—black, green and red
Black six-strand embroidery floss
Embroidery needle
Standard sewing supplies

Finished Size: The snowman applique measures 9 inches high x 6-1/2 inches wide and will fit on most garments for either children or adults. The design can be enlarged or reduced on a copy machine to fit other sizes of apparel.

Directions:
Pre-wash fabrics without fabric softeners, washing colors separately. If the water from any fabric is discolored, wash again until rinse water runs clear. Machine-dry and press fabrics.

Wash and dry sweatshirt following manufacturer's instructions.

Remove ribbing from bottom of purchased sweatshirt and, if desired, open side seams for ease in appliqueing. If you choose to make your own sweatshirt, applique the design onto garment front before stitching side seams.

Trace patterns at right onto paper side of fusible web, leaving a 1/2-in. margin between shapes. Cut shapes apart.

Following manufacturer's directions, fuse shapes to wrong side of fabrics as directed on patterns. Transfer inside design lines for mouth, holly and scarf by machine-stitching on lines traced on paper backing. Cut out shapes along outside traced lines. Remove paper backing.

Center appliques on front of sweatshirt as shown in photo at left and fuse, following manufacturer's directions.

Position tear-away stabilizer or typing paper on wrong side of garment behind design. Using black thread and a medium satin stitch, applique around shapes in the following order: top edge of hatband, crown and brim of hat, holly leaves, neck edge of scarf, gold band on scarf, end of scarf (starting and ending at neck edge), outer edge of head, eyes and nose.

Using black thread and a narrow satin stitch, stitch over inside design lines on holly and scarf.

Using red thread and a narrow satin stitch, applique around holly berries.

Remove tear-away stabilizer or typing paper. Pull all threads to wrong side and secure.

Separate six-strand black embroidery floss and use three strands to stem-stitch mouth. See Fig. 1 for stitch illustration.

Fold a 1-1/4-in. hem to wrong side on bottom of garment. Top-stitch hem, using green thread. ●

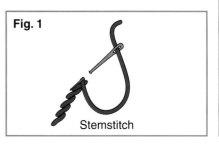

Fig. 1

Stemstitch

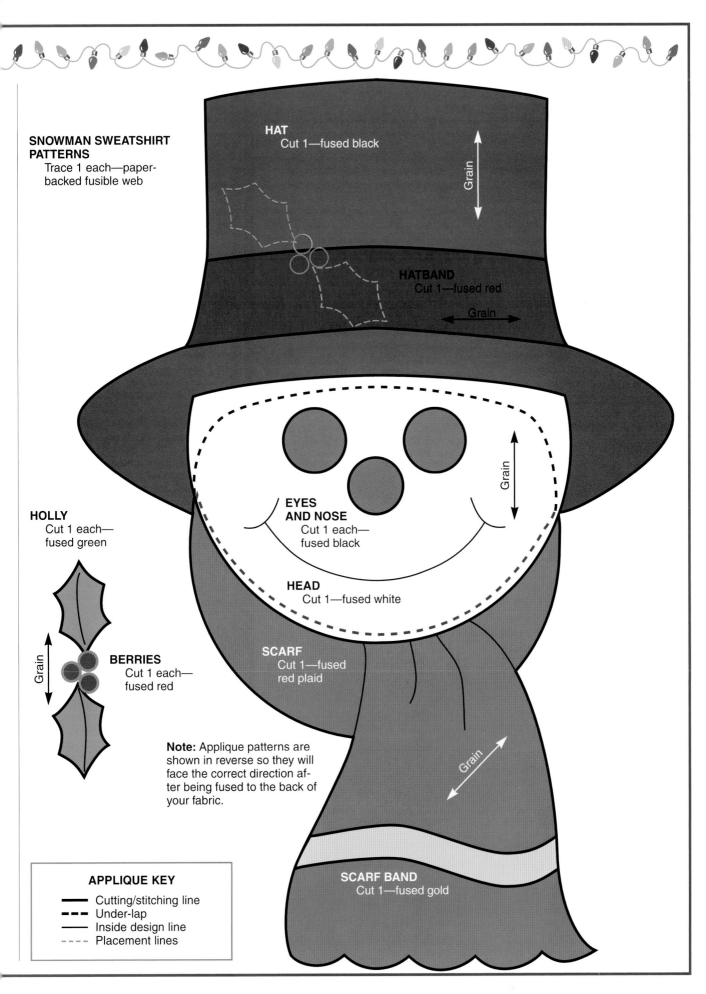

SNOWMAN SWEATSHIRT PATTERNS
Trace 1 each—paper-backed fusible web

HAT
Cut 1—fused black

Grain

HATBAND
Cut 1—fused red

Grain

Grain

EYES AND NOSE
Cut 1 each—fused black

HEAD
Cut 1—fused white

HOLLY
Cut 1 each—fused green

Grain

BERRIES
Cut 1 each—fused red

SCARF
Cut 1—fused red plaid

Grain

Note: Applique patterns are shown in reverse so they will face the correct direction after being fused to the back of your fabric.

APPLIQUE KEY
—— Cutting/stitching line
■■■ Under-lap
— Inside design line
- - - Placement lines

SCARF BAND
Cut 1—fused gold

Little Tree Skirt Makes Big Impact

SIZED RIGHT for a petite pine, this colorful cover will spread Christmas cheer in any setting, according to Linda Whitener of Glen Allen, Missouri.

"Sometimes, folks don't have room for a big evergreen. Or they might want to display a tabletop model in addition to a large one," she comments. "This skirt suits either situation."

Materials Needed:
44-inch-wide 100% cotton or cotton-blend fabrics—3/4 yard each of green print and white solid and 1/4 yard of red print
20-inch square of lightweight quilt batting
4-1/2 yards of 1/8-inch-wide green satin ribbon
Seven 1-inch two-hole white buttons
Matching all-purpose thread
Quilter's ruler
Quilter's marking pen or pencil
Rotary cutter and mat (optional)
Compass
Standard sewing supplies

Finished Size: The tree skirt measures about 22 inches across.

Directions:
Pre-wash all fabrics, washing colors separately. If the water from any fabric is discolored, wash again until rinse water runs clear. Machine-dry and press all fabrics.

CUTTING: Cut strips using rotary cutter and quilter's ruler or mark fabrics using ruler and marker of choice and cut with scissors.

Cut a 20-in. green print square. Fold square in half lengthwise, then fold in half crosswise. Measure and mark an arc with pins or quilter's pen or pencil 9 in. from point of folds as shown in Fig. 1. Cut along marking and open for an 18-in. circle. In the same way, cut an 18-in. circle from white backing fabric and from batting.

From remaining green print, cut one 2-in. x 20-in. crosswise strip.

From remaining white fabric, cut two 2-in. x 20-in. crosswise strips, one 2-in. x 36-in. crosswise strip and eight 5-in. squares.

From red print, cut two 2-in. x 36-in. crosswise strips.

QUILTING: Place circle of batting on a flat surface and smooth out all wrinkles. Center white backing circle right side up on top of batting and smooth out. Place green print circle wrong side up on top of white backing fabric and smooth out. Pin or hand-baste to hold all three layers together securely.

From center of circle, draw a straight line to outside edge. Use compass to draw a 1-in. circle in center of skirt.

Machine-stitch around outside edge of circle 1/2 in. from edge. Also stitch 1/2 in. from each side of traced straight line to center circle, leaving an opening for turning along one straight edge. See Fig. 2. Then stitch on line of inner circle as shown in Fig. 2.

Cut on traced straight line between seams from outside edge to inner circle. Trim seams to 1/4 in. from stitching. See Fig. 2. Clip curves and trim corners.

Turn right side out through opening so batting is between white and green print fabrics. Turn raw edges of opening in and hand-stitch opening closed. Press as needed.

PIECING: Do all piecing with accurate 1/4-in. seams and right sides of fabric together. Press seams toward darker fabrics unless otherwise directed.

Sew a 36-in.-long red print strip to each long edge of 36-in.-long white strip, making a 5-in.-wide x 36-in.-long pieced strip. The width of the center strip should be 1-1/2 in. along its entire length and the ends of all strips should be even.

Sew a 20-in.-long white strip to each

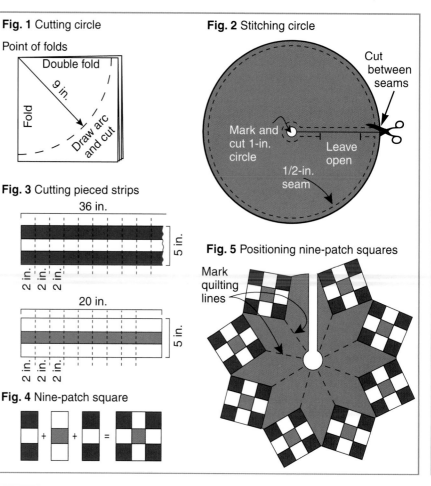

Fig. 1 Cutting circle

Point of folds

Double fold

Fold

9 in.

Draw arc and cut

Fig. 2 Stitching circle

Cut between seams

Mark and cut 1-in. circle

Leave open

1/2-in. seam

Fig. 3 Cutting pieced strips

36 in.

5 in.

2 in. 2 in. 2 in.

20 in.

5 in.

2 in. 2 in. 2 in.

Fig. 4 Nine-patch square

Fig. 5 Positioning nine-patch squares

Mark quilting lines

long edge of a 20-in.-long green print strip, making a 5-in.-wide x 20-in.-long pieced strip.

Referring to Fig. 3, cut each pieced strip into 2-in.-wide sections to make 16 red print and white combination strips and eight green print and white combination strips.

To make a nine-patch square, stitch a red print and white combination strip to each long edge of a green print and white combination strip, carefully matching corners (see Fig. 4). Repeat, making a total of eight nine-patch squares. Press each square.

With right sides together and raw edges matching, sew a 5-in. white square to each nine-patch square, leaving an opening for turning. Trim corners and turn right side out. Turn raw edges of opening in and hand-stitch opening closed. Repeat, making a total of eight nine-patch squares lined with white.

FINISHING: Referring to Fig. 5, place the nine-patch squares on right side (green print side) of tree skirt so corners of squares meet at outside edge of circle. Hand-baste squares to tree skirt.

Place quilter's ruler diagonally (from corner to corner) across a nine-patch square to center of circle and use quilter's pen or pencil to mark a quilting line to center circle. Repeat for each square, marking eight quilting lines to center of tree skirt as shown in Fig. 5.

Machine-stitch with green thread and a straight stitch on marked lines, ending stitching at the inside corner of each nine-patch square.

Using green thread, stitch around the outside edges of each nine-patch square, stitching as close as possible to the outside edge of the square and stitching the two inside edges of each square to tree skirt.

Cut seven 18-in.-long pieces of ribbon. Hand-stitch the center of each length of ribbon to tree skirt where corners of nine-patch squares meet. Thread ends of each ribbon through holes of a button and tie ends in a bow as shown in photo.

Cut remaining ribbon into four equal pieces. Hand-stitch an end of two of the ribbons to each side of back opening at center. Hand-stitch an end of remaining ribbons to corners of nine-patch squares along back opening.

Place tree skirt around base of tree and tie ribbons into bows to close. 🌢

Cherubs Stem from Evergreens

THE SEED for this idea didn't fall far from the tree. To make her spirited trims, Betsy Davis of Jamestown, North Dakota combined tiny pinecones with bits of lace, paper twist and other easy-to-find supplies. "They take no time at all to make," she comments.

Materials Needed (for one angel):
1-1/2-inch- to 2-inch-long pinecone—fully opened and dry
5/8-inch natural round wooden bead or wooden ball with center hole
3-1/2-inch-long piece of paper twist for wings in color of choice
30 inches of 4-ply brown yarn and size 3 all-metal knitting needle or 1/8-inch wood dowel
5 inches of 3/8-inch-wide white or ecru lace
6 inches of coordinating pearl cotton or embroidery floss for bow
10 inches of white pearl cotton or embroidery floss for hanger
2 inches of gold embroidery floss or metallic thread for halo
Acrylic craft paints—brown for eyes, mauve for mouth and coordinating color to highlight pinecone "dress"
Small paintbrush
Toothpick
Hand-sewing needle and white thread
Powdered blush and cotton swab
Tacky (white) glue
Scissors

Finished Size: Pinecone angel mea-

sures about 2 inches high x 3 inches across.

Directions:
Knot ends of 10-in. piece of pearl cotton or embroidery floss and glue knot to base of pinecone for hanger. Thread loop of hanger through hole in wooden bead or ball for head and glue to secure head to pinecone.

Use toothpick and brown paint to dab tiny eyes on head. In the same way, add a tiny mauve heart for the mouth. Let dry.

Use cotton swab to apply powdered blush for cheeks.

Dab paintbrush into dress color and wipe excess from brush. Lightly paint the tips of the scales on the pinecone for angel's "dress". Let dry.

Hand-sew running stitches along straight edge of lace, leaving long thread ends. See Fig. 1 for stitch illustration. Place lace around neck of angel. Pull up threads to gather and knot thread ends. Spot-glue lace to pinecone to secure.

Wrap brown yarn around size 3 knitting needle or 1/8-in. wood dowel for 5 in. Wet yarn with water and blot to remove excess. Place yarn-wrapped needle or dowel on cookie sheet and bake in oven at 225° until yarn is dry (about 30-40 minutes). Remove from oven and let cool.

Cut curled yarn into short ringlets and separate the plies. Glue yarn to head for hair as shown in photo, being careful not to cover hanger.

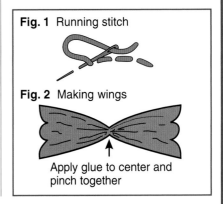

To make wings, cut a 2-in.-high x 3-1/2-in.-long piece of untwisted paper twist. Use scissors to cut scallops along each short edge as shown in photo. Place a bead of glue down the center and pinch paper twist together as shown in Fig. 2. When dry, glue wings to back of angel as shown in photo above.

Tie pearl cotton or floss into a small bow and glue to lace in front. Bring ends of gold floss or metallic thread together and glue into a circle for halo. Slip halo over hanging loop and spot-glue halo to top of angel's head. 🌢

Fig. 1 Running stitch

Fig. 2 Making wings

Apply glue to center and pinch together

Mix-and-Match Wall Banners Are Bright for Christmas!

YOU'LL FIND this well-worded holiday wall hanging is a piece of work that's fun to put together—one way or the other.

Julie Todd stitched up the red version first for her Aurelia, Iowa abode. "That looked so nice I thought I'd try a green one, too," she spells out.

Materials Needed (for each):

Patterns on this page
44-inch-wide 100% cotton or cotton-blend fabrics—1/2 yard of green or red print for outside border, hanging tabs, letters, backing and optional bow; 1/2 yard of contrasting red or green print for sash-ings and inside border; and 1/8 yard of light Christmas print for blocks
1/4 yard of paper-backed fusible web
8-inch x 19-1/4-inch piece of quilt batting
Rotary cutter and mat (optional)
Quilter's marking pen or pencil
Quilter's ruler
Four 3/8-inch black buttons
Six-strand embroidery floss—black for both mini-quilts and red for green mini-quilt or green for red mini-quilt
Embroidery needle
Six inches of 1/8-inch-wide red satin ribbon for green mini-quilt
7 inches of 1/4-inch wooden dowel
Two dowel end caps or wooden spools to fit dowel
Brown acrylic craft paint and small paintbrush or brown stain and soft cloth
14 inches of 19-gauge black craft wire (optional)
Pinking shears (optional)
Standard sewing supplies

Finished Size: Each mini-quilt is 7-1/2 inches wide x 18-3/4 inches high, excluding hanging tabs.

Directions:

Pre-wash and dry all fabrics without fabric softeners, washing colors separately. If the water from any fabric is discolored, wash again until rinse water runs clear. Machine-dry and press all fabrics.

CUTTING: Cut fabrics using rotary cutter and quilter's ruler or mark fabrics using ruler and marker of choice and cut with scissors. Cut strips crosswise from selvage to selvage.

From light Christmas print, cut four 3-1/2-in. squares for blocks.

From red or green print, cut five 1-1/4-in. x 3-1/2-in. strips and two matching 1-1/4-in. x 16-1/4-in. strips for sashing and inside borders.

From contrasting red or green print, cut two 2-in. x 19-1/4-in. strips for outside side borders and two 2-in. x 5-in. strips for outside top and bottom borders. Cut two matching 2-1/2-in. x 4-in. rectangles for hanging tabs.

Trace letter and ornament patterns at left onto paper side of fusible web, leaving a 1/2-in. margin between shapes. Cut apart shapes.

NOEL PATTERNS

Trace 1 each—paper-backed fusible web
Cut 1 each—red or green fused print

Add red French knots and red bow or green cross-stitches to ornament.

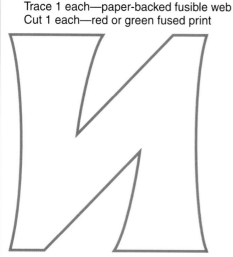

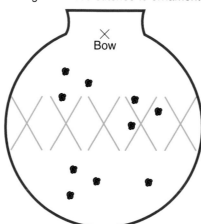

× Bow

Note: The letters are given in reverse so they will face in the correct direction after being fused to the back of the fabric.

Following manufacturer's directions, fuse shapes to wrong side of same print fabric used for outside borders. Cut out shapes along traced lines and remove paper backing. Center each shape on a 3-1/2-in. light Christmas print square and fuse into place.

PIECING: Do all piecing with accurate 1/4-in. seams and right sides of fabric together. Press seams toward darker fabrics when possible.

Lay out pieces right side up as shown in photo at far left. Making sure all letters and the ornament are running in the same direction, sew a 1-1/4-in. x 3-1/2-in. sashing piece between each block as shown in photo.

Stitch a 1-1/4-in. x 3-1/2-in. inside border strip to the top and bottom edges of pieced strip. Then stitch a matching 1-1/4-in. x 16-1/4-in. inside border strip to one side edge of pieced strip. Add a matching inside border strip to opposite side edge of pieced strip.

Stitch one 2-in. x 5-in. outside border strip to top edge of mini-quilt and a matching outside border strip to bottom edge. Then stitch a matching 2-in. x 19-1/4-in. outside border strip to each side edge.

ASSEMBLY: With right sides together, stitch long edges of each hanging tab together. Turn tabs right side out through

one end. Center seams and press tabs. Fold tabs in half with seams on the inside and raw edges matching. With all raw edges matching, pin each tab to right side of top edge of mini-quilt about 1 in. from side edges as shown in photo.

Cut a piece of batting and a piece of backing fabric to match the size of the pieced mini-quilt. Place batting on a flat surface and smooth out. Place backing centered right side up over batting, smoothing out wrinkles. Place pieced mini-quilt centered on top of backing with wrong side up and hanging tabs facing the center. Pin all layers together with edges matching.

Machine-stitch 1/4 in. from the raw

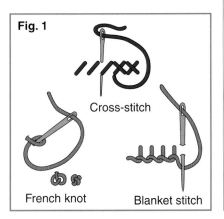

Fig. 1

Cross-stitch

French knot

Blanket stitch

edges, leaving an opening for turning along one edge. Remove pins. Clip corners diagonally. Turn right side out through opening so batting is on the inside. Turn raw edges of opening in and hand-stitch closed.

FINISHING: Separate six-strand black embroidery floss and use three strands to blanket-stitch around the outside edges of each letter and the ornament. See Fig. 1 for stitch illustration. Hand-sew a button on each corner of the inside border as shown in photo.

Use three strands of red embroidery floss to stitch French knots on the green ornament. Or use three strands of green floss to stitch large cross-stitches on the red ornament as shown on pattern. See Fig. 1 for stitch illustrations.

Tie red ribbon into a small bow and stitch bow onto the green ornament as shown in photo.

Apply brown paint or stain to dowel and end caps or spools. Let dry. Insert dowel through tabs and attach end caps or spools to dowel.

For optional wire hanger and bow, coil wire loosely around pencil. Remove pencil. Loop ends around dowel as shown in photo. Use pinking shears to cut a 1-in. x 12-in. strip of green print. Tie strip in a bow around coiled wire hanger as shown in photo. ◗

Frolicsome Fridgies Will Put Yule Pieces Together

IF YOU'RE GAME for a good time, you'll want to give Joanna Randolph Rott's engaging idea a try. She turned a Christmas greeting card into magnets that are practical *and* playful.

"I cut the card into squares, glued them onto wood pieces to craft a puzzle and added magnets to the puzzle pieces so they could hold notes on the fridge," she pens from Fort Washington, Pennsylvania.

Materials Needed:
Christmas card
Six 1/8-inch-thick x 1-1/2-inch-square wooden pieces or size appropriate for card (Joanna used Woodsies)
Six 1/2-inch magnet buttons
Four small coordinating buttons (Joanna used 3/8-inch square buttons)
Black thread and hand-sewing needle
Ruler and pencil
Scissors

Black permanent fine-line marker
White (tacky) glue

Finished Size: The size of the puzzle will vary, depending on the size of the wooden squares used.

Directions:
Cut card along fold and discard back section.

Place the six wooden squares on the front (picture side) of the card to determine the portion of the card you wish to include in your puzzle. Mark outside edges of card lightly with pencil. Cut on this line and discard outside edges.

Use marker to draw a broken line about 1/8 in. from edge on right side of card for "stitches".

Turn card over and divide the back of the card into six equal pieces, using pencil and ruler. Cut on lines.

Glue a wooden square centered on

the back of each card piece. Glue a magnet button to the center of each wooden square.

Thread needle with black thread. Stitch thread through the holes of each button and tie ends in a small bow. Trim ends to desired length. Glue a button to each outside corner of the assembled puzzle as shown in photo above. ◗

Well-Dressed Candy Jar Is Filled with Brisk Character

'SNO KIDDING! Homemade holiday treats somehow taste even better when they're stored in this dapper container.

Verna Dodson reports that the snowman takes center stage each Christmas in her Newport, Pennsylvania kitchen. "It all started with a pint jar and some loopy chenille I had handy," she recounts. "I've since received lots of compliments on my speedy design."

Materials Needed:
Pint-size canning jar with regular-size metal band and metal lid
2-inch Styrofoam ball for head
3 yards of white jumbo loopy chenille (available where pipe cleaners or chenille stems are sold)*
Black felt top hat to fit Styrofoam ball head
12 inches of 1/8-inch-wide red satin ribbon
Two 1/2-inch black animal eyes
Three straight pins with black plastic heads for mouth
Toothpick
1-inch-long piece of corncob for pipe
Small foam carrot for nose or orange pipe cleaner (chenille stem) to make nose
Three 3/4-inch black buttons
21 inches of 1-1/2-inch-wide red and green plaid ribbon

6 inches of yellow yarn
Craft scissors
Glue gun and glue sticks
Craft pins

*If you can't find jumbo loopy chenille, cut quilt batting into long strips, then wrap the strips around the jar and Styrofoam ball for a similar look.

Finished Size: Jar is 9 inches tall x 6 inches across.

Directions:
Wrap about 30 in. of loopy chenille around Styrofoam ball to cover ball for head. Glue each row as you wrap it. Secure loopy chenille with craft pins as needed to hold it until glue has set.

Wrap about 70 in. of loopy chenille around sides of pint jar as shown in photo above right, gluing each row as you wrap it and being sure not to glue loopy chenille to the rim of the jar.

Insert metal lid into metal band and glue head centered on top of lid. Glue hat to top of head. Glue red ribbon to hat as shown in photo, overlapping ends and trimming excess as needed.

If desired, make nose by wrapping orange pipe cleaner around finger, forming a tight coil. Remove coil and form it into a 1-in.-long carrot shape.

Glue foam carrot or pipe cleaner carrot nose, eyes and straight pins for mouth onto head as shown in photo.

Glue corncob to end of toothpick for pipe. Glue pipe to side of mouth as shown in photo.

Screw metal band onto top of jar and glue buttons onto snowman as shown in photo.

Cut two 3-in.-long pieces of loopy chenille. Form each into a circle and glue one to each side of the body for arms as shown in photo.

Tie ribbon around metal rim for scarf as shown in photo and spot-glue to secure. Cut yellow yarn into 1/2-in.-long pieces. Glue yarn to ends of scarf for fringe. ◗

Jolly Old Elf Has Lots of Rural Pull

FOLKS may be driven to grin when they spot this fresh-from-the-field ornament hanging on the tree.

Aside from accenting branches, the happy craft from Linda Lover of Byron, Michigan can also serve as a clever present for your favorite farmer. (To turn the trim into a *real* keepsake, paint the date onto the tractor's fender.)

Materials Needed:
Patterns on next page
Tracing paper and pencil
Stylus or dry ballpoint pen
3-inch x 4-inch piece of 1/4-inch-thick basswood

5-inch square of 1/2-inch-thick basswood or pine
Two 3/4-inch-long pieces of 1/8-inch dowel
1/2-inch wooden wheel for steering wheel
1/2-inch wooden spool for muffler
Black buttons—one 3/8 inch and one 5/8 inch
Scroll or band saw
Drill with 1/16-inch and 3/16-inch bits
Sandpaper and tack cloth
1 inch of 19-gauge craft wire
Acrylic craft paints—black, flesh, gold, gray, green, red and white
Paintbrushes—No. 8 and No. 2 flat and No. 1 liner

Palette or paper plate
Black permanent fine-line marker
Wood or craft glue
10 inches of 2-ply jute string

Finished Size: Tractor trim measures 4-1/4 inches across x 4-1/4 inches high.

Directions:
Trace patterns at right onto tracing paper as directed. Turn tracing paper patterns over and rub flat side of pencil lead over traced lines to darken.

Place arm, fender and star patterns right side up on 1/4-in.-thick wood. Trace over patterns with stylus or dry ballpoint pen to transfer pattern onto wood. Place Santa body and tractor pattern onto 1/2-in.-thick wood and trace over pattern in the same way.

Cut out wood pieces with scroll or band saw. Sand lightly and wipe with tack cloth to remove sanding dust.

Drill holes in tractor and arm where shown on patterns, drilling holes in one arm only.

PAINTING: Place small amounts of paint on paper plate or palette as needed. Paint as directed below, continuing paints around side edges. Apply a second coat as needed for complete coverage, allowing drying time between coats.

Using No. 8 flat brush, paint the fender and tractor green as shown on pattern. Paint entire back of tractor green. Paint tires, dowels, wooden spool and 1/2-in. wooden wheel black. Paint stars gold. Let dry.

Using No. 2 flat brush, paint Santa's leg red. Using larger flat brush, paint all sides of his body, hat and arms red as shown on patterns. Let dry.

Using No. 2 flat brush, paint Santa's boot and all sides of his mittens black as shown on pattern. Let dry.

Using No. 2 flat brush, paint Santa's face flesh. Let dry.

Add a bit of red to white to make light pink. Use liner to paint Santa's nose light pink.

Using No. 2 flat brush, paint Santa's beard, mustache and fur trim on his hat and suit white. Paint fur trim on all sides of his mittens white as shown on pattern. Let dry.

Using liner, paint lettering on tractor gold. Let dry.

Using liner, paint the pedal on the tractor under Santa's boot gray and the lines above and below the lettering black. Let dry.

Use black marker to dot on black eyes and add detail lines on Santa's beard, mustache and suit.

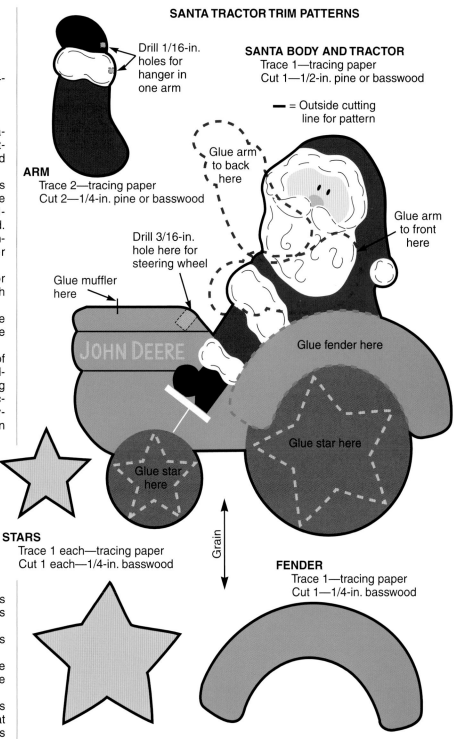

SANTA TRACTOR TRIM PATTERNS

Drill 1/16-in. holes for hanger in one arm

SANTA BODY AND TRACTOR
Trace 1—tracing paper
Cut 1—1/2-in. pine or basswood

ARM
Trace 2—tracing paper
Cut 2—1/4-in. pine or basswood

━ = Outside cutting line for pattern

Glue arm to back here

Glue arm to front here

Drill 3/16-in. hole here for steering wheel

Glue muffler here

Glue fender here

JOHN DEERE

Glue star here

Glue star here

Grain

STARS
Trace 1 each—tracing paper
Cut 1 each—1/4-in. basswood

FENDER
Trace 1—tracing paper
Cut 1—1/4-in. basswood

When dry, sand the outside edges lightly to expose the wood as shown in photo at far left.

FINISHING: Glue fender to tractor where indicated on pattern. Glue stars to centers of tires as shown on pattern and buttons centered over stars as shown in photo.

Glue the end of dowel into the hole of spool. Then glue spool to front of tractor for muffler as shown on pattern. Glue

wooden wheel to end of other dowel for steering wheel. Then glue dowel end into drilled hole on tractor. Glue arms to Santa as shown on pattern and in photo, gluing arm with drilled holes to the back.

Bend the 1-in. piece of craft wire to form a U shape. Glue the ends of wire into holes of arm to make a hanger. Thread jute string through wire hanger and tie ends together.

Manger Threads Meaning into Merriment

THE REAL STORY of Christmas unwinds movingly with this Nativity scene from Leslie Hartsock of Bartlesville, Oklahoma. Peopled by figures fashioned from empty spools of thread and fabric scraps, the project is easy enough for crafters of all skill levels.

Materials Needed (for all):

Patterns on next page
Tracing paper and pencil
100% cotton or cotton-blend fabrics—scraps or 1/4 yard each of five different prints for adult figures' garments (Leslie used earth tones for Joseph and the shepherds and pastels for Mary and the angel); four coordinating prints for head coverings for Mary, Joseph and shepherds; and white for baby's blanket
Plastic all-purpose empty thread spools—10 large (two for each adult figure) and one small for baby
Wooden balls—five 1-1/4-inch for heads of adult figures and one 1-inch for baby's head
Acrylic craft paints—blue, flesh, brown and pink
Paintbrushes—small flat and small round
Paper plate or palette
Ten 1-1/2-inch-long x 1/8-inch-thick wooden ovals for hands of adult figures (Leslie used Woodsies)
Curly doll hair in colors of choice (one package each of desired colors will be more than enough)
16 inches of 1/4-inch-wide gold metallic braid for trim on Mary's and Joseph's head coverings
Two 6-inch plastic canes for shepherds

16 inches of 2-ply jute string for shepherds' head coverings
6-inch heart-shape Battenburg doily for angel's wings
6 inches of 1-1/2-inch-wide pre-gathered lace for angel's collar
6 inches of 1/8-inch-wide gold metallic ribbon for angel's halo
Small coordinating rosebud for angel
Fine multicolored glitter
Gold spray paint
Small amount of polyester stuffing
Glue gun and glue sticks
Standard sewing supplies

Finished Size: Mary, Joseph, the shepherds and the angel are each about 6 inches tall x 4 inches across. Baby Jesus is about 2-1/2 inches tall x 1-1/2 inches across.

Directions:

Coat large spools with gold spray paint. When dry, stack two spools and glue the ends together, making five sets of two spools each for bodies of adult figures.

Fold tracing paper in half lengthwise and then in half crosswise. With foldlines matching, trace garment pattern onto tracing paper and cut out. Open tracing paper for a complete pattern.

Fold tracing paper in half. With foldlines matching, trace head covering pattern onto tracing paper and cut out. Open for a complete pattern.

Cut garments and head coverings from fabrics as directed on patterns, cutting each garment and head covering from a different fabric.

Stitch a 1/4-in. hem to the wrong side of each sleeve and the bottom edge of each garment. Fold each garment along

shoulder line with right sides together. Stitch each underarm/side seam with a 1/4-in. seam. Clip underarms as shown on pattern. Turn right side out.

Slip a garment over set of spools for each figure. Glue neck edge of each garment to top of spool, distributing fabric evenly around spools.

Use flat brush and flesh to paint all wooden balls and ovals for the heads and hands of figures. Let dry.

Glue a large painted head to the top of each garment-covered set of spools. Glue the small painted head to one end of the small spool.

Use round brush or handle of brush to dab dots of paint on heads for eyes, painting angel's eyes blue and remaining figures' eyes brown. Let dry.

Use round brush or dip eraser of pencil into paint and dab pink cheeks on each figure. While paint is still wet, sprinkle cheeks with glitter. Let dry.

Glue desired color of hair onto each figure's head.

Glue wooden oval hands into the sleeves of each garment as shown in photo above left. Glue a small amount of stuffing inside each sleeve.

FINISHING: Mary: Fold about 1/2 in. along straight edge of Mary's head covering to wrong side. Glue braid to right side along edge of fold. Glue head covering onto Mary's head, overlapping front edges as shown in photo.

Baby: Wrap a 6-in. square of white fabric around small spool and head for blanket. Glue baby in Mary's arms as shown in photo.

Joseph: Fold about 1/2 in. along straight edge of Joseph's head covering to wrong side. Glue head covering onto Joseph's head, draping front edges as shown in photo. Glue gold braid around head covering as shown in photo, overlapping ends in back.

Shepherds: Fold about 1/2 in. along straight edge of each shepherd's head covering to wrong side. Glue a head covering onto each shepherd's head with front edges draped over arms as shown in photo. Wrap a piece of jute around top of head covering and tie in back. Glue a cane to shepherds' hands.

Angel: Glue lace around neck of angel, overlapping ends in the back. Glue rosebud to front of lace.

Glue ends of ribbon together for halo. Glue halo to top of angel's head.

Glue doily to back of angel with rounded portion of heart forming the top of the wings.

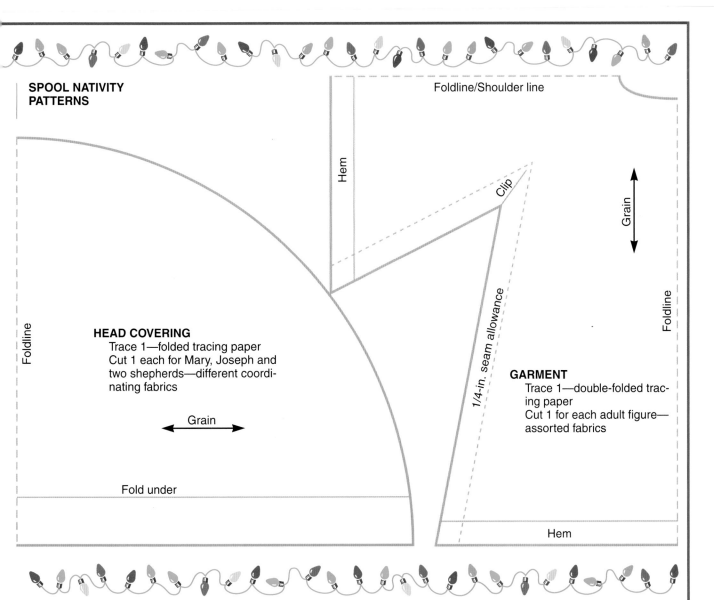

SPOOL NATIVITY PATTERNS

Foldline/Shoulder line

Hem

Clip

Grain

1/4-in. seam allowance

Foldline

Foldline

HEAD COVERING
Trace 1—folded tracing paper
Cut 1 each for Mary, Joseph and
two shepherds—different coordinating fabrics

Grain

Fold under

GARMENT
Trace 1—double-folded tracing paper
Cut 1 for each adult figure—
assorted fabrics

Hem

Snazzy Sequins Fall on Limbs

YOUR CHRISTMAS TREE will shine brighter than ever when you craft a pile of these sparkly snowflakes.

Karen Taylor of Redding, California says gluing together sequins into trims is so easy that kids and adults alike will be stuck on the idea. So get ready for a flurry of fun!

Materials Needed:
*Assorted sequin shapes—1-inch
    leaves, 5/8-inch spokes and 1-inch
    snowflake spangles
Quick-drying clear glue
Scrap of cardboard
Plastic wrap
Masking tape
Toothpick
Six-strand embroidery floss in color of
    choice for hangers
Embroidery needle
Scissors*

Finished Size: Sequin trims measure 3-1/2 inches to 4-1/2 inches across. Size will vary depending on the design and the size and shape of sequins used.

Directions:
Cover piece of cardboard with plastic wrap. Tape plastic wrap to the back of cardboard to secure.

Arrange sequins on the plastic wrap-covered cardboard as shown in photo at right or create your own design.

Glue sequins together, using toothpick to apply a small amount of glue where sequins overlap.

When glue is dry, carefully peel ornament from plastic wrap.

If needed, make a hole for hanger by inserting a needle through top sequin. Cut a 6-in. piece of embroidery floss. Separate strands and thread one or two strands through hole. Tie ends in an overhand knot for hanger.

Have a Ball with Bedecked Sweatshirt

**PAINTED SWEATSHIRT
ORNAMENT PATTERN**
Trace 5—tracing paper
Paint as directed

ROOTED in Christmas-tree style is this sweatshirt from Jean Devore of Jackson, Missouri. It features painted-on branch accents! (For another of Jean's pine-inspired projects, see the next page.)

Aside from fashions, the design can also be used to dress up table linens, tree skirts, curtains—or whatever unadorned fabric item catches your fancy.

Materials Needed:
Pattern on this page
Tracing paper and pencil
Quilter's marking pen or pencil
White cotton/polyester-blend
  sweatshirt
Acrylic fabric paints (or acrylic craft
  paints and textile medium)—blue,
  red, brown, dark green, gold,
  medium green and white
Paintbrushes—small flat and small
  round
Paper plate or palette
T-shirt board or heavy cardboard to fit
  inside sweatshirt

Waxed paper
Paper towels
Acrylic flat-backed rhinestones—two
  10mm round red, eight 8mm round
  blue, five 8mm round green, two
  8mm round red, two 6mm round
  red and two 5mm x 9mm oval red
Fabric glue
Scissors
Straight pins

Finished Size: Design area measures 20 inches across x 8 inches high and is shown on an Adult size Medium sweatshirt.

Directions:
Pre-wash and machine-dry sweatshirt. Do not use detergents with built-in stain resistors or fabric softeners. Press if needed.

Place a piece of waxed paper over T-shirt board or cardboard to protect surface. With right side out, slip sweatshirt over T-shirt board or cardboard. Smooth sweatshirt and pin sleeves out of the

way. Place on a flat surface.

Trace ornament pattern onto tracing paper five times and cut out each on traced line.

Pin ornament patterns onto sweatshirt, positioning them around the neckline in a semicircle with the center of each ornament about 5 in. from the neck edge as shown in Fig. 1 and in photo at left.

Use quilter's marking pen or pencil to trace around outside edge of each ornament. Also draw an arc to mark the placement of each branch above and below each ornament as shown in Fig. 1. The pine needles will be painted freehand later.

PAINTING: Place small amounts of each paint on paper plate or palette as needed. If necessary, mix paints with textile medium prior to use.

Using flat brush, paint two ornaments blue, two red and one gold as shown in Fig. 1. Extend paints to outside edge of each ornament, covering pattern lines completely. Let dry.

Referring to pattern and using flat brush, shade outside edges of each ornament with brown. To shade, dip flat brush in clean water. Remove excess water by touching the brush to a paper towel. Touch one corner of brush in brown paint and brush it back and forth on waxed paper to blend paint into brush. Apply paint with loaded edge of brush along outside edges of ornaments. Let dry.

Paint the hanger of each ornament

brown. Let dry.

With a nearly dry flat brush, paint white highlights on each ornament as shown on pattern. Let dry.

Use round brush and dark green to paint branches above and below ornaments as shown in Fig. 1, extending branches across each shoulder seam. While paint is still wet, shade edges of each with brown as directed for ornaments. Let dry.

Use round brush to add medium and dark green pine needles to each branch as shown in Fig. 1. Let dry.

Use flat brush to add gold or brown highlights to branches and needles as desired. Let dry.

Set the paints as directed by the paint manufacturer.

FINISHING: Referring to Fig. 1 for placement, glue rhinestones onto center of each bough.

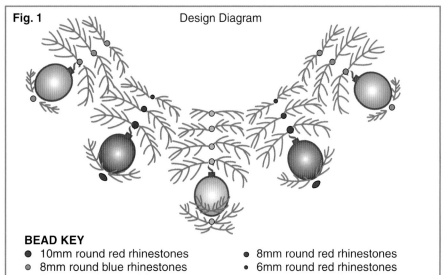

Fig. 1   Design Diagram

BEAD KEY
- ● 10mm round red rhinestones
- ● 8mm round blue rhinestones
- ○ 8mm round green rhinestones
- ● 8mm round red rhinestones
- • 6mm round red rhinestones
- ◗ 5mm x 9mm oval red rhinestones

Fir Array Glows for Holidays

JUST LIKE the spruced-up shirt she designed at left, Jean found the idea for this holiday swag waiting in the boughs.

"Our whole house receives evergreen treatment during December, so it seemed natural to turn to the tree to create this decoration," she confirms.

There's more to Jean's handcraft than meets the eye. Aside from dressing up a door, the swag can also top a table or enhance an exterior window.

Materials Needed:
4 feet of artificial wired pine garland
Five 2-inch gold liberty bells
1-1/2 yards of heavy gold metallic cord
3 yards of 2-1/2-inch-wide wire-edge gold metallic mesh ribbon
Assorted Christmas picks (Jean used gift boxes and gold berries)
Gold spray paint
Craft wire
Craft scissors

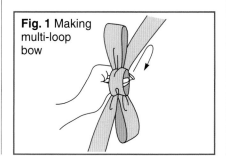

Fig. 1 Making multi-loop bow

Finished Size: Pine swag is about 26 inches long x 14 inches wide.

Directions:
Fold length of pine garland in half. Use craft wire to wire garland together at intervals along its length. Arrange boughs of pine garland as shown in photo at right, making sure one side of garland remains very flat.

Cut an 8-in. piece of floral wire and attach it to the flat side at one end for hanging loop.

Spray tips of boughs with gold paint. Let dry.

Cut gold cord into five pieces of varied lengths as shown in photo. Attach a gold bell to one end of each piece of cord. Wire other ends of cord together and then wire the entire group to the front, about 5 in. from the top.

Form ribbon into a multi-loop bow measuring about 12 in. across as shown in photo. To make bow, leave an 18-in. streamer and then form a small center loop. Make a large loop on one side of small loop, twisting it as needed to keep right side facing out. Make a matching large loop on opposite side. See Fig. 1. Repeat one more time, making a total of two pairs of large loops and leaving another streamer the same length as the first. Wire bow to swag, covering wired ends of cord.

Position Christmas picks and secure them with wire as needed.

Merry Motifs Crop Up in Yule Patchwork!

IT'S the image of Christmas! Crafter Jeanne Prue made her merry mini-quilt to deck the walls of her Newport, Vermont home. "The appliqued symbols could also be used individually to dress up clothing or pillow tops," she suggests.

Materials Needed:

Patterns on next page
Tracing paper and pencil
44-inch-wide 100% cotton fabrics—scraps or 1/8 yard each of light green plaid for quilt block, gold print for candle flame and dark green print for tree and holly appliques; 1/3 yard each of white print for quilt block, black background print for quilt blocks and medium green print for quilt blocks and mitten appliques; 1/2 yard of red print for quilt blocks, bow and candlestick appliques and binding; 3/4 yard each of coordinating stripe for border and muslin for backing
1/4 yard of paper-backed fusible web
1/4 yard of tear-away stabilizer
Matching all-purpose thread
Monofilament thread
22-inch x 26-inch piece of lightweight quilt batting
Quilter's ruler
Quilter's marking pen or pencil
Rotary cutter and cutting mat (optional)
Red buttons—four 1/2 inch and three 5/8 inch
Standard sewing supplies

Finished Size: Mini-quilt measures 24 inches high x 20 inches wide.

Directions:

Pre-wash fabrics without fabric softeners, washing colors separately. If the water from any fabric is discolored, wash again until rinse water runs clear. Machine-dry and press all fabrics.

CUTTING: Cut quilt blocks and border strips using rotary cutter and quilter's ruler or mark fabrics using ruler and marker of choice and cut with scissors. Cut border strips following direction of stripes.

From light green plaid fabric, cut a 2-1/2-in. x 4-1/2-in. rectangle.

From medium green print, cut a 6-1/2-in. x 10-1/2-in. rectangle and a 6-1/2-in. x 2-1/2-in. rectangle.

From white print, cut a 6-1/2-in. square and a 2-1/2-in. x 10-1/2-in. rectangle.

From red print, cut a 6-1/2-in. square and a 6-1/2-in. x 8-1/2-in. rectangle for quilt blocks. Also cut a 4-in. x 1-in. rectangle for candlestick. For binding, cut two 2-1/4-in. x 44-in. strips.

From black background print, cut a 4-1/2-in. square and a 2-1/2-in. x 8-1/2-in. rectangle.

From coordinating stripe, cut four 3-1/4-in. x 26-in. border strips with stripes running the length of the strips.

From muslin, cut a 22-in. x 26-in. rectangle for backing.

APPLIQUES: Trace mitten pattern

onto tracing paper and cut out. Trace remaining patterns onto folded tracing paper. Cut out shapes and open each for complete patterns.

Trace one each of all of the patterns except mitten and holly patterns onto the paper side of fusible web, leaving 1/2 in. between shapes. Trace three sets of holly leaves and two mittens, reversing one, onto the paper side of fusible web. Also draw a 4-in. x 1-in. rectangle onto the paper side of the fusible web for the

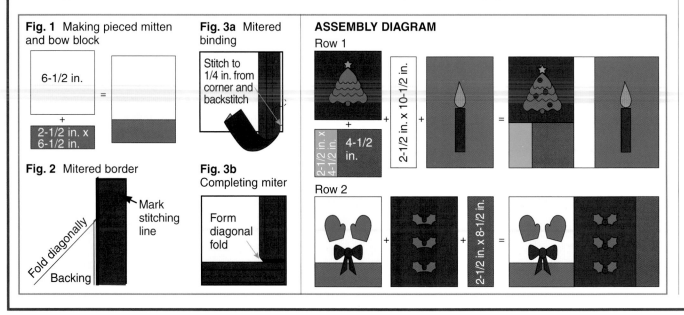

Fig. 1 Making pieced mitten and bow block

6-1/2 in.

2-1/2 in. x 6-1/2 in.

Fig. 2 Mitered border

Fold diagonally

Backing

Mark stitching line

Fig. 3a Mitered binding

Stitch to 1/4 in. from corner and backstitch

Fig. 3b Completing miter

Form diagonal fold

ASSEMBLY DIAGRAM

Row 1

2-1/2 in. x 4-1/2 in.

4-1/2 in.

2-1/2 in. x 10-1/2 in.

Row 2

2-1/2 in. x 8-1/2 in.

candlestick. Cut apart the shapes.

Following manufacturer's directions, fuse shapes to wrong side of fabrics as directed on patterns. Fuse candlestick to wrong side of red print. Transfer inside design lines of bow by stitching on lines traced on paper backing. Cut out shapes along outside lines.

To make the pieced mitten and bow block, stitch one edge of the 6-1/2-in. white square to one long edge of the 6-1/2-in. x 2-1/2-in. medium green print rectangle with a 1/4-in. seam. See Fig. 1.

Remove paper backing from the appliques and position on fronts of blocks as shown in the Assembly Diagram. Layer pieces for the tree in this order: trunk, bottom tier of tree, third tier, second tier, top tier and star. Fuse the appliques onto the blocks following the manufacturer's directions.

Position tear-away stabilizer on the wrong side of blocks behind designs. Using matching thread and a medium satin stitch, applique around each shape. For tree, applique around trunk, each tier of tree from bottom to top and then around star. For bow, applique around loops and ends first and then over inside design lines.

Remove tear-away stabilizer. Pull all threads to wrong side and secure. Hand-stitch 1/2-in. buttons randomly to tree and 5/8-in. buttons to base of holly leaves as shown in photo above left.

BLOCK ASSEMBLY: Do all piecing with accurate 1/4-in. seams and right sides of fabrics together. Press seams toward darker fabrics. Lay out all pieces as shown in the Assembly Diagram.

Stitch the 2-1/2-in. x 4-1/2-in. light green plaid rectangle to the left edge of the 4-1/2-in. black print square. Then stitch the top edge of this pieced block to the bottom edge of the tree block, making a pieced tree block.

Stitch 2-1/2-in. x 10-1/2-in. white print rectangle between pieced tree block and candle block as shown in Assembly Diagram, making Row 1.

To assemble Row 2, stitch the holly block between the pieced mitten and bow block and the 2-1/2-in. x 8-1/2-in. black print rectangle.

To complete piecing, stitch top edge of Row 2 to bottom edge of Row 1.

BORDER: With right sides together and raw edges matching, center one border strip along the top edge of pieced mini-quilt. Starting and stopping 1/4 in. from each end, stitch border to mini-quilt. Do not trim off the excess border fabric. Press border strip away from top edge of mini-quilt. Attach border strip to bottom edge in the same way.

Attach a border strip to each side of

mini-quilt in the same way, taking care not to catch the top and bottom border strips in your stitching.

To stitch mitered corners, fold mini-quilt diagonally with right sides together and raw edges and stripes of border strips matching. Pin in place.

Referring to Fig. 2, place quilter's ruler along diagonal fold and use quilter's marking pen or pencil to mark stitching line on border as shown. Sew on the marked line from inside corner to outside edge. Open and check for accuracy of miter before trimming seam to 1/4 in. Press seam open. Repeat miter on remaining corners of border.

QUILTING: Place muslin wrong side up on a flat surface and smooth out wrinkles. Center batting over backing and smooth. Center pieced mini-quilt over batting, right side up, and smooth. Hand-baste through all layers, stitching from center to corners, then horizontally and vertically every 4 in.

Using monofilament thread on top and thread to match backing in the bobbin, stitch-in-the-ditch of all seams and around outside of each applique. Stitch borders along the lines of the stripes if desired. Baste around outer edges.

HANGING SLEEVE: Cut a 5-in. x 19-in. strip of fabric for hanging sleeve. Stitch a 1/4-in. hem to wrong side of each short edge. Fold strip in half lengthwise with wrong sides together. Baste strip to back of top edge of mini-quilt, matching raw edges. Hand-stitch fold of hanging sleeve to backing only.

BINDING: Stitch short ends of bind-

ing strips together to make one long strip. With wrong sides together, fold binding in half lengthwise and press. Pin binding to quilt, matching raw edges. Beginning with a 1/2-in. fold to the wrong side, attach binding, mitering corners. Overlap binding 1 in. and trim excess binding. Fold binding to back and hand-stitch folded edge to backing, covering seam and mitering corners. See Figs. 3a and b. ●

APPLIQUED MINI-QUILT PATTERNS

BOW Fuse and cut 1— red print

Foldline

Foldline

CANDLE FLAME Fuse and cut 1— gold print

Grain

STAR Fuse and cut 1— gold print

Foldline

Foldline

TREE TIERS Fuse and cut 1 each—alternating medium and dark green prints

TOP TIER

SECOND TIER

THIRD TIER

BOTTOM TIER

Foldline

HOLLY Fuse and cut 3—dark green print

Foldline

MITTEN Fuse and cut 2, reversing 1— medium green print

APPLIQUE KEY

—— Outline/stitching line
- - - Under-lap
—— Inside design line

TREE TRUNK Fuse and cut 1—black background print

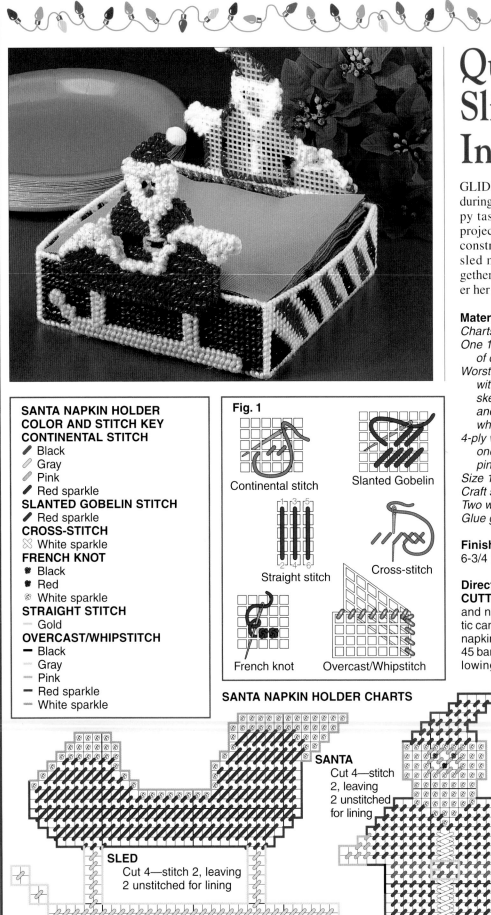

Quick Claus Slides Neatly Into Kitchen

GLIDING in glad tidings *and* tidiness during December mealtimes is the happy task of Emma Willey's practical project. The Winston, Oregon crafter constructed plastic canvas Santa and sled motifs first, then tied them together into a cheerful napkin container her family enjoys using.

Materials Needed:
Charts below left
One 13-1/2-inch x 22-1/2-inch sheet of clear 7-count plastic canvas
Worsted-weight sparkle yarn (yarn with a silver metallic thread)—one skein each of green, red, white and variegated green, red and white
4-ply worsted-weight yarn—scraps or one skein each of black, gold, gray, pink and red
Size 16 tapestry needle
Craft scissors
Two white 1/2-inch pom-poms
Glue gun and glue sticks

Finished Size: Santa napkin holder is 6-3/4 inches square x 6 inches high.

Directions:
CUTTING: Remembering to count bars and not holes, cut four pieces of plastic canvas 13 bars x 45 bars for sides of napkin holder. Cut one piece 45 bars x 45 bars for bottom of napkin holder. Following charts at left, cut four Santas and four sleds.

STITCHING: Working with 18-in. to 20-in. lengths of yarn, follow charts and individual instructions that follow to stitch each piece. See Fig. 1 for stitch illustrations.

Do not knot yarn on back of work. Instead, leave a 1-in. tail on the back of the plastic canvas and work the next stitches over it. To end a strand, run yarn on back of canvas under completed stitches of the same color and clip yarn close to work.

Sled (make two): Use gray to fill in the center bar of

SANTA NAPKIN HOLDER COLOR AND STITCH KEY

CONTINENTAL STITCH
- Black
- Gray
- Pink
- Red sparkle

SLANTED GOBELIN STITCH
- Red sparkle

CROSS-STITCH
- ⊠ White sparkle

FRENCH KNOT
- Black
- Red
- White sparkle

STRAIGHT STITCH
- Gold

OVERCAST/WHIPSTITCH
- Black
- Gray
- Pink
- Red sparkle
- White sparkle

Fig. 1

Continental stitch

Slanted Gobelin

Straight stitch

Cross-stitch

French knot

Overcast/Whipstitch

SANTA NAPKIN HOLDER CHARTS

SANTA
Cut 4—stitch 2, leaving 2 unstitched for lining

SLED
Cut 4—stitch 2, leaving 2 unstitched for lining

the runners with Continental stitch. Use red sparkle and slanted Gobelin stitch to fill in the base of the two sleds, leaving outside edges of each unstitched. Use white sparkle to stitch French knots along top of each sled as shown on chart.

Place a matching unstitched sled on back of each stitched sled and whipstitch outside edges together, using matching yarn as shown on chart.

Santa (make two): Use white sparkle to cross-stitch fur trim down center of suit. Use red sparkle to fill in Santa's suit and hat with Continental stitch. Use black and Continental stitch for belt. Straight-stitch belt buckle with gold. Stitch face and hand with pink and Con-

tinental stitch. Use black to add French knot eyes and red to add French knot nose. Use white sparkle to stitch French knots around Santa's face.

Place a matching unstitched Santa on back of each stitched Santa and whipstitch the outside edges together, using matching color of yarn as shown on chart.

Napkin holder: Use green to fill in two napkin holder sides with Continental stitch, leaving outside edges unstitched. Stitch remaining two sides of napkin holder with variegated green, red and white sparkle yarn and Continental stitch, leaving outside edges unstitched. The bottom of the napkin holder is not stitched.

ASSEMBLY: Using white sparkle, whipstitch a bottom edge of each green napkin holder side to opposite edges of napkin holder bottom, making sure all wrong sides face the inside of the napkin holder.

Whipstitch bottom edges of variegated sides to remaining edges of bottom of napkin holder in the same way. Use white sparkle to whipstitch corners together and to overcast top edges.

Glue one sled to the front of one green side of napkin holder as shown in photo at far left. Glue one Santa to inside behind the sled as shown in the photo. Repeat on other green side of napkin holder. Glue the white pom-poms to the tips of the hats. ◗

Poinsettia Ring Wraps Napkin in Holiday Appeal

IF YOU PLANT this blooming beauty all around your Christmas table, soon you'll see a bright bouquet of smiles burst forth!

Janna Britton of Firebaugh, California raised the simple idea. "I painted and glued together wooden shapes to form the petals, then added seed beads to the center and ribbon for the leaves," she details.

Materials Needed (for one):
1/8-inch-thick wooden shapes—twenty 7/8-inch-long wooden teardrops and one 1-1/4-inch-diameter wooden circle (Janna used Woodsies)
14 yellow giant seed beads
17 inches of 1-1/4-inch-wide green satin ribbon
5 inches of 1/4-inch-wide red satin picot ribbon
Acrylic craft paints—red and yellow
Small paintbrush
Palette or paper plate
Tacky (white) glue
Scissors

Finished Size: Poinsettia measures about 3 inches across. Napkin ring measures about 2-1/2 inches across.

Directions:
POINSETTIA: Leaving a center opening of about 5/8 in. across, glue 10 teardrop shapes to edge of wood circle with points facing outward and edges of teardrops touching on the inside. Let dry.

Glue remaining teardrops in a second layer so the points of the second layer are between the points of the first layer and the inside edges of each layer are even as shown in the photo at left. Let dry.

Fig. 1 Making ribbon leaves

Paint the center circle yellow and all sides of each teardrop shape red. Let dry.

Glue yellow beads to yellow center as shown in photo.

Cut three 4-in. pieces of green ribbon. Fold and glue each as shown in Fig. 1 for leaves.

Glue each ribbon leaf to back of poinsettia so points extend just beyond tips of flower petals as shown in photo. Let dry.

NAPKIN RING: Cut a 5-in. piece each of red picot ribbon and green ribbon. Glue red ribbon centered lengthwise over green ribbon. Overlap ends of ribbon 1/2 in. to form a ring and glue ends to secure. Let dry.

Glue poinsettia centered over glued ends of ribbon ring. Let dry. ◗

Sweet Christmas Style Is Knit into Peppermint Set

ANY GIRL WHO dons this scrumptious knit pair from designer Jana Trent of Colleyville, Texas is sure to savor jolly Christmas festivities all the more.

The pullover sweater and hat feature fun stitch combinations and tasteful candy-striped trimming. "It's a project that experienced knitters will enjoy making," Jana assures.

Materials Needed (for both):

4-ply worsted-weight yarn—three 3-1/2-ounce skeins of white and one 3-1/2-ounce skein of red*

Size 6 knitting needles—straight, double pointed, 24-inch-long circular and 16-inch-long circular or size needles needed to obtain correct gauge

Four large stitch holders

Stitch markers

Tapestry needle

*Jana used Patons Canadiana yarn with 246 yards per 100-gram (3-1/2-ounce) skein. If you use a different yarn, be sure to purchase the amount based on yardage per skein not ounces per skein.

Gauge: When working in DM pattern on size 6 needles, 18 sts and 28 rows = 4 inches.

Finished Size: Oversized sweater is a Child's size 4. Actual chest measurement is 30 inches and sweater is about 15 inches long. Hat measures about 19 inches around and is about 4 inches high.

Notes/Stitches Used:

Working in rounds: Cast on sts on circular needle, being careful not to twist sts. Place marker after last cast-on st and move marker with each round worked. Pull up yarn firmly when joining last st of round to first st of next round.

DOUBLE MOSS PATTERN (DM pattern):

Round 1: * K 2, p 2; repeat from * around.

Round 2: Repeat Round 1.

Round 3: * P 2, k 2; repeat from * around.

Round 4: Repeat Round 3.

DOUBLE DECREASE (dbl dec):

Slip 2 sts, k 1, pass 2 slipped sts over knit st.

Directions:

SWEATER: With 24-in. circular needle and ivory, cast on 120 sts. Place marker and work in rounds, being careful not to twist stitches in cast-on row.

Rounds 1-8: Purl each round.

Round 9: * K 4, k 2 tog, yo; repeat from * to end of round.

Rounds 10-60: Work in DM pattern for 50 rows (about 7 in.).

Place 60 sts for front of sweater on a stitch holder. On remaining 60 sts for back of sweater, use straight needles to continue in established DM pattern for 6 in., ending with an odd-numbered row. Place sts on three stitch holders as follows: 17 sts for one back shoulder seam, 26 sts for back neck edge and 17 sts for other back shoulder seam.

Place the 60 sts for front of sweater onto straight needle and work in established DM pattern for 26 rows (about 3-1/2 in.).

FRONT NECK SHAPING: Working in DM pattern on straight needles shape front neck edge as follows:

Row 1: Work 25 sts in established DM pattern and place remaining 35 sts on a stitch holder.

Row 2: Dec 1 st at neck edge with k or p 2 sts tog as DM pattern requires, work in DM pattern to end: 24 sts.

Row 3: Work row in DM pattern until last 2 sts, dec 1 st at neck edge with k or p 2 tog as DM pattern requires: 23 sts.

Row 4: Repeat Row 2: 22 sts.

Row 5: Repeat Row 3: 21 sts.

Rows 6 and 8: Work in established DM pattern.

Rows 7 and 9: Repeat Row 2: 19 sts at end of Row 9.

Rows 10-11: Work in established DM pattern.

Row 12: Repeat Row 3: 18 sts.

Rows 13-14: Work in established DM pattern.

Row 15: Repeat Row 2: 17 sts.

Work neckline dec on 25 sts of other side of front, reversing shaping and keeping the 10 center sts on stitch holder.

Turn sweater inside out and join front and back shoulder seams, working a joinery seam as follows: With right sides of garment facing each other, place sts of matching front and back shoulder seams on dp needles. Hold the two needles parallel to each other with tips aligned. With third dp needle, bind off in DM pattern, working the first st from each needle together as one. Repeat with second st from each needle and then pass the first st over the second to bind off. Repeat to end of seam and fasten off. Join other shoulder seam in the same way.

NECK EDGING: With 16-in. circular needle, pick up and knit or purl in established DM pattern the 26 sts from holder at back neck edge, 18 sts along one front neck edge, 10 sts from holder at front neck and 18 sts along remaining front neck edge. Place marker and join round: 72 sts.

Round 1: * P 4, p 2 tog, yo; repeat from * to end of round.

Rounds 2-9: Purl each round.
Bind off in purl.

SLEEVES: With right side of work facing and beginning at center of one underarm, use 16-in. circular needle to

ABBREVIATIONS

dec	decrease
dp	double pointed
k	knit
p	purl
st(s)	stitch(es)
tog	together
yo	yarn over
*	Instructions following asterisk are repeated as directed.

pick up 52 sts. Place marker and work in rounds in established DM pattern for armhole as follows:

Rounds 1-74: Work in DM pattern for 74 rounds (about 10-1/2 in.), dec 4 sts evenly on last row: 48 sts.

Round 75: * P 4, p 2 tog, yo; repeat from * to end of round.

Rounds 76-84: Purl each round.

Bind off in purl in Round 84.

Repeat for other sleeve.

Make and attach red I-cords as directed below right.

HAT: With 16-in. circular needle and ivory, cast on 84 sts. Place marker and work in rounds.

Rounds 1-8: Purl each round.

Round 9: * K 4, k 2 tog, yo; repeat from * to end of round.

Rounds 10—31: Work in DM pattern for 22 rounds (about 2 in.).

Round 32: * P 4, p 2 tog, yo; repeat from * to end of round.

Rounds 33-40: Purl each round.

Bind off in purl and fasten off.

TOP OF HAT: Using 16-in. circular needle, pick up and k 84 sts from inside (wrong side) of hat on last row of DM pattern. Place marker and join round.

Rounds 1-4: Knit each round.

Round 5: * K 5, dbl dec, k 4; repeat from * to end of round.

Round 6 and all even rounds: Knit each round.

Round 7: * K 4, dbl dec, k 3; repeat from * to end of round.

Round 9: * K 3, dbl dec, k 2; repeat from * to end of round.

Round 11: * K 2, dbl dec, k 1; repeat from * to end of round.

Round 13: * K 1, dbl dec; repeat from * to last 2 sts, k 2 tog.

Thread tapestry needle with yarn end and close top.

FINISHING: I-CORD: Using red and dp needle, cast on 4 sts. Without turning work, place right-hand needle in left hand, slide sts to right edge and knit sts, pulling the yarn behind the sts from left edge of knitting to right edge as you

begin each row. As you knit, the four sts will close and make a tube. Make approximately 6 yds. of I-cord.

Thread I-cord over neck edge of sweater and through yarn-over eyelets around neck. Adjust tension as desired. Cut cord about 1/2 in. from desired seam and ravel cord to that point.

Use tapestry needle to thread end of yarn through open sts on one end of cord and through open sts on other end of cord. Pull yarn to join sts. Fasten off and weave in loose ends. Adjust seam so it is hidden. Repeat for sleeve edges and bottom of sweater.

Insert I-cord through eyelets along top and bottom edges of hat as shown in photo at far left, following instructions for I-cord above.

Tie 4-in. length of I-cord into overhand knot. Hand-stitch ends together and stitch knot to center top of hat as shown in photo. Weave in loose ends and block if needed, following yarn manufacturer's instructions. 🌢

Tree-Slice Trim Leaves Lasting Impression

A MEMENTO in the making is this evergreen branch brightener shared by Karen Wittkop of Duluth, Minnesota. To create it, you use a section cut from your family's Christmas tree trunk!

For extra sentiment, add the date and your clan's last name around the fir you glue onto the wood. Or saw a bunch of trunk slices and fix personalized ornaments for members of your family.

Materials Needed:
Patterns at left
Tracing paper and pencil
3/4-inch-thick angled slice of pine with bark on it from 3-1/2-inch-diameter tree trunk or branch
Scraps of green and brown felt
10 inches of 2-ply jute string
Spray snow or textured snow paint and small paintbrush
Tacky (white) glue
Sandpaper
Scissors

Finished Size: Tree slice ornament measures about 3-1/2 inches across.

Directions:
Trace patterns onto tracing paper. Cut each tier of the tree and the trunk from felt as directed on patterns.

Sand front of pine slice until smooth.

Glue trunk to pine slice as shown in photo above right. Glue bottom tier, middle tier and top tier to pine slice, overlapping edges as shown on patterns.

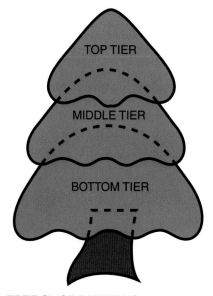

TREE SLICE PATTERNS
Cut 1 each—color of felt shown

Note: Dashed lines indicate that piece is overlapped by another piece.

Spray lightly with spray snow or use paintbrush to add textured snow paint to tree, trunk and bottom edge of pine slice.

Cut a 4-in.-long piece of jute string and tie it into a small bow. Glue bow to top of tree. Glue ends of remaining jute string to top center back of pine slice for hanging loop. 🌢

Snappy, Scrappy Stocking Fits the Season Perfectly

STUFFING this stocking is no short assignment—thanks to the *very* generous nature of its design!

Mary Ayres of Boyce, Virginia constructed her jumbo fabric version with her enthusiastic loved ones in mind. "Digging into stockings on Christmas morning is a favorite activity in my family," she grins.

Materials Needed:
Pattern on next page
19-inch x 24-inch piece of tracing paper
44-inch-wide 100% cotton or cotton-blend fabrics—scraps or 1/8 yard each of several different red and green print fabrics, 5/8 yard of red corduroy or coordinating heavy fabric for stocking back and 5/8 yard of coordinating print for lining
Purchased piping—1-3/4 yards of light green for side and bottom edges of stocking and 20 inches of dark green for top edge of stocking
Rotary cutter and mat (optional)
Quilter's ruler
Quilter's marking pen or pencil
Matching all-purpose thread
Standard sewing supplies
Pencil

Finished Size: Stocking measures about 17-1/2 inches across x 19-1/2 inches long without hanging loop.

Directions:
Mark tracing paper with a 1-in. grid. (An easy way to create the grid is to lay tracing paper on top of a rotary cutting mat that has a grid with 1-in. squares

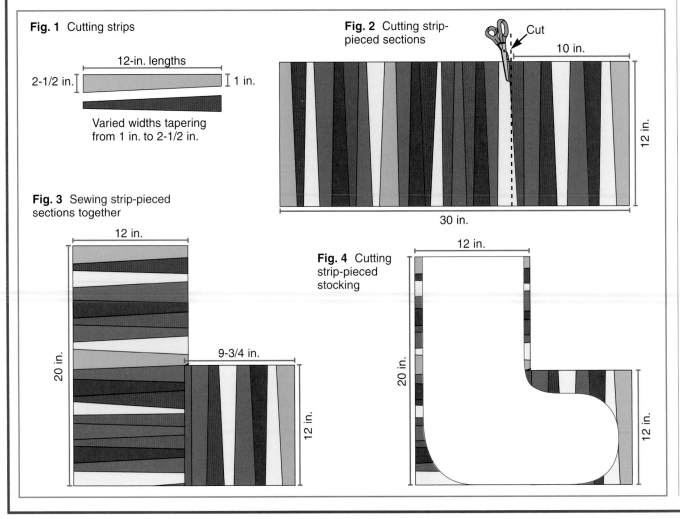

Fig. 1 Cutting strips

12-in. lengths
2-1/2 in. · · 1 in.
Varied widths tapering from 1 in. to 2-1/2 in.

Fig. 2 Cutting strip-pieced sections

Cut
10 in.
12 in.
30 in.

Fig. 3 Sewing strip-pieced sections together

12 in.
20 in.
9-3/4 in.
12 in.

Fig. 4 Cutting strip-pieced stocking

12 in.
20 in.
12 in.

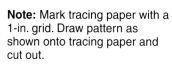

printed on it and trace over the lines.) Draw pattern on this page onto tracing paper as shown. Cut out pattern and set aside.

PIECING: Use rotary cutter and quilter's ruler or scissors to cut red and green print fabrics into 12-in.-long strips of varied widths, tapering from about 1 in. to 2-1/2 in. See Fig. 1. You will need to cut about 27 strips.

Sew one long edge of two strips together with a 1/4-in. seam, placing the widest edge of each strip at opposite ends. Press seam toward darker fabric. Continue to add strips in this way until you have a pieced rectangle about 12 in. x 30 in.

CUTTING: From the 12-in. x 30-in. rectangle, cut a 10-in. x 12-in. rectangle as shown in Fig. 2.

Sew 10-in. x 12-in. rectangle to bottom right edge of remaining 12-in. x 20-in. rectangle as shown in Fig. 3. Press seam toward smaller piece.

Place stocking pattern on right side of pieced strips as shown in Fig. 4. Cut out stocking. Place pattern on wrong side of backing fabric and cut out stocking back.

Fold lining fabric in half with right sides together. Place pattern on top and cut out stocking lining.

ASSEMBLY: With raw edges matching, baste light green piping to sides and bottom of pieced stocking.

With right sides together and raw edges matching, sew pieced stocking to backing, concealing basting stitches. Clip curves and turn right side out.

With raw edges matching, baste dark green piping to top edge of stocking, overlapping ends on backing near back seam.

For hanging loop, cut a 2-1/2-in. x 11-in. rectangle from a scrap of red or green print. Fold hanging loop in half lengthwise and stitch long edges together with a 1/4-in. seam. Turn loop

right side out through one open end. Center seam and press flat. With raw edges matching and right sides together, pin one end of loop to top edge of stocking front and the other end to top edge of stocking back along back seam of stocking.

Sew sides and bottom of lining pieces together with a 1/4-in. seam, leaving a 4-in. opening centered along one seam for turning. Clip curved seam. Do not turn right side out.

Slip stocking (right side out) into lining. Right sides of stocking and lining will be together and hanging loop will be sandwiched in between. Pin top edges together with raw edges matching. Sew top edge of lining and stocking together, concealing basting stitches.

Turn the stocking right side out through the opening in seam of the lining. Hand-stitch the opening closed. Insert the lining into the stocking and press as needed.

JUMBO STOCKING PATTERN
Enlarge pattern as directed
Each square = 1 in.
Cut 1—pieced strips
Cut 1—backing fabric
Cut 2—lining fabric

Note: Mark tracing paper with a 1-in. grid. Draw pattern as shown onto tracing paper and cut out.

Hot Pads Warm Kitchen at Christmas

MARK the season in a tasteful way with these toasty decorative pot holders from Winnie Malone of Westerville, Ohio. They're covered in appliqued and quilted motifs, then accented with an assortment of trinkets that'll sparkle on a kitchen wall.

(Pssst…it's easy to turn these into usable holders—just substitute embroidered details for the beads and other trims.)

Materials Needed (for both):

Patterns on next page
Template plastic or lightweight cardboard
Tracing paper and pencil
100% cotton fabrics—1/4 yard each or scraps of white solid for background of appliques, Christmas print for back of pot holders, red solid and green solid for bell appliques and green solid for tree applique
1/4 yard of cotton batting
1/4 yard of paper-backed fusible web
1/4 yard of tear-away stabilizer
12 inches of 1/4-inch-wide green satin ribbon for bell
Assorted bead and sequin trims for tree (Winnie used gold and silver 3/8-inch oval beads, 1/4-inch red sequins, small gold and silver round beads and pearls and a larger pearl for the top of the tree.)
Two 1/4-inch gold jingle bells, eight 1/4-inch gold sequins and eight 3mm gold beads for bell
Two plastic rings for hangers

1/2-inch-wide double-fold bias tape— 1 yard each of green and red
Matching all-purpose sewing thread
Quilting thread—green for trees and red for bells
Quilter's marking pen or pencil
Standard sewing supplies

Finished Size: Each pot holder is about 8 inches square.

Directions:

Pre-wash all fabrics without fabric softeners, washing colors separately. If the water from any fabric is discolored, wash again until water runs clear. Machine-dry and press all fabrics.

Trace patterns onto paper side of fusible web as directed on patterns, leaving 1/2 in. between shapes. Cut shapes apart.

Fuse shapes onto wrong side of fabrics as directed on patterns, following manufacturer's directions. Transfer inside design lines by straight-stitching on traced lines through paper backing. Cut out shapes along outside traced lines.

For each pot holder, cut one 8-in. square each from white solid fabric and Christmas print fabric. Cut two 8-in. squares from batting.

APPLIQUE: Remove paper backing from shapes. Center shapes for each pot holder at an angle on the right side of the white fabric as shown in photo below, overlapping shapes where shown on patterns. Fuse shapes into place.

For each pot holder, place a single layer of batting over tear-away stabilizer. Place a fused pot holder top over batting

Fig. 1 Running stitch

with right side up and edges matching. Pin or baste the two layers together.

Applique around shapes of each with matching thread and a medium satin stitch, stitching around red parts of bells first and then around the green areas. Remove stabilizer. Bring all threads to back and secure.

QUILTING: Trace bell and tree templates onto template plastic and cut out. Or trace templates onto tracing paper and cut from lightweight cardboard.

Referring to photo for placement, use quilter's marking pen or pencil to trace around bell templates four times and around tree template three times onto right side of matching appliqued pot holder. Hand-stitch over the traced lines of bells and around appliqued bells using red quilting thread and running stitch. See Fig. 1. In the same way, hand-stitch over traced lines of trees and around appliqued tree with green quilting thread.

FINISHING: Referring to photo for placement, hand-stitch jingle bells to bells as shown. Center beads on sequins and hand-stitch them onto bells where desired. Tie green ribbon in a bow and hand-stitch bow onto top of bells.

String beads for garland as shown in photo. Hand-stitch garland and remaining trims to tree as desired.

Place a backing piece for each pot holder right side up over a piece of batting, matching raw edges. Machine- or hand-quilt together, stitching a 1-in. grid or pattern of choice.

Place each pot holder top and back together with batting sides together and edges matching. Baste around outside edges.

With right sides together and raw edges matching, pin green bias tape to outside edges of bell pot holder and red bias tape to outside edges of tree pot holder. Starting with 1/4-in. fold to wrong side, stitch bias tape to each pot holder with 1/4-in. seam, mitering corners. Overlap ends of bias tape and trim excess. Fold tape to back and hand-stitch to backing, covering seam line. Remove basting.

Sew plastic ring to back of top corner of each pot holder. ●

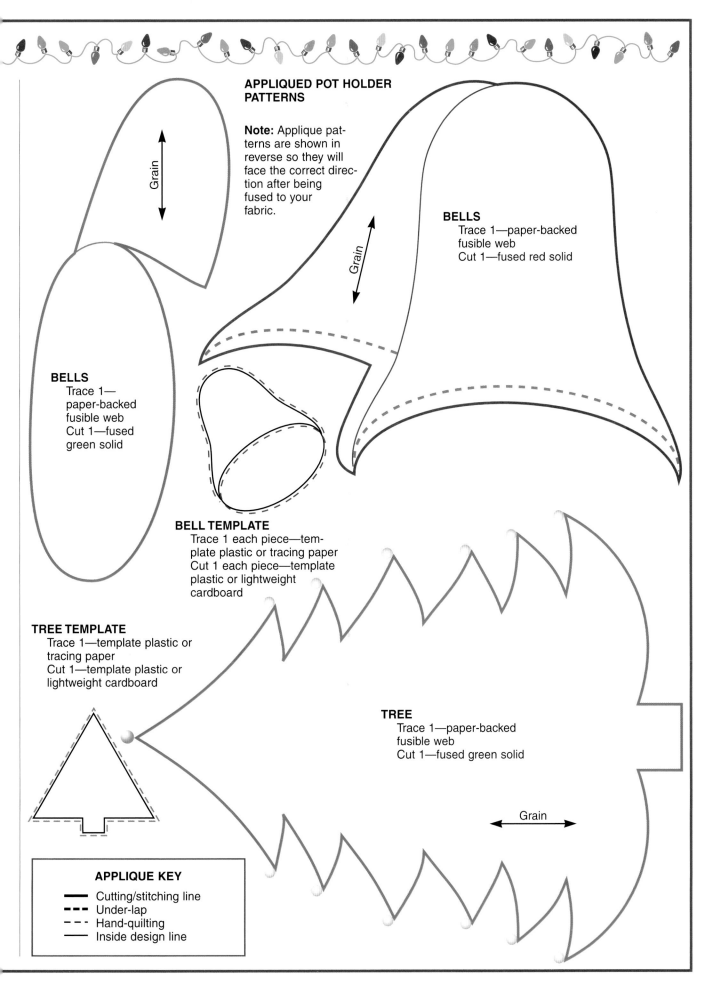

APPLIQUED POT HOLDER PATTERNS

Note: Applique patterns are shown in reverse so they will face the correct direction after being fused to your fabric.

Grain

BELLS
Trace 1—paper-backed fusible web
Cut 1—fused red solid

Grain

BELLS
Trace 1—paper-backed fusible web
Cut 1—fused green solid

BELL TEMPLATE
Trace 1 each piece—template plastic or tracing paper
Cut 1 each piece—template plastic or lightweight cardboard

TREE TEMPLATE
Trace 1—template plastic or tracing paper
Cut 1—template plastic or lightweight cardboard

TREE
Trace 1—paper-backed fusible web
Cut 1—fused green solid

Grain

APPLIQUE KEY
—— Cutting/stitching line
▬ ▬ ▬ Under-lap
- - - Hand-quilting
—— Inside design line

Well-Heeled Trims Are in Step with Season

CHOCK-FULL of festive intentions, these colorful stocking ornaments from Chris Pfefferkorn easily keep pace with Christmas.

The scrappy design is ideal for using up fabric left over from other projects, confides the crafter from New Braunfels, Texas. And because the top of the stocking isn't stitched shut, it's a perfect place to stick a candy cane or other merry little treat.

Materials Needed (for each):
Patterns on this page
Tracing paper and pencil
Scraps of 100% cotton or cotton-blend fabrics—green and white or red and white stripe for stocking and green or red pin-dot for cuff, heel and toe
Scrap of paper-backed fusible web
Scrap of green felt for holly
Six-strand embroidery floss—green or red for hanger and red for holly berries
Embroidery needle
Polyester stuffing
Pinking shears
Standard sewing supplies

Finished Size: Each stocking measures 5 inches high x 4 inches across.

Directions:
Trace stocking pattern onto tracing paper and cut out. Trace cuff pattern onto folded tracing paper. Cut out and open for a complete pattern. Cut stocking and cuff

FABRIC STOCKING TRIMS

Note: The heel and toe patterns are given in reverse so they will face in the correct direction after being fused to the back of the fabric.

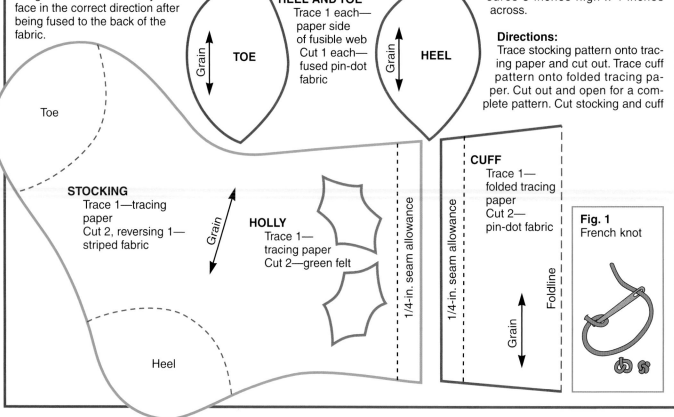

HEEL AND TOE
Trace 1 each—
paper side
of fusible web
Cut 1 each—
fused pin-dot
fabric

Grain

TOE

Grain

HEEL

Toe

Heel

STOCKING
Trace 1—tracing
paper
Cut 2, reversing 1—
striped fabric

Grain

HOLLY
Trace 1—
tracing paper
Cut 2—green felt

1/4-in. seam allowance

1/4-in. seam allowance

CUFF
Trace 1—
folded tracing
paper
Cut 2—
pin-dot fabric

Grain

Foldline

Fig. 1
French knot

from fabrics as directed on patterns.

Trace heel and toe patterns onto paper side of fusible web and cut out, leaving a 1/2-in. margin around shapes. Fuse heel and toe to wrong side of pin-dot fabric, following manufacturer's directions. Cut out shapes on traced lines.

Remove paper backing and fuse heel and toe to right side of one stocking piece where indicated on stocking pattern and as shown in photo at far left.

Sew one long edge of cuff to top of one stocking piece with right sides together and a 1/4-in. seam. Press seam toward cuff. Fold cuff along foldline with wrong sides together and press. Repeat with remaining cuff and stocking pieces.

Trace holly pattern onto tracing paper and cut out. Trace around holly onto green felt two times and cut out along traced lines.

Using unseparated six-strand red floss, stitch each holly leaf to right side of stocking below cuff with a French knot. See Fig. 1 for stitch illustration. Stitch one more French knot between holly leaves as shown in photo.

Pin stocking pieces with wrong sides together and edges matching. Straight-stitch around raw edges of stocking 3/8 in. from raw edges. Do not stitch across top of cuff.

Using pinking shears, trim around raw edges of stocking a scant 1/4 in. from stitching.

Use unseparated red or green floss to stitch a hanging loop to top edge of cuff as shown in photo. Lightly stuff stocking.

Clay Pot Pokes Figure Fun Among Bright Blossoms

THIS PAIR of plant enhancers you can quickly fix are sure to grow on all who see them during the holidays.

Barbara Matthiessen of Port Orchard, Washington raised her Christmas tree and gingerbread man figures by embellishing mini clay pots with paint, beads, string and other accents. "Just use whatever's on hand," she advises.

Materials Needed (for each):
2-inch clay pot
Small paintbrush
White (tacky) glue
Clear acrylic spray sealer
14 inches of 3/8-inch dowel
Scissors

Materials Needed (for Christmas tree):
1-1/2-inch wooden flowerpot
Two 1/4-inch wooden hearts
1-inch-high x 1/2-inch-thick wooden star
Acrylic craft paints—brown, green, red and yellow
Thirteen 3mm red pom-poms
Ten 6mm natural wooden beads
Black permanent fine-line marker
Red six-strand embroidery floss
13 inches of 2-ply jute string
Scrap of yellow print fabric

Materials Needed (for gingerbread man):
1-inch wooden ball for head
1/4-inch wooden heart
Acrylic craft paints—black, brown, light brown, pink and red
12 inches of 1/4-inch-wide red satin ribbon
12 inches of white baby rickrack
Four 10mm black beads for hands and feet
18-gauge black craft wire
Toothpick
Cotton swab
Wire cutters

Finished Size: Christmas tree is 4-1/4 inches tall x 2 inches across. Gingerbread man is 3-3/4 inches tall x 2 inches across.

Directions:
CHRISTMAS TREE: Paint clay pot and wooden flowerpot green, hearts red, star yellow and dowel brown. Let dry.

Glue hearts to center of each side of star. Glue star to bottom of wooden pot.

Invert wooden pot and glue over bottom of larger clay pot to form tree shape as shown in photo above right.

Cut nine small patches from yellow fabric and glue randomly onto tree as shown in photo.

Glue dowel to inside center of clay pot. Spray tree and dowel with acrylic sealer. Let dry.

Wrap jute string in spiral around tree and glue in place. Glue pom-poms onto jute string as shown in photo.

Cut five 6-in. pieces of floss and tie each into a small bow. Glue bows and natural wooden beads randomly onto tree.

Use marker to add stitches to patches and rays to star as shown in photo.

GINGERBREAD MAN: Paint clay pot and wooden ball light brown. Paint dowel brown and heart red. Let dry.

Cut a 7-in. piece of craft wire for legs. Slip a bead onto each end of wire and then bend ends of wire back into a small loop, securing bead. Fold wire in half. Insert fold of wire into clay pot and thread it through hole in bottom of clay pot.

Cut 5-in. piece of craft wire for arms. Center wire under fold of wire legs. Glue wires to bottom of clay pot. Glue wooden ball head over wires. Add a bead to each end of wire arms as for legs.

Referring to photo for placement, use handle of brush to dab three black dots on clay pot for buttons. Use toothpick and black to paint eyes and mouth on wooden ball as shown in photo. Use cotton swab and pink to paint cheeks.

Spray gingerbread man and dowel with acrylic sealer. Let dry.

Glue rickrack around head as shown in photo, trimming ends as needed. Glue remaining rickrack around rim of clay pot the same as for head. Glue heart to one side of buttons.

Tie ribbon in a bow below head as shown in photo. Trim as desired.

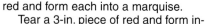

Put a Spin on Limbs with Paper Trim

GRIN AND BEAR IT. That's what you'll be doing when you turn out this quilled trim for the family fir!

The charming decoration comes from Jody Ondrus of Maple Heights, Ohio. "It may look intricate, but the technique's easy to master," she notes.

Materials Needed:
Patterns at right
1/8-inch-wide quilling paper or construction paper cut into 1/8-inch-wide strips—red, tan and white
Corsage pin, round toothpick or slotted quilling tool for rolling paper
Straight pin or toothpick
White (tacky) glue
Waxed paper
Ruler and pencil
Black fine-line marker
Scissors
Clear monofilament thread

Finished Size: Quilled trim is about 3-3/4 inches long x 2-1/4 inches across.

Directions:
BASIC QUILLING INSTRUCTIONS:
To roll paper coils, tear off strip of 1/8-in.-wide quilling paper or construction paper to the length specified in the instructions. Moisten one end of the strip slightly and press it to the center of the corsage pin or toothpick. If using a quilling tool, place end of paper in the crevice.

Roll the remaining length of the strip tightly between your thumb and forefinger, keeping the strip's edges as even as

possible. Slide the pin/toothpick/tool out and allow the coil to open to desired size, then glue end in place. Strive for uniformity between like shapes.

Prepare the coils as directed, noting that the lengths given represent the lengths of paper strips to tear, not the lengths or widths of rolled shapes.

When gluing quilled shapes together, use pin or toothpick to place drop of glue wherever shapes touch each other.

The following shapes are used, as shown in Fig. 1:

Tight Coil: Roll paper to end of strip and glue the end before removing it from the tool.

Loose Coil: Roll a tight coil without gluing end. Slip off the tool and let it expand to desired size. Glue the end.

Teardrop: Roll and glue a loose coil. When dry, tightly pinch one side of the coil to a point, allowing the opposite side to stay rounded.

Marquise: Roll and glue a loose coil as for teardrop. When dry, pinch opposite sides.

Pressed Heart: Roll and glue a loose coil. When dry, push coil into center while pinching bottom of coil.

Square: Roll and glue a loose coil. When dry, pinch opposite sides, then pinch remaining sides to form a square.

Ball: Cut paper strip from corner to corner. Roll wide end toward narrow end. Glue end before removing from tool.

U Shape: Roll and glue a loose coil. Flatten top portion of coil while pushing in sides slightly.

Cone: Roll and glue a tight coil. Gently push out center of coil, making cone shape. See arms on pattern. Spread glue inside cone to hold the shape.

MITTEN: Tear twenty 6-in. pieces of

red and form each into a marquise.

Tear a 3-in. piece of red and form into a teardrop.

Tear three 6-in. pieces of white and form each into a square.

Mitten Assembly: Place a piece of waxed paper over mitten pattern and glue red shapes together following pattern. Glue a strip of red around outside of red shapes to outline. Let dry.

Glue white squares across mitten top for cuff as shown on pattern. Let dry.

BEAR: Head: Tear two 24-in. strips of tan and glue together end to end, making a strip about 47 in. long. Roll strip into a tight coil. Gently push out center of coil to make rounded or domed shape. Spread glue inside dome to hold the shape. Repeat for back of head.

Nose: Cut a 1-1/2-in. strip of tan from corner to corner. Discard one piece and make a tight coil ball shape from the remaining piece.

Ears: Tear two 9-in. pieces of tan and roll each into a tight coil.

Body: Tear a 12-in. piece of tan and form into a U shape.

Arms: Tear two 6-in. pieces of tan

QUILLED BEAR TRIM PATTERNS
BEAR

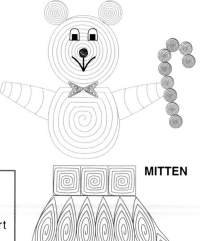

MITTEN

Fig. 1 Quilling shapes

⊙ Tight Coil		⋁ Pressed Heart
◎ Loose Coil		▣ Square
◊ Teardrop		● Ball Shape
◊ Marquise		◎ U Shape

and shape each into a 1/2-in.-long cone.

Candy Cane: Tear five red and four white strips each 3 in. long. Roll each strip into a tight coil.

Bow Tie: Tear two 1-in. pieces of red and form each into a pressed heart.

Bear Assembly: Tie ends of 8-in. piece of monofilament thread together in overhand knot for hanging loop. Spread glue onto inside rim of half of head.

With outside edges matching and knot of hanging loop sandwiched in between, glue the rims of the two dome-shaped pieces together to form the bear's head.

Referring to photo at far left, glue nose to center of one side of head. Glue bits of white paper above nose for eyes. Add black pupils with marker as shown in photo. Draw mouth on with pencil as shown in photo.

Referring to photo, glue ears to top of head. Glue body to the base of the head and arms to sides of body. Glue bow tie at neck.

Make candy cane by gluing alternating red and white tight coils together as shown in photo. Let dry. Glue candy cane to end of one arm.

Glue bear to back of mitten cuff as shown in photo. Let dry. ◗

Fanciful Gingerbread Fellow Dances a Merry Jig for Kids

YOUNGSTERS will kick up their heels when you set this lively gingerbread man in motion for them. Crafted from poster board and rickrack and held together by paper fasteners, the plaything takes no time to make, assures Susie Mintert of West Alton, Missouri.

Materials Needed:
Patterns at left
Tracing paper and pencil
8-inch square of poster board
8-inch square of brown kraft paper or grocery sack
> Four brass paper fasteners
> Round hole punch
> 8 inches of white rickrack
> Satin ribbon—12 inches of 1/4-inch-wide green and 24 inches of 1/8-inch-wide red
> 15 inches of white yarn
> Medium-point permanent markers—black and red
> Black ballpoint pen
> Glue stick
> White (tacky) glue
> Scissors

Finished Size: Dancing gingerbread man is 9 inches long x 8 inches across.

Directions:
Spread glue stick on one side of poster board and glue kraft paper or grocery sack onto poster board with edges matching. Carefully smooth out any wrinkles and let dry.

Trace patterns onto tracing paper as directed. Cut out and open. Trace around body pattern onto poster board. Trace around arm and leg patterns twice onto poster board. Cut out pieces on traced lines.

Glue rickrack across arms and legs as shown in photo above right. Trim even with edges.

Use hole punch to make holes at each "X" on patterns. Place arms and legs behind body piece as shown in photo above, aligning punched holes. Attach each with a paper fastener.

Use black ballpoint pen to add smile and outlines of cheeks and heart as shown on pattern.

Use black marker to add dots for eyes and red marker to fill in cheeks and hearts.

Cut red ribbon in half. Thread one end of each ribbon through punched holes of hands. Tie ribbons to hands with an overhand knot.

Tie the green ribbon into a small bow. Glue the bow under chin as shown in photo.

To make hair, cut a 12-in. piece of white yarn and wrap it around two fingers. Remove yarn from fingers. Thread remaining piece of yarn through loops as shown in Fig. 1 and tie ends in an overhand knot. Cut loops opposite knot and trim strands to 3/4 in. from knot. Glue hair to top of gingerbread man's head as shown in photo. ◗

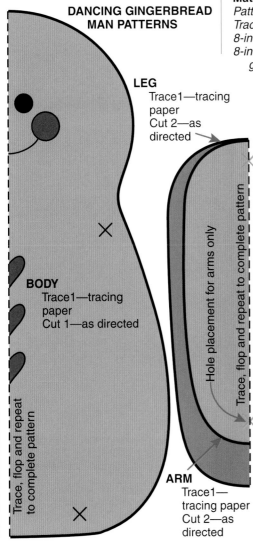

DANCING GINGERBREAD MAN PATTERNS

LEG
Trace1—tracing paper
Cut 2—as directed

BODY
Trace1—tracing paper
Cut 1—as directed

Trace, flop and repeat to complete pattern

Hole placement for arms only

Trace, flop and repeat to complete pattern

ARM
Trace1—tracing paper
Cut 2—as directed

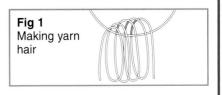

Fig 1 Making yarn hair

Sturdy Stitched Sack Has Merry Gift-Giving Covered

DELIVERING presents is in the bag …this tree-trimmed plastic canvas Christmas tote, that is! It's the jolliest of ways to wrap up handcrafted goodies for the folks on your list.

The design, from Shirley Wiskow of Jackson, New Jersey, is packed with purpose. Aside from its gift-giving role, it can hold greeting cards, store holiday craft supplies, top a table or do whatever else you dream up.

Materials Needed:
Charts on next page
Three 13-1/2-inch x 22-1/2-inch sheets
*   of stiff clear 7-count plastic canvas*
Worsted-weight yarn—15 yards of
*   dark green, 1 yard of brown, 154*
*   yards of red and 72 yards of white*
2 yards of silver metallic cord
Thirteen 5mm pearl beads
Thirteen 10mm silver sequins
Size 16 tapestry needle
Hand-sewing needle
Nylon monofilament thread
Craft scissors

Finished Size: Gift bag measures 10-1/2 inches high x 8 inches wide x 4 inches deep without handles.

Directions:
CUTTING: Remembering to count bars and not holes, cut the following from plastic canvas: One 54-bar x 69-bar piece for front, one 54-bar x 25-bar piece for bottom, one 54-bar x 57-bar piece for top section of back and one 54-bar x 13-bar piece for bottom section of back. (The back of the gift bag is seamed to allow it to fold flat.)

For the sides, follow charts at far lower right and cut two each of triangles A and B. Cut two front sides, following chart. Also cut two 57-bar x 13-bar pieces for the back sides.

For handles, cut two 69-bar x 4-bar pieces.

Lay out pieces as shown in Layout Diagram at left.

STITCHING: Cut 18-in. to 20-in. lengths of yarn. Follow charts and individual directions to stitch each piece, leaving outside edges of each piece unstitched. Do not knot yarn on back of work. Instead, leave a 1-in. tail on the back of the plastic canvas and work the next stitches over it. To end a strand, run yarn on back of canvas under completed stitches of the same color and clip yarn close to work.

Following charts and referring to Fig. 1 for stitch illustrations, fill in tree on front with green and leaf stitch. Fill in tree trunk with brown cross-stitches. Stitch tree stand with the silver cord and cross-stitches.

Stitch background of front with red slanted Gobelin and white Continental stitches, leaving shaded areas on chart unstitched for handle.

For trim on tree, use

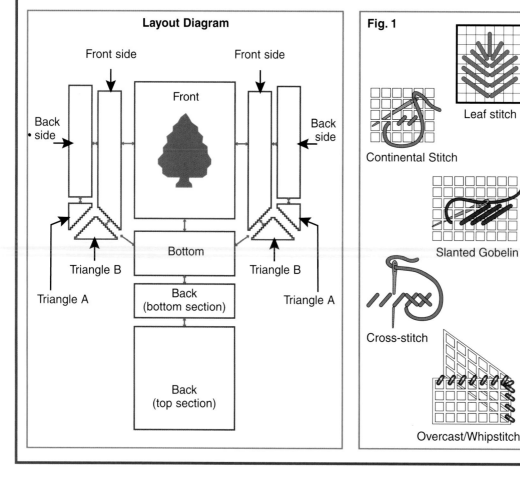

96

monofilament thread to hand-stitch a pearl on top of a sequin where indicated on the chart.

Fill in front sides and triangles A and B as shown on charts with red Continental stitches. Then stitch rest of front sides with red slanted Gobelin and white Continental stitches as shown on chart. Fill in back sides with red slanted Gobelin and white Continental stitches to match front sides.

Overlap one bar of the short edges of top back and the bottom back sections, making the back 54 bars x 69 bars to match the front. Stitch the pieces together along the overlapped bars, using white Continental stitches. Repeat Rows 1 and 2 on the Front chart throughout to complete the back, matching the

red slanted Gobelin stitches and white Continental stitches with the front and leaving outside edges and shaded areas unstitched.

Stitch bottom with red slanted Gobelin and white Continental stitches, repeating Rows 1 and 2 across the long edge and leaving outside edges unstitched.

Stitch the handles with red Continental stitches over the length of the center bar. Overcast the outside edges of the handles with red.

Referring to the Layout Diagram and with right sides facing out, use red to whipstitch triangle A to the bottom edge on a back side. Then whipstitch that back side to a front side. Next whipstitch a triangle B to base of joined

sides. Repeat, using the remaining sides and triangles.

With right sides facing out and red yarn, whipstitch a joined side to each side of the front piece. Stitch sides of the joined back piece to other side edge of attached sides. Next use white to whipstitch outside edges of bottom to bottom edges of front, back and sides of gift bag.

Overcast the top edge of the gift bag with white.

Place one end of handle flat against inside of top of gift bag front where indicated on chart and attach with matching yarns and Continental stitch. Repeat with other end of handle. In the same way, attach remaining handle to top edge of gift bag back.

GIFT BAG CHARTS

FRONT CHART
54 bars x 69 bars

Attach handles

FRONT SIDE
13 bars x 69 bars
Make 2—reversing 1

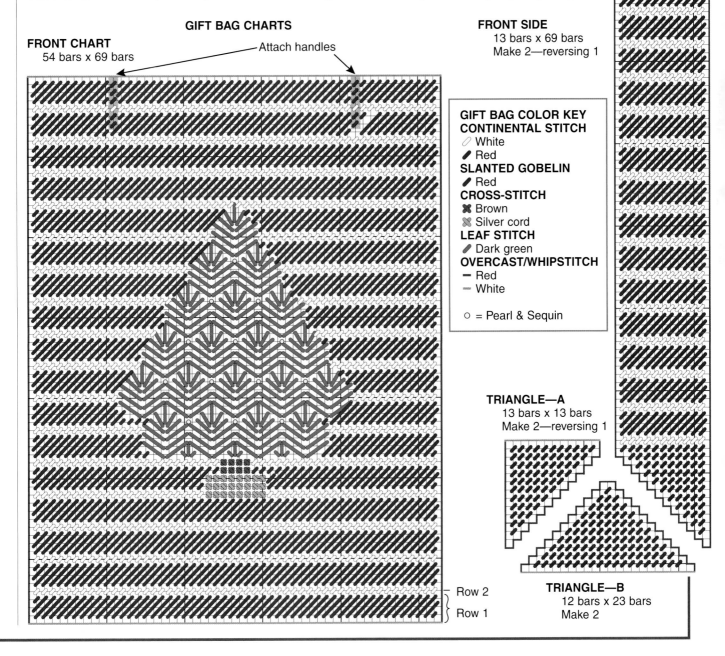

Row 2
Row 1

GIFT BAG COLOR KEY
CONTINENTAL STITCH
⊘ White
❚ Red
SLANTED GOBELIN
❚ Red
CROSS-STITCH
✖ Brown
✖ Silver cord
LEAF STITCH
❚ Dark green
OVERCAST/WHIPSTITCH
— Red
— White

○ = Pearl & Sequin

TRIANGLE—A
13 bars x 13 bars
Make 2—reversing 1

TRIANGLE—B
12 bars x 23 bars
Make 2

Her Festive Figures Point The Way to Lively Attire!

TO ANIMATE outfits for the holidays, Verlyn King went "shopping"—among her craft supplies. "I found wood shapes that I thought might make fun pins," she pens from Tremonton, Utah.

"Each took just a short time to make. I get lots of compliments whenever I wear one."

Materials Needed (for each):
Patterns below
Tracing paper and pencil
1-1/2-inch-long wooden split egg
Paintbrushes—small flat and liner
Paper plate or palette
Glue gun and glue sticks
Drill with 1/8-inch bit
1-1/2-inch pin back
Craft scissors
Needle-nose pliers

Materials Needed (for Santa pin):
One 6mm red pipe cleaner (chenille stem)
Pom-poms—one 6mm red for nose and one 10mm white for hat
Pony beads—six black and four white
Acrylic craft paints—black, flesh, red and white

Materials Needed (for reindeer pin):
One 3mm brown pipe cleaner (chenille stem)
6mm red pom-pom for nose
Scrap of brown felt or plastic art foam for ears
Four small black heart pony beads
Acrylic craft paints—black, brown, red and white

Finished Size: Santa pin is about 3 inches high x 2-1/2 inches across. Rein-

deer pin is about 3-1/2 inches high x 2-1/2 inches across.

Directions:
SANTA: Drill two holes through egg about 5/8 in. from narrow end and 3/4 in. apart for Santa's arms. Drill two holes through wide end of the egg about 1/4 in. from end and 3/8 in. apart for Santa's legs. See Fig. 1.

Trace painting pattern onto tracing paper. Turn traced pattern over and rub flat side of pencil lead over traced lines to blacken. Place painting pattern right side up on curved side of egg and trace over lines of painting pattern to transfer pattern to egg. Remove pattern.

Using flat brush, paint face flesh. Let dry. Next, paint beard, mustache, hair and hatband white. Let dry.

Paint flat side of egg, top of hat, mouth and body red. Let dry. Paint belt black. Let dry.

Using liner and black, paint eyebrows and outline of hat, hair, beard, mouth and mustache as shown on painting pattern. Let dry.

Using red and a nearly dry brush, lightly paint Santa's cheeks. Let dry.

Glue red pom-pom onto face for nose and white pom-pom onto tip of hat. Glue pin back centered along the length of the back of the egg, taking care not to cover drilled holes. Let dry.

Cut a 3-in. piece of red pipe cleaner for arms. Gently fold pipe cleaner in half and insert ends from back to front over opened pin back and through holes drilled for arms. Cut a 3-1/2-in. piece from red pipe cleaner for legs. Gently fold in half and insert into holes drilled for legs in the same way.

Slip one white and one black pony

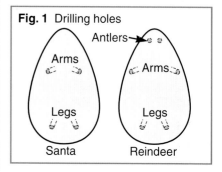

Fig. 1 Drilling holes

Antlers

Arms

Legs

Santa

Arms

Legs

Reindeer

bead over the end of each arm and one white and two black pony beads over each leg as shown in photo above. Use needle-nose pliers to bend tips of pipe cleaners so wires are not exposed, making arms about 3/4 in. long and legs about 1-1/4 in. long. Slide beads to ends of pipe cleaners. Apply glue to ends to secure beads.

REINDEER: Drill holes for arms and legs through egg as directed for Santa. Also drill two holes through narrow part of egg 1/4 in. apart and about 1/4 in. from end for antlers.

Trace painting pattern and transfer pattern to curved side of egg as directed for Santa.

Using flat brush, paint entire egg brown. Let dry.

Referring to painting pattern, use liner to paint eyes white. When dry, use liner to paint black pupils, eyebrows and mouth. Let dry.

Using red and a nearly dry brush, paint cheeks. Let dry.

Glue red pom-pom onto face for nose. Glue pin back centered along length of back of egg, taking care not to cover drilled holes. Let dry.

Trace ear pattern onto tracing paper and cut out. Cut ears from felt or plastic art foam as directed. Glue ears onto

---

SANTA PIN PAINTING PATTERN
Trace 1—tracing paper
Paint as directed

REINDEER PIN PAINTING PATTERN
Trace 1—tracing paper
Paint as directed

REINDEER PIN EAR PATTERN
Trace 1—tracing paper
Cut 2—brown felt or art foam

back of egg along edge of pin back, positioning them as shown in photo.

Cut a 3-in. and a 4-in. piece of brown pipe cleaner. Gently fold each in half. Insert ends of 3-in. piece from back to front over opened pin back and through top holes for "arms". In same way, insert 4-in. piece through holes for legs.

For antlers, cut one 1-1/2-in. piece and two 1-in. pieces of brown pipe cleaner. Gently fold 1-1/2-in. piece in half. Insert ends through drilled holes at narrow end of egg from front to back over the opened pin back. Fold remaining 1-in. pieces into V shapes and glue them to antlers as shown in the photo.

Slip one heart bead point first over ends of arms and legs as shown in photo. Use needle-nose pliers to bend tips of pipe cleaners so wires are not exposed, making arms about 1 in. long and legs about 1-1/4 in. long. Slide beads to ends of pipe cleaners. Apply glue to ends to secure beads. ●

Farm Container Is Place to Herd Yule Greetings

FILLED with rural ingenuity is this handy barn Evie Reece constructed from Christmas cards sent to her Pittsburgh, Pennsylvania home.

You can use it to hold mail or fill it with candy and set it out during the holidays. "It's a fun craft for kids to tackle themselves," Evie adds.

Materials Needed:
Six assorted Christmas cards (Evie used four same-size cards for the front, back, roof and bottom and two cards 2 inches taller for the sides)*
Hole punch
Bulky-weight yarn in color of choice
Tapestry needle
Ruler and pencil
Scissors

*It may be necessary to trim the cards to get the proper sizes. If possible, use cards with horizontal folds for the front, back, roof and bottom. Use cards with vertical folds for the sides.

Finished Size: The card barn pictured is 7 inches high x 7 inches long x 5 inches wide. The finished size will vary depending on the size of cards used.

Directions:
Cut along the fold of front, back, bottom and side cards and discard backs of each card. Do not cut along the fold of the roof card.

Trim tops of side cards as shown in Fig. 1, making sure height of each side card is 2 in. longer than the height of the front and back cards.

Place cards right side down on a flat surface as shown in Fig. 2. Using a pencil, lightly mark placement of holes about 1/2 in. apart and about 1/2 in. from outside edges of the cards as shown in Fig. 2. Make holes with hole punch.

Thread tapestry needle with yarn and insert through matching holes of the cards as follows: With right sides facing out, join one side card to the bottom card. Knot yarn loosely on inside and cut excess yarn. Continue to tie matching holes in the same way, attaching the

front, back and remaining side card to the bottom card.

Bring one side card and the front card up and insert a length of yarn through matching holes. Tie yarn in a bow on the outside to join corners as shown in photo below left. Trim ends as desired. In the same way, join remaining corners.

Place roof card on top of card box with right side out. Align holes of roof card with holes of side cards and join cards with yarn as before. ●

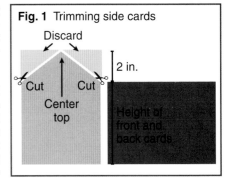

Fig. 1 Trimming side cards

Discard

Cut   Cut

Center top

2 in.

Height of front and back cards

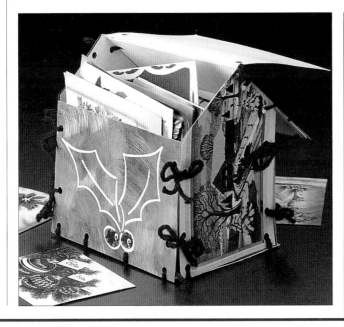

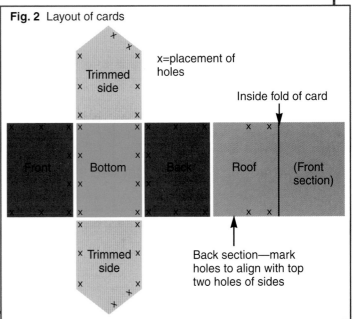

Fig. 2 Layout of cards

x=placement of holes

Trimmed side

Inside fold of card

Front   Bottom   Back   Roof   (Front section)

Trimmed side

Back section—mark holes to align with top two holes of sides

Woven Sleigh Basket Adds Old-Time Twist to Decor!

LET good times slide right in on the runners of this fun-to-weave container! The sleigh, with its look of yesteryear, will bring cheer into any setting.

Gerda Shebester of Milan, Michigan suggests filling the basket with candy or stocking it with potpourri or heirloom trims and placing it on the mantel.

Materials Needed:
Patterns on next page
Tracing paper and pencil
Natural reed—No. 2 round
Red-dyed reed—No. 3 round and 1/4-inch flat for weavers*
Green-dyed reed—1/4-inch flat for weavers*
12-inch x 4-inch piece of 1/4-inch-thick basswood
Drill with 1/8-inch bit
Scroll or band saw
Sandpaper and tack cloth
Wood glue
Brown stain and soft cloth
Heavy scissors or side cutters
Tape measure
Container for soaking reed
Old towel
Spring-type clothespins
Needle-nose pliers
14 inches of 2-ply jute string

*To dye your own reed, use red and green Rit dye and follow the instructions included in the package.

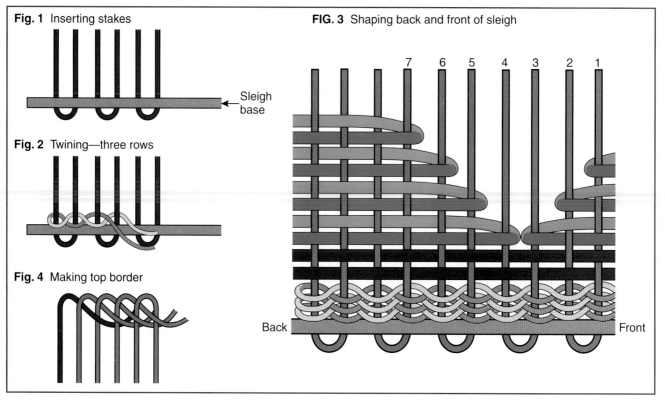

Fig. 1 Inserting stakes

Sleigh base →

Fig. 2 Twining—three rows

Fig. 4 Making top border

FIG. 3 Shaping back and front of sleigh

7   6   5   4   3   2   1

Back   Front

Finished Size: The sleigh basket is 7-5/8 inches long x 4-1/4 inches across x 6 inches high.

Directions:

SLEIGH BASE: Trace sleigh runner pattern onto tracing paper and cut out. Trace around pattern twice onto basswood. Use scroll or band saw to cut out.

Trace pattern for sleigh base onto folded tracing paper. Cut out and open for a complete pattern. Trace around pattern onto basswood once. Mark placement for drilling holes. Cut out sleigh base with band or scroll saw.

Drill holes in sleigh base and runners where indicated on patterns. Sand pieces smooth and wipe with tack cloth to remove sanding dust.

Wipe stain on base and runners with soft cloth and let dry.

SLEIGH BASKET: Cut twelve 22-inch-long stakes from No. 3 round red reed. Soak reed in warm water until pliable. Remove from water. Wipe with towel to remove excess dye from reed.

Carefully bend the stakes in half and insert them into the drilled holes of the base. See Fig. 1. Use clothespins as needed to hold materials in place.

Twining: Soak natural No. 2 round reed until pliable. Place ends of reed together to find center. Use needle-nose pliers to crimp reed 3 in. from center. Loop the crimped spot around one of the stakes. Begin twining with the longer end, taking it over one stake and under the next. See Fig. 2. Twine with natural round reed for three rows.

Sleigh base: Soak 1/4-in. flat red reed until pliable and wipe with towel to remove excess dye.

Starting over second stake from front of sleigh, weave one row of red above the twining, alternating under and over the stakes. When beginning stake is reached, continue under and over next few stakes, clipping end of weaver in the middle of the stake.

Starting on opposite side, weave another row of red in same way.

Shaping back: Soak 1/4-in. flat green reed until pliable and wipe with towel to remove excess dye.

Taper one end of green reed and bend 2 in. from end. Starting with tapered end, begin weaving the back of sleigh by starting bend of reed over fourth stake from the front on one long side. See Fig. 3.

Continue weaving, alternating under and over the stakes to the fourth stake from the front on the other side of the sleigh. Turn and weave back to the fifth stake from the front on the other side.

Turn and weave back in the same way, decreasing one stake every turning until you have four stakes left and have woven 13 rows of green. End row at back of sleigh, tucking end under a stake.

Shaping front: Using a tapered 1/4-in. flat green reed as before, begin weaving front of sleigh by starting bend of reed over third stake from front. See Fig. 3.

Continue weaving, alternating under and over the stakes to third stake from front on opposite side of sleigh. Turn and weave back to the second stake from front. Turn and weave back in the same way until you have four stakes left and have woven five rows of green. End row, tucking the end under a stake.

Twining top: Soak No. 2 natural round reed and twine top of sleigh for two rows.

Top border: Dampen all stakes. Take any stake and wrap it behind a neighboring stake, then bring it to front over next neighboring stake. See Fig. 4. Do this with all remaining stakes.

Next, start with any stake and pass it under the neighboring stake to the inside above the twining.

Inside border: Take any three stakes in your hand and, working in the inside of the border, place the far left stake under the second stake and then over the third. Now take the second stake and place it under the third stake and over the fourth. Continue in this way, using the far left stake as the worker and completing one or two rows as desired. Tuck ends to inside.

FINISHING: Glue runners to underside of the sleigh base where shown on pattern.

Thread ends of jute string through holes of runners and tie each end in a knot. ◆

RUNNERS
Trace 1—
tracing paper
Cut 2—
basswood

SLEIGH BASKET PATTERNS

SLEIGH BASE
Trace 1—tracing paper
Cut 1—basswood

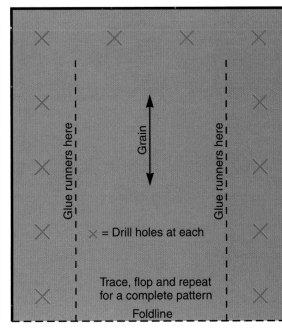

Festive Fingertip Towel Is Twice as Nice to Make

THROW IN this towel and you're sure to double the delight that handcrafting brings during December. How so? Designer Nancy Hearne of Marysville, California turned to two techniques—crochet and cross-stitch—to dress up the terry cloth piece.

(If you prefer, Nancy points out, you can simplify this project by skipping the crocheted trim and just doing the cross-stitching.)

Materials Needed:
Chart below
Fingertip towel with a 2-1/2-inch-wide 14-count Aida cloth insert
Size 24 tapestry needle
DMC six-strand embroidery floss in colors listed on color key
DMC Light Gold Metallic embroidery thread
One 50-gram ball of size 30 cotton crochet thread
Size 11 steel crochet hook
Scissors

Finished Size: The design is 103 stitches wide x 31 stitches high and measures 7-3/4 inches wide x 2-1/4 inches high.

Directions:
CROSS-STITCHING: Fold towel in half lengthwise, then fold it in half crosswise to determine center and mark this point. To find center of chart, draw lines across chart connecting arrows. Begin stitching at this point so design will be centered.

Working with 18-in. lengths of six-strand floss, separate strands and use two strands for all cross-stitches and one strand for backstitches. Use one strand of metallic thread for letters. See Fig. 1 for stitch illustrations.

One cross-stitch is worked over each set of threads on the Aida cloth with the needle passing through the holes. Each square on the chart equals one stitch worked over a set of fabric threads. Use colors indicated on color key to complete cross-stitching, then backstitching.

Do not knot floss on back of work. Instead, leave a short tail of floss on back of work and hold it in place while

ABBREVIATIONS	
ch(s)	chain(s)
dc(s)	double crochet(s)
lp(s)	loop(s)
sc(s)	single crochet(s)
sl st	slip stitch
sp(s)	space(s)
st(s)	stitch(es)
yo	yarn over
* or [ ]	Instructions following asterisk or between brackets are repeated given number of times.
( )	Instructions in parentheses are all worked in one space.

Fig. 1
Backstitch

Cross-stitch

SEASON'S GREETINGS COLOR KEY	DMC
⊡ White	000
◼ Black	310
◉ Light Navy Blue	322
◼ Dark Coral Red	817
▤ Christmas Green	890
⊞ Very Light Peach	3818
⊠ Light Gold Metallic	282Z
BACKSTITCHING	
— Black	310

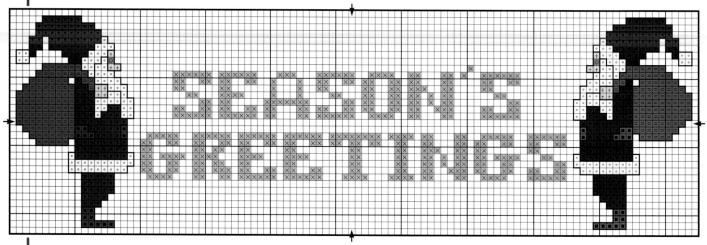

working first few stitches around it. To end a strand, run needle under a few neighboring stitches in back before cutting floss close to work.

CROCHETED TRIM: Edging is worked with size 30 crochet cotton across top and bottom of Aida cloth insert. The first row of sts is worked into the edge row of the insert. Crochet trim is worked so it extends over terry cloth portion of towel.

Top Border Edging: Row 1: With towel right side up and slip knot on hook, bring hook under the first set of fabric threads at top right corner of Aida cloth insert and sl st over that set of threads; ch 3 for first dc, work 1 dc over next set of fabric threads; * ch 3, skip 2 sets of fabric threads, [dc over next set of fabric threads] twice; repeat from * across top edge of Aida insert to last three sets of fabric threads, ch 3, skip 2 sets of fabric threads, dc over last set of fabric threads; ch 7, turn.

Row 2: Work (1 dc, ch 5, 1 sc, ch 5, 1 dc) in each ch-3 sp across; ch 1, turn.

Row 3: Sl st into first ch-5 sp; ch 6, draw up lp in each of next two ch-5 sps, yo and draw through all three lps; * ch 5, draw up lp in each of next two ch-5 sps, yo and draw through all three lps; repeat from * across; turn.

Row 4: * Sl st into next ch-5 sp, ch 5 and sl st in fourth ch from hook, ch 1, sl st in same ch-5 sp; repeat from * across. Fasten off.

Bottom Border Edging: Repeat Top Border Edging, turning the towel to begin in the lower left corner of the Aida cloth insert.

Hand-stitch ends of trim to side hem with a single strand of white floss. ●

Sole Goal of Cozy Slippers Is to Pamper

COLD FEET are a thing of the past with these comforting crocheted slippers from country crafter Yvonne Hostler of Bellevue, Nebraska.

The snug warmers are quick as a wink to finish, so you have time to stitch sets for friends and family in all sorts of holiday hues. Just make sure to hang on to a pair so you can also snuggle your toes into them!

Materials Needed:
2-ply bulky-weight yarn—approximately 275 yards of red and 35 yards of white
Size H/8 (5mm) crochet hook or size needed to obtain gauge
Stitch marker
Yarn needle or large tapestry needle

Gauge: Working in sc, 4 sts and 4 rows = 1 inch.

Finished Size: Women's size Medium slippers measure about 10 inches from toe to heel.

Directions:
With red, ch 25 loosely.

Round 1 (sole): Sc in second ch from hk and in each of next 22 chs; work 2 scs in end ch. Working on opposite side of ch, sc in each of next 23 chs; join with sl st to first sc: 48 scs. Mark last sc with a stitch marker. (Move stitch marker to the last sc at the end of each round.)

Round 2: Ch 1, work 2 scs in same st; sc in each of the next 22 scs; work 2 scs in each of the next 2 scs; sc in each of next 22 scs, work 2 scs in last sc; join with sl st to first sc: 52 scs.

Round 3: Ch 1, work 2 scs in same st, sc in each of next 24 scs, work 2 scs in each of next 2 scs; sc in each of next 24 scs, work 2 scs in last sc; join with sl st to first sc: 56 scs.

Round 4: Ch 1, work 2 scs in same st; sc in each of next 26 scs; work 2 scs in each of next 2 scs; sc in each of next 26 scs, work 2 scs in last sc; join with sl st to first sc: 60 scs.

Round 5: Ch 1, work 2 scs in same st; sc in each of next 28 scs; work 2 scs in each of next 2 scs; sc in each of next 28 scs, work 2 scs in last sc; join with sl st to first sc: 64 scs.

Round 6: Ch 1, work 2 scs in same st; sc in each of next 30 scs; work 2 scs in each of next 2 scs; sc in each of next 30 scs, work 2 scs in last sc; join with sl st to first sc: 68 scs.

Round 7: Ch 1, work 2 scs in same st; sc in each of next 32 scs; work 2 scs in each of next 2 scs; sc in each of next 32 scs, work 2 scs in last sc; join with sl st to first sc: 72 scs.

Round 8: Ch 1, work 2 scs in same st; sc in each of next 34 scs; work 2 scs in each of next 2 scs; sc in each of next 34 scs, work 2 scs in last sc; join with sl st to first sc: 76 scs.

Rounds 9-11: Ch 1, work 1 sc in same st and in each sc around; join with sl st to first sc: 76 scs.

Round 12: Ch 1, decrease by pulling up a lp in the same st and in each of the next 2 scs, yo and draw yarn through all four lps on hk; [work 1 sc in each sc] around to last 3 scs, decrease by pulling up a lp in each of the next 3 sts, yo and draw yarn through all four lps on hk: 72 sts.

Rounds 13-20: Ch 1, decrease by pulling up a lp in the same st and in each of the next 2 scs, yo and draw yarn through all four lps on hk; [work 1 sc in each sc] around to last 3 scs, decrease by pulling up a lp in each of the next 3 sts, yo and draw yarn through all four lps on hk. Fasten off at end of Round 20: 40 sts at end of Round 20.

Round 21: With right side facing, join white with sl st in any sc; ch 6, [sl st in next sc, ch 6] around; end with sl st in joining st. Fasten off. ●

ABBREVIATIONS

ch(s)	chain(s)
hk	hook
lp(s)	loop(s)
sc(s)	single crochet(s)
sl st	slip stitch
st(s)	stitch(es)
yo	yarn over
[ ]	Instructions between brackets are repeated a given number of times or as instructed.

Midwesterner Puts Jolly Face on December Decor

THERE'S no doubt Marilyn Barnett is a heads-up holiday crafter. Just take a look at the very merry visages she makes up for this time of year!

"I paint papier-mache Santa faces, then style flowing beards and mustaches from raffia," she details from White Heath, Illinois. "For the final touch, each trim is topped off with a colorful fabric stocking cap.

"Friends tell me the life-size St. Nicks add such a warm look to doors and walls they keep the characters up well beyond December 25."

The Noel fellows have a hand in keeping up Christmas appearances for Marilyn and husband Paul as well. "At least one is always on display at our

MINDING merry matters year-round is Marilyn Barnett (bottom left with husband). She fixes St. Nick noggins at shop, teaches others how.

craft and holiday shop in nearby Monticello.

"Although we carry items for all seasons, supplies and finished Yuletide handmades make up most of the stock. The St. Nick trims fit in with other projects brightening the space."

The jovial Kris Kringles turn the most heads, however. In fact, Marilyn has been inundated with requests for the elves almost from the moment she first made them.

"The store's front counter is my favorite crafting spot—folks are used to seeing me elbow-deep in a design. Still, the Santas seemed to catch people's eyes and get them talking," she recalls.

The first few Marilyn gussied up with acrylic paints alone…but the results were ho-hum. "Not until I began gluing on the raffia hairdos did the characters come to life.

"Then the comments really started to flow," Marilyn beams. "Everyone loved my elves!

"While a good number were interested in the finished figures, quite a few crafters wanted to make their own. Because I regularly teach other techniques in the shop, offering a session on St. Nick was easy—and fun besides."

For a Good Claus

This North Pole noggin's good nature is more than skin deep, according to its creator. "He raises spirits, too," Marilyn attests.

"The best example is the time our

church needed funds for an important construction project. To help, we decided to offer finished Santas and do-it-yourself kits through the mail.

"Little did we know we'd soon have orders pouring in from all over. When Paul and I couldn't keep up with the volume, we got several friends from church to help," Marilyn smiles. "St. Nick sure seemed heaven-sent!"

Several years later, the Barnetts still receive excited inquiries. "That large version proved so popular that we've branched out a bit by creating Santas in other sizes, including a little pin Paul shapes in plaster and I decorate."

Winks this happy hobbyist, "Making these jolly gents puts smiles on our faces, no matter what the season!"

Editor's Note: *For more details on Marilyn's crafts, classes and shop, send a self-addressed stamped envelope to Creative Crafts, 208 W. Washington St., Monticello IL 61856. Or call 1-217/762-7024.*

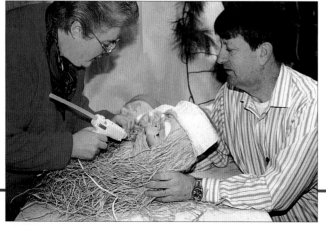

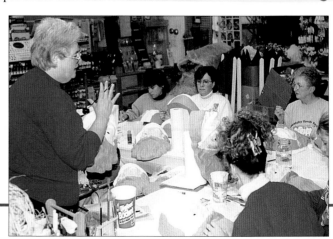

Country Designer Keeps Yule in Stitches

THERE'S a pattern to Donna Henton's craftiness…characterized by Christmas! The Blair, Nebraska resident maps out plans and creates kits for festive sewn dolls and trims she routinely dreams up.

"December 25 is often on my mind," admits Donna. "I can hardly keep up with the motifs that pop into my head."

When an idea sprouts forth—a calico-garbed Santa dubbed "Irving Mc-Klaus", or "Hannah", an angel whose curls are bound by bright rag bows—Donna charts the figure's features.

"Then I start stitching—but things don't always turn out as planned. Sometimes the project will change shape right on the sewing table! One time, I thought I was creating a cow…and ended up with a merry bear cub instead.

"After I have the details all worked out, I draw patterns and write instructions, then check and recheck until I'm sure everything is foolproof and easy to follow," she concludes.

Styling a helpful elf or a clever spool wreath is like second nature for Donna. "I've been making things as long as I can remember," she confirms.

"My grandmother was a wonderful seamstress who taught me to sew at an early age. Over the years, I've mastered other techniques, but working with fabric will always be my favorite."

Crafting's in the Bag

While the pattern packages contain ready-to-use blueprints and instructions, Donna's kits hold the whole caboodle—directions, schematics, plus all the supplies necessary to bring the accent to life.

"Some are simple, others are more complicated," she reveals. "My 'Angel Babies' kit is one of the most appealing. It comes with lumber to make a tree and trims, doll hair and the like for the lacy cherubs that hang on the 'branches'."

As busy as she is offering nifty notions for others to try, Donna finds time to do some family-style fixing up for husband John and two grown children.

"Each year, I put together presents for everyone," she attests. "One I'm most proud of is the pair of homespun teddy bears sewn from an old quilt my grandmother made. Our children just loved the critters.

"It was so rewarding to see their happy faces," sighs Donna contentedly. "I'm just as pleased whenever I hear from folks who've enjoyed making my creations. Those 'gifts' keep me in festive form!"

Editor's Note: *For a brochure listing Donna's patterns and kits, send $2 to Donna's Country Crafts, 13092 U.S. Hwy. 30, Blair NE 68008; or call 1-800/886-8907. And, if you'd like to try a holiday project that characterizes how adorable her designs are, turn the page…* ●

SEW MERRY. Donna Henton pins down festive stitched trimmings for folks with easy-to-follow Christmas patterns, kits she creates.

Scrappy Santa Claus Will Add Cheer to Decor

WANT to try your hand at a Christmas pattern created by craft designer Donna Henton (see article on page 105)? You can without delay—thanks to the jolly project she happily shares!

This clever fellow Donna calls Kountry Klaus needs only simple supplies and the instructions here to make him. In an afternoon, you'll have a lively guy who'll figure fun into any setting.

Materials Needed:

Patterns on next page
Tracing paper and pencil
44-inch-wide 100% cotton or cotton-blend fabrics—1/4 yard or scraps of red Christmas print and 1/8 yard each or scraps of white Christmas print and black solid
Matching all-purpose thread
9-inch x 12-inch piece of cotton quilt batting
2-inch flat-bottom wooden ball for head
Two 3/8-inch gold metallic star buttons
1-inch-high wooden star
Acrylic craft paints—black, dark green and pink
Small flat paintbrush
Toothpick
Three 12mm gold jingle bells
Eight 1-1/8-inch-high wooden spools
Several strands of white curly wool roving or one package of white curly doll hair
1 cup of plastic doll pellets or uncooked rice
Polyester stuffing
Compass
Glue gun and glue sticks
Standard sewing supplies

Finished Size: Kountry Klaus is about 7 inches across x 14-1/2 inches tall when seated.

Directions:

Trace patterns onto folded tracing paper as directed on patterns. Cut out and open each for complete patterns. Cut shapes from fabrics as directed on patterns.

For mitten and boot patterns, use compass to draw a 3-in. circle and a 4-1/4-in. circle onto tracing paper. Then from black solid, cut two 3-in. circles for mittens and two 4-1/4-in. circles for boots.

Do all sewing with right sides of fabrics together and a 1/4-in. seam unless instructed otherwise.

BODY: From red print, cut two 3/4-in. x 17-in. strips for legs and two 3/4-in. x 6-in. strips for arms. Fold strips in half lengthwise with wrong sides together, leaving edges unfinished. Press.

Baste leg and arm strips to right side of one body piece where indicated on pattern with one short edge of each strip matching a raw edge of body piece. Sew two body pieces together with outside edges matching and arms and legs sandwiched in between, leaving top open for turning.

Match bottom seam of body with adjoining side seam and stitch across corner as shown in Fig. 1. Repeat with other end of bottom seam and adjoining side seam to create a flat bottom for Santa's body.

Turn body right side out through top opening.

Hand-sew around top of body 1/4 in. from raw edge with running stitch, leaving thread attached. See Fig. 2 for stitch illustration.

Pour plastic doll pellets or uncooked rice into body. Stuff rest of body firmly with polyester stuffing.

Draw up thread to close top. Fasten off thread.

JACKET: Sew jacket front and back together along shoulder and underarm seams. Clip underarm seam where shown on pattern. Cut down center fold-line of one jacket piece only for center front opening.

From quilt batting, cut a 2-in. x 12-1/2-in. strip for trim on bottom of jacket and a 2-1/4-in. x 6-in. strip for trim down front of jacket.

Fold the 12-1/2-in.-long strip in half lengthwise and pin to hold. Sew strip to right side of bottom edge of jacket with long cut edges matching. Trim ends even with center front edge of jacket.

Fold 1/2-in. hem to inside on one short end of 2-1/4-in. x 6-in. strip. Fold strip in half lengthwise, encasing hem. Pin to hold. Sew strip to right edge of center front opening of jacket with long cut edges matching and hemmed end even with bottom edge of trim on bottom edge of jacket.

Lap trimmed edge over left edge of opening, concealing raw edges. Glue or hand-sew trim to hold in place.

Hand-sew buttons to trim on jacket as shown in photo at left.

Place jacket right side out over Santa's body, aligning underarm seams on jacket with side seams on body. Glue neck opening of jacket to top of Santa's body, easing in fullness as needed.

Turn raw edge of one sleeve opening 1/4 in. to wrong side. Hand-sew around opening of sleeve with running stitch, leaving thread attached. Pull a fabric-strip arm through sleeve opening and draw up thread around strip. Fabric-strip arm will extend beyond sleeve. Fasten off thread. Repeat on other sleeve opening.

HEAD: Glue flat side of wooden ball centered on top of Santa's body.

Referring to photo for placement, use a nearly dry brush and a circular motion to paint pink cheeks on front of ball head. Dip toothpick into black and dab on two tiny dots for eyes. Let dry.

Glue wool roving or doll hair to head for Santa's hair, beard and mustache as shown in photo.

HAT: Paint all sides of wooden star dark green. Let dry.

Sew hat pieces together along the curved top edge. Turn right side out.

Cut a 2-in. x 9-in. strip of quilt batting for trim on hat. Fold strip in half lengthwise and pin. Sew strip to right side of bottom edge of hat with long cut edges matching and short ends overlapped on back of hat.

Glue star and hand-sew jingle bell to front of hat as shown in photo.

Place a small amount of stuffing inside hat. Place hat on Santa's head with star and bell in front. Spot-glue hat to head as needed.

SPOOLS: Cut four 3/4-in. x 3-in. pieces each of white Christmas print and quilt batting.

Wrap a strip around each spool and overlap ends, adding glue as needed to secure.

MITTENS AND BOOTS: With matching thread, hand-sew a running stitch 1/4 in. from outside edge of one mitten fabric circle and leave thread attached. Draw up thread slightly to gather fabric a bit. Stuff inside of the mitten firmly. Draw up thread tightly and fasten off. Repeat with remaining fabric circles.

FINISHING: Arms: Take one end of a fabric-strip arm and thread through hole of one spool wrapped with batting. Slide spool up to end of sleeve and knot strip close to spool. Trim excess fabric. Glue gathered area of a mitten to bottom of spool, covering knot. Repeat for other arm.

Legs: Thread a fabric-strip leg through two fabric-covered spools. Then add a batting-covered spool and knot strip, making leg about 6 in. long from body to bottom of last spool. Trim excess fabric. Glue gathered area of boot to bottom spool, covering knot. Repeat for other leg.

Cut two 1/2-in. x 9-in. strips of red Christmas print. Tie each in a bow between last two spools of each leg as shown in the photo. Trim ends to desired length.

Hand-sew a jingle bell to each boot as shown in photo.

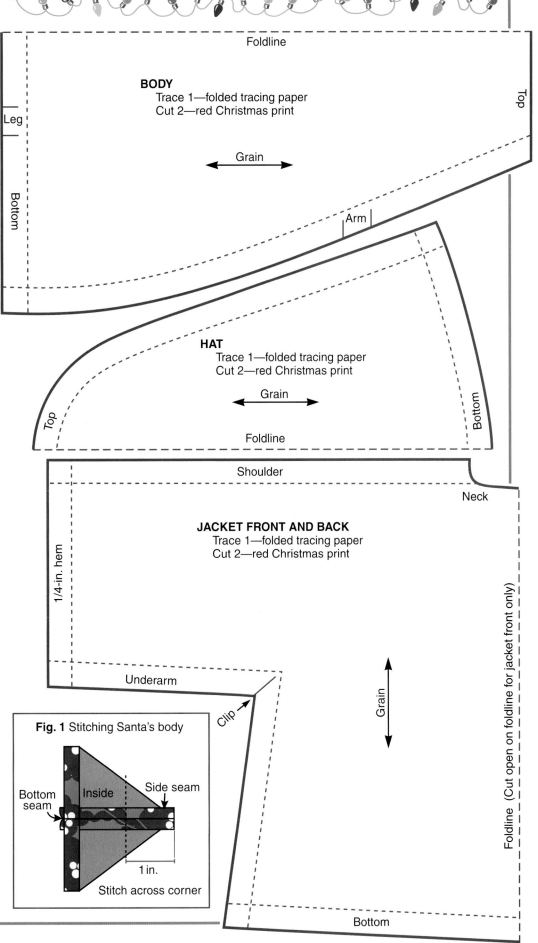

Foldline

BODY
Trace 1—folded tracing paper
Cut 2—red Christmas print

Leg

Bottom

Grain

Top

Arm

HAT
Trace 1—folded tracing paper
Cut 2—red Christmas print

Grain

Top

Bottom

Foldline

Shoulder

Neck

JACKET FRONT AND BACK
Trace 1—folded tracing paper
Cut 2—red Christmas print

1/4-in. hem

Grain

Underarm

Clip

Foldline (Cut open on foldline for jacket front only)

Bottom

Fig. 1 Stitching Santa's body

Bottom seam

Inside

Side seam

1 in.

Stitch across corner

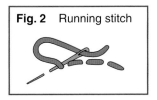

Fig. 2 Running stitch

She Highlights North Pole Personalities!

MAKING spirits bright is what Marilyn Crouch delights in doing. The Oolitic, Indiana grandma enhances branches, mantels and more with Yuletide figures she paints…on burned-out light bulbs!

A glance around the workroom of her craft and antiques shop located in nearby Bedford highlights the scope of Marilyn's holiday habit. Bright Santas—large and small, fat and skinny—cover most surfaces.

"I also fix up flocks of penguins and piles of snowmen," Marilyn mentions.

"Easter bunnies, Halloween cats and everyday critters figure into my crafting, too, although Christmastime is what sparks my imagination most often."

Another inspirational beacon is the size and shape of each light. "How big or small a bulb is will determine what

CREATIVE OUTLET for Marilyn Crouch involves brushing bright images on burned-out light bulbs. She uses all sizes and shapes to paint Santas, snowmen and penguins.

it becomes—an ornament, shelf-sitter or a piece of jewelry.

"I've brushed figures on teeny-tiny night-lights, bulbs as big as 23 inches wide and everything in between. Each new style gets me fired up to make more," she says.

"In the past, I painted on ceramic shapes and other dimensional surfaces, but nothing like this. Still, it didn't surprise my family when I started brightening bulbs.

"After all, my motto is 'If it doesn't move—paint it,' " Marilyn chuckles.

The task of finding the unusual materials doesn't dim Marilyn's enthusiasm one bit. "That's because I get lots of help," she admits.

"Ever since our friends and neighbors found out that I paint old light bulbs, they've kept me well-stocked.

"Once in a while, I'll spot one in a store that's different and bring it home. My husband, Merrill, sometimes does

the same. But mostly I work with lights that'd otherwise be thrown away. I paint them freehand, using acrylics."

Aside from the occasional shopping trip, Marilyn's spouse regularly plugs in ideas, as do their three grown daughters. "Our 11 grandchildren and one great-grandchild make suggestions as well," she proudly points out.

"Merrill gives support in another way—he cuts bases to hold large bulbs.

"We often offer the decorations at area craft shows and give them as gifts each Christmas," Marilyn adds.

"For the last several years, we've decked a Christmas tree with the bulbs for a local charity auction. Folks seem to take a shine to those pines we've gussied up," she beams herself.

Editor's Note: *For a brochure about Marilyn's painted light-bulb creations, send $1 and a self-addressed stamped envelope to Marilyn's Light House, 711 R St., Bedford IN 47421.*

Frugal Farm Wife Rounds Up A Thrifty Little Christmas

BECAUSE of Sharon Egger's bent for "wreath-cycling", Christmas is an all-around more decorative season.

"I enjoy decking our family homestead for the holidays…both inside and out," allows the Nebraska farm wife about the acres near Hickman she shares with her husband, Denny, and their two growing children.

"In fact, for years, I'd wanted to garnish our granary with a great big Christmas wreath. But I always figured that would be much too expensive."

Finally, this do-it-yourselfer found her way around the problem—with a priceless solution. Using two old artificial Christmas trees that she and a friend were planning to discard, she brought a homemade wreath full circle.

"First, Denny welded metal rods into two circular forms—one 20 inches, the other 54 inches in diameter," she recounts. "Then he connected the smaller 'hub' to the outer 'rim' with more rods, like the spokes of a wheel.

"Next, I laid 16 individual branches from a 7-foot artificial tree side by side around the front of the base. I wired the bottom of the limbs to the inner hub and the bushy tops to the outer rim with baler twine. The finished product turned out to be 7-1/2 feet across!"

To give her wreath a seasonal twist, Sharon added a bow fashioned from gold wire foil ribbon and brightened it up with 200 white light bulbs.

The final cost of the wreath—under $20—has a *very* nice ring to it, Sharon notes. What's more, the economical but enduring greenery has spruced up the granary without bowing to brisk winds or blizzards for several years now.

In addition, Sharon's Yule ingenuity is merrily making the circuit among her friends and neighbors. Many of them are rounding up artificial trees from flea markets to recycle into wreaths of their own.

"Not only is the wreath fun to craft," Sharon affirms, "it preserves our holiday spirit all through winter."

In keeping Christmas evergreen, what goes around truly comes around for this country woman! ●

WREATHED in smiles is Sharon Egger! Her centsible craft wraps granary in holiday cheer.

'Edible Tree' Is Perfect Gift for Backyard Buddies

IF YOU'D LIKE to share holiday spirit with the birds, squirrels and other critters that inhabit your yard, try this—a tastefully trimmed tree they can sink their teeth—or beaks—into!

Janet Walker, who runs the Critter Alley Wildlife Care Center in Grand Ledge, Michigan, passes along the "recipe" she uses to keep the feathered and furry friends who live around her home merry all winter long.

Here's what you will need:

- A small tree in your yard that's close to other shrubs or trees
- String and needle
- Dried cranberries, apples, apricots, raisins and other dried fruit
- Oranges and grapefruit, cut in half
- Whole peanuts in shells
- Pinecones
- Peanut butter
- Birdseed

Begin by threading a needle with string. Pierce peanuts and dried fruits with the needle and push them onto the string to create a garland. Make several to hang on the branches of your tree.

Scoop out the orange and grapefruit halves (you can leave a little fruit inside) and fill them with a mixture of peanut butter, birdseed and raisins.

Fasten the filled citrus halves securely to the tree branches with string.

Spread peanut butter onto pinecones.

Then roll in birdseed and raisins or other dried fruits. Hang on the tree with string just as you would for traditional ornaments.

"The birds and small animals love all of these homemade treats—plus it's a joy to watch from the kitchen window as they nibble away," Janet reports.

Christmas in the Country

Christmas in the country is a really grand affair—
Pine trees shine, bright candles gleam and sleigh bells fill the air.
My porch is swagged with green boughs tied up with bows of red,
And holly sprigs with brass bells adorn my antique sled.

The door greets all who enter with a wreath of red and gold
That welcomes friends and family to a haven from the cold.
Inside, they're met with warm smiles and hearts that overflow
With country love and friendship wrapped up in Christmas glow.
            —*Bess Michael, La Jose, Pennsylvania*

Hostess Opens The Door to a Crafty Holiday

GREETING the season with homespun hospitality has turned into a crowd-pleasing habit for Joanne Miller. During November, she welcomes thousands into her Janesville, Wisconsin dwelling—for a holiday craft fair!

"Lots of people come year after year because the atmosphere, they say, is so warm and cozy," Joanne smiles.

"I got the idea after a pal suggested I hold a craft fair in our barn. Herm, my husband, wasn't too keen on that idea. The barn's *his* space. So I decided to try it in the next best place—the first floor of our old farmhouse.

"Besides, displaying accents in real rooms is the best way to show how they can be used. Most any kind of trim can be found decking our halls!"

That's apparent the moment visitors step inside. From the foyer on are Santas, woven baskets, rural wreaths, merry centerpieces and more.

Christmas trees are a key to the decorating scheme—each area features at least one. Many spots sport themes, too. For instance, the living room dons traditional tones and features old-time ornaments on the grove of evergreens planted there, while the dining room's done in Victorian frills.

In the den are birdhouses, holiday figures and other baubles. The kitchen, of course, showcases sweet treats such as cookie trims on a tabletop pine and potpourri pies. Free for the taking are cups of cider and oven-fresh cookies.

"I make sure it smells like Christmas

throughout the house," notes this Midwestern Mrs. Claus.

Aside from the unusual setting, Joanne's show has a freshness that helps it stand apart. Most of the 40-plus artisans sending their wares her way reside outside the area. "That allows us to feature designs folks aren't likely to find locally," she says.

Boxes of handcrafts begin arriving in October. "It's the signal we need to start our 'redecorating'," details Joanne. "Our six grown kids and their families come the first weekend to help us move the large furniture out to the corncrib. Meanwhile, Herm and I 'relocate' upstairs, our living quarters during the fair.

"Then everyone pretties the porches, windows and wagon parked out front with bows and boughs."

Joanne stays inside, though. "This is also our Thanksgiving celebration," she explains. "I time my preparations so the feast is complete just as the exterior 'face-lift' is finished.

"After the meal, we head out to the

SPREADING hands-on cheer is what Joanne Miller (above left) does during the holiday craft fair she hosts in her turn-of-century farmhouse.

barn to haul the artificial firs stored there back to the house for trimming."

The flurry of activity doesn't let up for weeks. "Family, friends and neighbors all help," Joanne acknowledges. "We couldn't do it without them."

By December, the Millers' house is quiet as can be. "It's almost lonely," this happy hostess admits.

"I love the hustle and bustle of the fair, and the garnishes…but mostly, I enjoy meeting everyone who comes in for a bit of Christmas cheer!"

Editor's Note: *Christmas at the Miller farm runs from the end of October through November (closed on Thanksgiving Day). The doors are open 10 a.m.-6 p.m. Monday through Friday, 9 a.m.-5 p.m. Saturday and 11 a.m.-4 p.m. Sunday.*

For exact dates and directions, contact Joanne at 5709 N. State Rd. 184, Janesville WI 53545; 1-608/756-8579.

Visit by 'Father Christmas' Was the Best Gift of All!

By Verlene McOllough of Clarion, Iowa

OF ALL the holidays I've ever celebrated, none stands out in my mind like the Christmas when I was 6. That was the year I got to meet Santa Claus …thanks to a loving family connection.

It was in the throes of the Great Depression, and money was scarce. My sister and I were blissfully unaware, though.

We felt safe and loved by our parents. And we never went hungry. Dad saw to that with his big country garden.

When the air sharpened and leaves crisped to gold, Dad began preparing for the winter to come. All he had to do was open the doors to the dirt cellar to alert us it was time to pick, pull, dig and store baskets of succulent harvest.

Some of the pickings didn't make it into storage, of course. We'd snap the tail off an orange carrot, rub it clean and crunch its sweetness. Or we'd devour a juicy red tomato.

Not only did these activities signal the approach of winter, they also heralded the merriest of holidays—Christmas! Well before the first frost, I started anticipating our December festivities, especially the arrival of one person.

That year in particular, I couldn't get Santa Claus out of my mind. I'd

L. DZIK

drop off to sleep envisioning the miracle man from the North Pole gliding through the star-studded sky, steering a sleigh full of toys. And I'm sure I mentioned more than once how I'd love to meet Santa in person.

Well, the evening of December 24, my wish came true.

That night, my father herded everyone into the parlor to relax and enjoy each other's company. While my sister and I started a game of "Hide the Thimble" and Mother settled into the rocker, Dad nonchalantly rose from his chair and sauntered into the basement.

Soon, we all heard a hearty "Ho, ho, ho" and a sweet jingling coming from the front porch, followed by several snappy raps on the door. Mother opened it, revealing a rotund red figure bearded up to his eyebrows.

Came Calling for Her

"Is this where Verlene lives?" a voice I didn't quite recognize boomed.

For one wondrous moment, I hid behind the door. Then, as with every other important event in my life, I turned toward my father. But he wasn't there!

Remembering that he had gone downstairs just moments before, I dashed to the basement door, all the while keeping my eye on Santa Claus. "Daddy! Daddy!" I hollered. "Come quick! Santa is here!"

Before Dad could reply, Mother steered me away from the door so Santa could quiz me. Had I been a good girl? Would I sit on his lap? I answered excitedly—hoping Santa could stay until Dad came back upstairs.

Finally, though, Santa explained he had more children to visit. With two shakes of a bell, he disappeared into the icy night.

Minutes after Santa's departure, my father emerged from the cellar.

"Oh, Daddy, you missed Santa Claus," I sighed. Then I breathlessly told him all about the unforgettable visit.

If Santa brought a toy that night, I don't remember. And years later, when I realized why Dad had disappeared during Father Christmas' appearance, I was far from disappointed.

On the contrary, that night taught me Christmas is about much more than brightly wrapped packages and store-bought trinkets. Since then, no present has ever measured up to the one Dad gave—the priceless gift of himself. 🌰

May the sights and sounds of the season fill you and your family with wonder...the whole year through.

INDEX

Food

Appetizers & Snacks
Bacon-Wrapped Scallops with Cream Sauce, 22
Chocolate-Raspberry Fondue, 23
Cinnamon Granola, 47
Creamy Shrimp Dip, 22
Elegant Cheese Torte, 21
Festive Cheese Bites, 22
Homemade Smoked Almonds, 21
Nutty Caramel Popcorn, 46
Olive Cheese Nuggets, 23
Piquant Meatballs, 22
Pizza Poppers, 21
Pretzel Wreaths, 46
Sausage-Filled Stars, 21
Savory Mushroom Tartlets, 23
Sesame Ham Pinwheels, 23
Spicy Pineapple Spread, 22

Beverages
Homemade Coffee Mix, 12
Pineapple Cranberry Punch, 23

Candy
Buttermilk Pralines, 38
Chocolate Caramel Wafers, 38
Chocolate Toffee Crunchies, 37
Cinnamon Hard Candy, 37
Coconut Surprise Candy, 39
Dandy Caramel Candies, 37
Dipped Peanut Butter Logs, 38
Festive Popcorn Bars, 38
Nutty Sandwich Treats, 39
Orange-Sugared Pecans, 39
Peanut Butter Mallow Candy, 38
Raspberry Truffles, 38
Speedy Oven Fudge, 39
Sugarplums, 39
Sugary Orange Peel, 37

Condiments
Cinnamon Cream Syrup, 11
Honey-Mustard Salad Dressing, 47
Plum-Apple Butter, 47
Rosy Cider Jelly, 45

Cookies & Bars
Almond Crescents, 35
Black Forest Oatmeal Crisps, 31
Caramel Date Pinwheels, 30
Cardamom Almond Biscotti, 34
Chewy Pecan Drops, 34
Chocolate Fruit 'n' Nut Cookies, 35
Coconut Raspberry Bars, 30
Frosted Spice Cutouts, 34
Gift-Wrapped Brownies, 45
Gingerbread Rings, 35
Lime Spritz Cookies, 31
Minty Chocolate Crackles, 30
Mocha Truffle Cookies, 30
Nutmeg Logs, 45
Raspberry Kisses, 35
Rich Chocolate Cream Bars, 34
Spumoni Slices, 31

Desserts (also see Cookies & Bars)
Almond Fruit Squares, 41
Caramel Custard, 24
Coffee Cream Pie, 41
Cranberry Dream Pie, 28
Fudgy Walnut Sauce, 46
Holiday Cranberry Cobbler, 41
Marbled Peppermint Angel Cake, 43
Mincemeat Trifle, 42
Nutcracker Sweet, 42
Pumpkin Mousse Cheesecake, 43
Snowflake Pudding, 42
Spice Cake Bars, 42
Swedish Fruit Soup, 29
Walnut Apple Cake, 43
White Christmas Cake, 41

Main Dishes
After-Christmas Turkey Potpie, 25
Bacon Potato Omelet, 11
Blueberry Blintz Souffle, 13
Christmas Breakfast Casserole, 11
Confetti Bean Soup Mix, 46
Flavorful Lamb Chops, 28
Ham and Mushroom Toast, 13
Herbed Rib Roast, 28
Jack Cheese Oven Omelet, 13
Orange-Cream French Toast, 12

Muffins
Cheesy Bacon Muffins, 12
Glazed Lemon Muffins, 14
Old-Fashioned Molasses Muffins, 15
Traditional English Muffins, 12

Quick Breads
Caramel Orange Ring, 14
Crispy Almond Strips, 18
Danish Coffee Cake, 47
Golden Fruitcake, 45
Orange-Chip Cranberry Bread, 18
Savory Onion Corn Bread, 19
Strawberry Nut Bread, 19

Rolls & Sweet Rolls
Butterscotch Crescents, 18
Cloverleaf Rolls, 18
Cranberry Almond Sweet Rolls, 15
Pecan Pumpkin Biscuits, 14
Special Long Johns, 11

Salads
Fluffy Pink Fruit Salad, 12
Greens with Creamy Celery Dressing, 29
Snow-White Salad, 25

Side Dishes
Cheesy Rosemary Potatoes, 24
Citrus Carrots and Sprouts, 29
Curried Rice Mix, 46
Festive Peas and Onions, 29
Herbed Vegetable Squares, 24
Home-for-Christmas Fruit Bake, 13
Perfect Scalloped Oysters, 29
Potato Stuffing, 24
Savory Wild Rice Casserole, 25

Yeast Breads
Cinnamon Swirl Bread, 14
Herbed Yeast Bread, 15
Holiday Tree Bread, 19
Swiss Cheese Bread, 28

Crafts

Appliqued Snowman Sweatshirt, 70
Appliqued Tablecloth, 60
Bright Lights Garland, 58
Candy-Striped Santas, 67
Card Puzzle Magnets, 75
Cheery Pinecone Trim, 63
Christmas Card Barn, 99
Country Claus Trim, 76
Crocheted Slippers, 103
Crocheted Star Place Mat Set, 68
Cross-Stitched Santa Trim, 66
Dancing Gingerbread Toy, 95
Evergreen Door Decor, 81
Fabric Candy Canes, 64
Fabric Stocking Trims, 92
Festive Hot Pads, 90
Jumbo Stocking, 88
Knit Sweater and Hat, 86
Kountry Klaus, 106
Kris Kringle Tea Towel, 102
Merry Plant Pokes, 93
Mini Tree Skirt, 72
Noel Bell Pulls, 74
North Pole Pins, 98
Painted Tree Trims Sweatshirt, 80
Pinecone Angels, 73
Plastic Canvas Gift Bag, 96
Poinsettia Napkin Ring, 85
Quilled Bear Ornament, 94
Santa and Mrs. Claus Mugs, 62
Santa Claus Napkin Holder, 84
Sequin Snowflakes, 79
Shining Star Ornament, 69
Signs of the Season Quilt, 82
Snowman Candy Jar, 76
Speedy Sock Reindeer, 59
Spool Nativity, 78
Sugar Cookie Sleigh, 48
Tree Slice Ornament, 87
Woven Sleigh Basket, 100

☀ Share Your Holiday Joy! ☀

DO *YOU* celebrate Christmas in a special way? If so, we'd like to know! We're already gathering material for our next *Country Woman Christmas* book. And we need your help!

Do you have a nostalgic holiday-related story to share? Perhaps you have penned a Christmas poem…or a heart-warming fiction story?

Does your family carry on a favorite holiday tradition? Or do you deck your halls in some festive way? Maybe you know of a Christmas-loving country woman others might like to meet?

We're looking for *original* Christmas quilt patterns and craft projects, too, plus homemade Nativities, gingerbread houses, etc. Don't forget to include your best recipes for holiday-favorite main-dish meats, home-baked cookies, candies, breads, etc.!

Send your ideas and photos to "*CW* Christmas Book", 5925 Country Lane, Greendale WI 53129. (Enclose a self-addressed stamped envelope if you'd like materials returned.)